LEARNING FROM THE LEAST

Learning
from the
Least

Reflections on a Journey in Mission
with Palestinian Christians

ANDREW F. BUSH

FOREWORD BY
ELAINE A. HEATH

CASCADE *Books* • Eugene, Oregon

Cascade Books
An Imprint of Wipf and Stock Publishers
199 W. 8th Ave., Suite 3
Eugene, OR 97401

www.wipfandstock.com

ISBN 13: 978-1-62564-256-1

Cataloguing-in-Publication data:

Bush, Andrew F.

Learning from the least : reflections on a journey in mission with Palestinian Christians / Andrew F. Bush, with a foreword by Elaine A. Heath.

xviii + 192 pp. ; 23 cm. Includes bibliographical references.

ISBN 13: 978-1-62564-256-1

1. Palestine—In Christianity. 2. Arab-Israeli conflict—Religious aspects—Christianity. 3. Missions—History. I. Title.

BT93.8 .B88 2013

Manufactured in the U.S.A.

Scripture taken from the NEW AMERICAN STANDARD BIBLE®, Copyright © 1960, 1962, 1963, 1968, 1971, 1972, 1973, 1975, 1977, 1995 by The Lockman Foundation. Used by permission.

Scripture taken from the New King James Version®. Copyright © 1982 by Thomas Nelson, Inc. Used by permission. All rights reserved.

Qur'anic quotations herein are taken from Saheeh International, *The Qur'an: English Meanings and Notes,* Riyadh: Al-Muntada Al-Islami Trust, 2001–2011; Jeddah: Dar Abul-Qasim 1997–2001.

Quotations from *Beyond Self: The Story of the Palestinian Bible Society, 1993–2005* (July 2006) by Labib Madanat are used with the permission of the author.

With the loving gratitude of her son, this book is dedicated to
Nancy Ferguson Bush,
whose courage in journeying from her West Virginia home to the halls
of the Library of Congress while giving so much to us along the way
has been an inspiration

And to my beloved wife,
Karen Mehl Bush,
who has never swerved in our journey from our one-room adobe in
the desert to lands beyond our dreams

See, my servant will act wisely;
he will be raised and lifted up and highly exalted.
Just as there were many who were appalled at him—
his appearance was so disfigured beyond that of any human being
and his form marred beyond human likeness—
so he will sprinkle many nations,
and kings will shut their mouths because of him.
For what they were not told, they will see,
and what they have not heard, they will understand.

ISAIAH 52:13–15

Contents

Illustrations

Foreword

IN WRITING THIS FOREWORD for *Learning from the Least*, I want to begin with character, for character is the most important credential in those who would guide the church. It has been forty years since I met Andrew Bush, the biblical nomenclature for a lifetime. Over the past four decades I have watched Professor Bush grow from a passionate, young, lay pastor of a diverse young church in Santa Fe, New Mexico, to a fruitful missionary and church planter in multiple international contexts, to the world of theological education where he now imparts missional wisdom to future generations of leaders. I cannot imagine anyone more qualified to have written this book. For as Professor Bush clearly describes in this volume, his inward journey has been just as deep and impactful as his outward vocation of ministry.

In this wonderful text of narrative theology Professor Bush invites the reader to walk with him through his own process of liberation from colonialistic, imperialistic forms of mission and evangelism. Here is the story of a young couple and their family setting out on a traditional missionary path, only to encounter Jesus in the "other." From impoverished railroad track villages in Manila to a university coffee house in Palestine, again and again the young family experienced prayer, hospitality, and compassion from those to whom they had been sent. They experienced the transforming love of God in, through, and from "the least of these." Everything had to change.

The journey has been marked with many thresholds—liminal space—opening unimagined vistas of God's presence in the world. As Andrew and his family increasingly learned from the least, no longer could uncritical Zionism in American churches go unchallenged. No longer could patriarchal constructs that have deformed the evangelical church be simply accepted, as the way things are. Denominational turf building had to be named for what it is—a force contrary to the gospel that makes little sense outside of the U.S.

No theological stone was left unturned as Andrew embraced the kenotic path of Philippians 2, finding solidarity with and learning from the least.

Here is a book that tells a deeply human, divinely breathed story of real people who have to an extraordinary degree entered into the truth of the Apostle Paul's words:

> But God chose what the world considers foolish to shame the wise. God chose what the world considers weak to shame the strong. And God chose what the world considers low-class and low-life— what is considered to be nothing—to reduce what is considered to be something to nothing. So no human being can brag in God's presence. It is because of God that you are in Christ Jesus. He became wisdom from God for us. This means that he made us righteous and holy, and he delivered us. (1 Cor 1:27–30, CEB)

May this beautiful story bring transformation of missional vision to many. May it bring conviction and conversion to a church that is still in bondage to consumeristic, militaristic ecclesiology. May it bring comfort to the new cadre of leaders whom God is calling forth to live among and learn from the least. For it is in the end a book that honors and blesses the least of these, who live always in the center of God's heart.

Elaine A. Heath
McCreless Professor of Evangelism
Southern Methodist University
Dallas, Texas
August 4, 2013
11th Sunday after Pentecost

Traditional feast day for the finding of the body of St. Stephen, the first martyr of the church, an appropriate day to pray for this theological text about the kenotic way.

Preface

CHRISTIAN MISSION IS THE endeavor of the followers of Jesus to participate in God's healing and redemptive work in the world in all of its creative expressions. Whereas the word *mission* is not found in the Bible, God's desire to reconcile all of humanity to himself—and the inclusion of the people of God in this reconciling work—is found in the warp and woof of scripture, from God's covering of the first man and woman in their shame (Gen 3:21), to the calling of Abraham through whom all nations were to be blessed (Gen 12:1–3), to the vision of the Hebrew prophets that all nations would someday be included in God's blessed kingdom (Ps 47:6–9).

This redemptive plan of God was most fully revealed and advanced in the life and teachings of the carpenter from Nazareth, Jesus. The central act in God's reconciling mission was the crucifixion and resurrection of Jesus. "Behold, the Lamb of God who takes away the sin of the world!" as John the Baptist proclaimed (John 1:29). The cross of Christ Jesus made possible the healing of humanity's brokenness through reconciliation with the Giver of Life. The wonderful message of this healing—both individual and corporate—was to be announced to all of humanity. Jesus commissioned his disciples to share the blessing of God's forgiveness with all peoples:

> Then He opened their minds to understand the Scriptures, and He said to them, "Thus it is written, that the Christ would suffer and rise again from the dead the third day, and that repentance for forgiveness of sins would be proclaimed in His name to all the nations, beginning from Jerusalem (Luke 24:45–47).

How the followers of Jesus have understood and acted on this instruction is a two thousand-year-old story that includes both the deepest failures as well as the realization of the highest ideals of the Christian faith. This account of how the global Christian community brings witness by word and deed to God's reconciling love in Christ Jesus is still being written; it is a story of discovery because, as the Christian community finds itself in continually changing contexts, what it means to participate in the mission of God must be reconsidered and redefined.

Today, as a result of the phenomenal expansion of Christianity during the last one hundred years it has become a truly global movement. In fact, more Christians now reside *outside* of those regions most associated with Christian tradition—Europe and North America—than *within* them. Consequently, Christian mission is developing a new face, a new dynamic character, as the bearers of Christ's love to their neighbors are no longer predominately from the West, but hail from nations such as Korea, Mexico, and the Philippines.

With this profound shift in Christian mission, it is being asked, What will the character of Christian mission be in the twenty-first century? Indeed, will the Christian West even continue to have a role in global mission? If it will, what role will it serve? Can the Christian West yield its long-held dominance to adopt a humbler place alongside—and under—its Indian, Chinese, Korean, and Middle Eastern sisters and brothers?

For those who long to see the pain of the world assuaged by the comfort of the love and healing life of God in Christ Jesus, these are critical questions. Answering them will not be painless, especially for the Christian West. The purpose of this book is to participate in this discussion. It argues that for the Christian West to find its place in global Christian mission will require a radical renewal of its spirituality by fresh reflection on the act from which mission first flowed—the cross of Christ. However, how can Christians overcome cultural norms and religious tradition in order to consider the cross afresh?

As I am a member of the Christian West, its aberrations have been my own, as well as its same urgent need for spiritual renewal. From twenty-five years of serving with Christians in Manila, the Philippines and in the Palestinian West Bank I have found that it has often been the least likely of brothers and sisters on the frontiers of Christian faith—those not molded by the West's long commingling of faith and secular power—who have led me through the clutter of extraneous concerns in mission praxis and of too easily accepted values more Western than Christian, back to the forgiveness, the mercy, the radical servanthood of the cross.

Learning from the Least offers a glimpse into the faith of several of these remarkable Christians. For those seekers in the West who are longing for the dawn of a new day in the spirituality of Western Christianity and its mission, the tough decisions these sisters and brothers have made to push more deeply into the radical servanthood of Christ in spite of the violence around them are like lights shining in darkness—lights that illuminate the path to renewal.

Andrew Bush
Bir Zeit, Palestine July 30, 2013

Acknowledgments

THE LONG ROAD OF *Learning from the Least* from its initial conception to completion has depended upon the hospitality and generosity of the Palestinian people, especially those whose stories the writer has told in part in these pages. I especially thank Jack Sara, the president of Bethlehem Bible College, a wonderful friend during the last eighteen years. I am most grateful to the Palestinian Bible Society, which has been a family to us during our years in Palestine, especially Labib Madanat, Nashat Filemon, and the Living Stones team. Their vital witness for Christ against all odds provides much of the inspiration for this book. I am deeply grateful for the honor of serving among them, and for the openness with which they have shared their stories with us. To all those who have opened their hearts and homes throughout the last fifteen years, thank you. It is my hope and prayer that this book may spark discussion that will make your way forward easier, however slightly. Although the Palestinian Bible Society is referred to several times, the ideas and convictions stated in *Learning from the Least* are entirely those of the author.

In respect for those who are mentioned in these pages, it should be noted that, other than the Palestinian leaders who are publicly known, pseudonyms are used throughout to protect their confidentiality. In one particular personal account minor details are also modified for the same purpose.

It is also important to acknowledge those other Christians from the margins who have been a source of fellowship and inspiration in the way of Christ for many years, especially the sisters and brothers of Harvesters Christian Fellowship in Manila, and Augustus Anthony, known as Brother Tony, and his wife Neelam of the Assembly of Believers Churches, based in Lucknow, India, who more than thirty years ago introduced the writer to the fervent worship and evangelism of their ministry.

Acknowledgments

Professor emeritus of English at Eastern University and a social activist in her own right, Betsy Morgan has been an invaluable critical reader from the first rough drafts. Her wise counsel at many turns helped me sort through the myriad of topics that thread their way through the book. Special thanks also to David Shenk, global consultant for Eastern Mennonite Missions, mission scholar, author, and pilgrim in the Muslim world, whose insightful comments have brought clarity and correction to many points in this discussion. Elaine Heath, McCreless Associate Professor of Evangelism and the Director of the Center for Missional Wisdom at Perkins Theological Seminary at Southern Methodist University, as well as a nationally recognized leader in the new discussion of spirituality and mission, offered invaluable advice, inspiration, and friendship throughout this project. She has also graciously contributed the foreword. Key ideas in the formation of this book were first presented in the Craven Wilson Evangelism Lectures, which she invited me to present at Perkins Theological Seminary in October, 2009. Indeed, the title of my lecture was "Learning from the Least." While acknowledging the valuable contribution these scholars have made to this book, it is important to state that all the shortcomings which remain are entirely the responsibility of the author.

The confidence that Wipf and Stock Publishers and its Cascade Books division have shown towards this project is greatly appreciated. Special thanks to Rodney Clapp for his adept editorial assistance in bringing the manuscript to publication, and to Sara Barnhurst, a recent graduate of Eastern University, who found the time and patience in the weeks before her wedding to help with the final formatting of the manuscript.

The writing of this book could never have been accomplished had it not been for the sabbatical leave in 2012 granted to the author by the Board of Directors of Eastern University, St. David's, Pennsylvania. I remain deeply appreciative to them for their gift of this time. The EU community's pursuit of faith, reason, and justice has provided an environment for open inquiry that has given me the freedom to explore some of the difficult topics in this book.

Friends too many to mention have been important voices of affirmation along the way, without whose guidance and affirmation at critical times in my life this book would never have been realized. Among these are the late Art Katz, the founder of Ben Israel Ministries, who introduced me to the prophetic perspective and sought us out to bring words of encouragement in our journey from New Mexico to Manila and then Palestine;

Jonathan Bonk, the long-time director of the Overseas Missions Study Center in New Haven Connecticut; Dennis Olson, Professor of Old Testament Theology at Princeton Theological Seminary; and Nigerian theologian Sister Teresa Okure, SHCJ, Professor of New Testament and Gender Hermeneutics at the Catholic Institute of West Africa, under whom I had the privilege of studying for a year from 1999-2000 at the Ecole Biblique et Archéologique Française in Jerusalem.

This project has been a spiritual task, and the writer thanks those men who have prayed for it on Wednesday nights, and for the support of Methacton Mennonite Church. Debby Rush and her brother John Mark Lindvall of Mission Ministries in Santa Ana, California, have made the writer's international service possible with their faithful administrative assistance. Special thanks also to our friends in churches throughout the country who have been partners in our journey and have been willing to listen even when we struggled to grasp our own changing perspectives.

Finally, words cannot express sufficient gratitude for the love and support of my wife, Karen, who has borne with all the trials of bringing this book to fruition, read every word, and made very helpful suggestions. A licensed midwife and clinical social worker, she has been a pillar in our more than one quarter century's sojourn in mission. Our children, who didn't choose our sojourning life but were faithful to walk with us through it, have been a constant source of encouragement, fun, and parental pride as they have gone on to excel in their own unique professions. To our youngest, who suffered the violence of the Intifada firsthand, and is now completing medical school with a hope to bring healing to other troubled places, bravo!

Abbreviations

SCRIPTURE ABBREVIATION

Hebrew Bible / Old Testament:

Gen	Judg	Neh	Song	Hos	Nah
Exod	Ruth	Esth	Isa	Joel	Hab
Lev	Sam	Job	Jer	Amos	Zeph
Num	Kgs	Ps (*pl.* Pss)	Lam	Obad	Hag
Deut	Chr	Prov	Ezek	Jonah	Zech
Josh	Ezra	Eccl (or Qoh)	Dan	Mic	Mal

New Testament:

Matt	Acts	Eph	Tim	Heb	1-2-3 John
Mark	Rom	Phil	Titus	Jas	Jude
Luke	1–2 Cor	Col	Phlm	Pet	Rev
John	Ga	1–2 Thess			

Introduction

WHEN THE DISCIPLES PETER and Andrew and James and John left their fishing nets on the shores of the Sea of Galilee, when Matthew walked away from his counting desk, and when at some point Mary left the family home in Nazareth, they had no way of knowing how surprising, perplexing, and transforming their journey with Jesus would be, how deeply it would challenge their assumptions about what really is of value in this world, and what it means to be part of the people of God. Jesus cautioned those who were over-enthusiastic to join his disciples. Following him would offer little earthly security. The Son of Man has nowhere to lay his head, Jesus warned (Matt 8:20).

When Jesus called his disciples to follow him, there was no promise that doing so would be convenient. In fact, Jesus made clear that following him would cost them their lives; he said, "He who has found his life will lose it, and he who has lost his life for My sake will find it" (Matt 10:39). Part of this "losing" of one's life meant a changed perspective concerning what disciples thought God was going to do in Israel, what sort of deliverance the Messiah would bring, who could be part of God's salvation, and more. In order to follow Jesus, they would have to make profound, fundamental shifts in their understanding of many of the foundations of their faith.

Today following Jesus remains a radical journey. The values that Christ Jesus challenged in the first century—making personal security a priority, the quest for personal advancement and prominence, claiming exceptional privilege for one's people, subjugating the weak to advance one's cause, harboring hatred for one's enemies—he challenges today. Jesus is calling his disciples to a radically different way of living in the world. He desires that God's love and compassion will as fully guide the affairs in this world as they do in heaven (Matt 6:10).

Every generation of Christians must face the temptation to domesticate Jesus, reducing him, as H. Richard Niebuhr in his classic text *Christ and Culture* states, to nothing more than a figurehead of culture, someone that simply affirms a culture's values and institutions.[1] Christ calls his disciples to challenge what is ungodly in culture. To do so requires a willingness to reevaluate the familiar. The journey of dislocation from a familiarly held conviction, to another perspective that may be only dimly perceived from the onset, can be frightening. Along the way spiritual pilgrims may question whether they are losing their faith, or perhaps worse for evangelicals, if they are becoming "liberals"!

The lessons Jesus taught were given in the midst of the flow of life in first-century Palestine, then occupied by the Roman Empire's forces. As the poor and outcast came to him, he taught his disciples and the religious leaders who challenged his associations that it is the sick who need a physician, not the well (Matt 9:12), that the one who claims to see is blind (John 9:39), that the one who seeks to glorify himself will be abased, and that the least is the greatest (Luke 9:48).

Although one's journey toward understanding the ways of God, which are so unlike our ways, certainly may be helped by the tools of academia and biblical scholarship, it may also be advanced through the insights gained by experiences that occur in the midst of the work of daily life, the pressures of family, the hurts of misunderstandings, the upheaval of ethnic and national conflicts, and interaction with people of other faiths and ethnicity. Experience can provide an avenue into new perspectives on biblical truths of God's compassion and grace. As an important mentor in my journey, and one of the majority world's most vital scholars of mission, Sister Teresa Okure, has stated, the experiences of Jesus's audiences became the interpretative key for discovering the meaning of the scriptures as it applied to their lives.[2]

These insights, which we can gather along the way of life's journey, are frequently unexpected. They reflect the continual surprise of God's grace, as unexpected as a treasure hidden in a field, of such value that the man in the parable of Jesus who finds it will sell all he has to purchase the field (Matt 13:44). Such unexpected discoveries of "the breadth and length and height

1. Niebuhr, *Christ and Culture*, xlvi.

2. Okure, "Enkindling Fire in the Mission," 7. I had the privilege of studying under Teresa Okure in 1999 at the Ecole Biblique et Archéologique Française in Jerusalem. It was as a result of her encouragement that I completed a thesis at the Ecole that greatly helped me in my theological and spiritual pilgrimage.

and depth" of God's love (Eph 3:19, NASB[3]) have marked the journey of my wife and I as we have sought to serve alongside brothers and sisters in Christ Jesus in the Philippines and Palestine for the last twenty-five years.

In 1987, my wife and our five children arrived with stacks of second-hand luggage in Manila, the Philippines. Our theological understanding of mission and the dynamics of cross-cultural life was rudimentary, but we were motivated by a zeal for serving God that had first been kindled in the small mountain evangelical churches we stumbled into when we were finding our way out of the confusion of "counter-cultural" life in northern New Mexico in the early 1970s. For the next eleven years we served alongside Filipino brothers and sisters in planting congregations in the upscale commercial district as well as the deepest slums of the inner city in Manila. These were years of learning as we sought to grasp the subtleties of Filipino culture and the implications of becoming bi-cultural.

They were also years of fresh hope and renewed faith as we began to explore new theological and spiritual paths that augmented the spirituality in which we had been discipled. That spirituality emphasized hearing God's voice personally through the scriptures and an expectancy of the presence of God in worship. Whereas graduate theological studies in an evangelical seminary in Manila were an important tool in opening new readings of scripture, it was the example of the very poor whom we met living along the railroad tracks that passed through the center of Manila—their generosity, their zeal to share the gospel of hope in Christ, and their warm hospitality—that kept nudging us toward the radical teachings of Christ. Those included the teachings about the need to loosen one's grip on the false security of wealth, the power of serving out of weakness instead of strength, and the need to value humanity regardless of its frailty.

These years in the eastern edge of Asia would prepare us for a transition to the westernmost edge of Asia, Israel and Palestine. In 1998, my wife and I moved—now with only two children with us—to the city of Ramallah, north of Jerusalem in the Palestinian Territories. This was quite a shift in the direction in our life journey, one that we never could have foreseen when we first left the United States as unlikely missionaries twelve years earlier. Working with several remarkable young Palestinian men, we established Living Stones Student Center in the village of Bir Zeit, several kilometers north of Ramallah. It was an oasis for the students who could

---

3. The New American Standard Bible (NASB), is used throughout unless otherwise noted.

not return to their families for several years during the worst years of the Second Intifada, or Uprising, from 2000–2005, which pitted Palestinian civilians and militants against the occupying Israeli military in the West Bank and Gaza. Living Stones, a project of the Palestinian Bible Society, has become a multi-faceted project that today serves the students of Bir Zeit University, families in Bir Zeit, the youth in the Muslim villages nearby, Christian congregations in the area, and more.

As I will describe in greater detail, two years after we made our new home on the West Bank, the violence of the Second Intifada was ignited. The fires of this conflict raged for more than four years, at the cost of hundreds of lives lost in both Israel and Palestine, and of many more casualties whose injuries will never be healed. Besides these external wounds, the violence inflicted internal wounds of hatred. Living in a war zone, often isolated in Bir Zeit where we were then living, we also struggled to resist the temptation of anger and bitterness as we witnessed the suffering of people around us.

It was in this context of intense conflict that our spiritual journey took an unexpected turn as we sought to answer pressing questions. How could we rise above the swells of hatred that were threatening to engulf us? In the midst of such violence, how could the reality of Christ Jesus's love become relevant, something more than simply more religious talk? The answer to these questions would be found through the example of the Palestinian Christians who, in spite of the violence that formed a constant background to their daily lives, were making radical decisions to walk in the way of Christ. These were Christians many in the West did not even know existed. They were living under restrictions on their daily lives that made the pursuit of every day's work and school almost impossible; yet, in spite of this, they were choosing the way of life, forgiveness, and servanthood. Insights into God's grace gleaned from their lives opened new possibilities in our personal spiritual journey and in our understanding of the mission of God, his full-orbed redemptive purposes in the world. Essentially, they led me to a fresh understanding of the cross of Christ, to the way of servanthood in humility and weakness. Here was a sure foundation for being a Christian in the world, for being sent into the world as Jesus was sent (John 20:21).

During the years of the Intifada and afterward, when I had the opportunity to speak to Christian groups in the United States, I found that there was often a sharp disparity between what we were experiencing in Palestinian society, especially what we were learning from Palestinian

Christians, and the perceptions many American Christians had of the Palestinian people. For some conservative evangelicals it seemed that God's will in Israel and Palestine had more to do with national triumph than with the grace of God that values all of humanity.

These misguided and still prevalent convictions about God's will for Israel and Palestine express, however unintentionally, a conviction about the mission of God and how God's redemptive purposes are worked out in the world: it will succeed when allied with power, even if such power is exerted to subjugate a weaker people. Apparently, power and the use of it are both acceptable if they advance "God's will." As will be discussed, whereas such ideas would seem obviously to contradict the values of Christ, they are in fact commonplace in popular end times theologies that talk casually about which nations will soon be destroyed by God, the national triumph of the modern State of Israel, and so forth.

Such triumphalism is problematic for Western mission. Although Western mission is seeking to forge a new partnership with the majority world church, it is at the same time largely ambivalent about theologies that equate God's purpose in Israel to nationalism, a nationalism promoted by power.

The fact that Western Christianity can remain oblivious to profound contradictions in its expressions of mission suggests that the renewal that it seeks in order to find its place in the new era of global mission cannot merely be a reordering of programs, organizational charts, or financial policies. If Western mission is going to remain relevant and tolerated, it will require a profound spiritual renewal. That mission is now initiated from the margins of the Christian world, often by the powerless, the unknown, and the unlettered, underscores the realization that such spiritual renewal will require a reacquaintance with the way of Christ. This indeed is the way of the cross, the way of radical service out of weakness, which seeks to serve those whom Jesus called "the least of these My brethren" (Matt 25:40, NKJV). The way of Christ is the antithesis of triumphalism toward the "Other."

Renewal of the Western Church's missional spirituality is critical, particularly as it concerns Israel and Palestine, because a new generation of progressive evangelicals—twenty and thirty-year-olds—are repelled by the triumphal theology of their parents' generation. I recall the disdain of a very bright Christian university student from a Jewish background for the ideas of Christians who uncritically support the most reactionary policies of the Israeli government toward the Palestinians. With a look of shock on her face she asked how anyone could believe that such repressive policies are God's will. If evangelical mission is going to maintain relevance to this new generation of progressive evangelicals—its own children—it must be willing to re-examine its unquestioning affirmation of popular theology that enthusiastically promotes the marginalization of an indigenous people.

This book then is a call for spiritual renewal in Western mission. This renewal cannot be achieved as a conversation within Western Christianity's own familiar circles. We cannot extricate ourselves from the web in which we are entangled. I argue that this renewal must be facilitated by learning from the non-Western Christians who are seeking to walk in the way of Christ as they bring the reality of God's life and love in Christ Jesus to their communities. Their insights are valuable as their perspectives are from outside Western tradition with its merging of Christianity and secular power. This is not to say that majority-world, formerly known as third-world, Christians are above reproach, or that their churches are not prone to the same difficulties of those in the West. Nevertheless, living outside of the sphere of the West, majority-world Christians may, even unintentionally, help us find our way back to the radical call of Jesus upon his disciples characterized by the laying aside of every prerogative of power and privilege, and the embracing of servanthood out of humility; in short, they may help us find our way back to the cross. As eminent historian of Christian mission Andrew Walls succinctly states, "It is now the churches of the non-Western world that have the accumulated and ripened experience of God's salvation."[4]

In short, this book is about the renewal of missional spirituality by listening to and learning from "the least of these" of global Christianity. Where should learning from the least begin? It should begin with those who are presently still being wounded by Western mission. How can Western mission find its place in the new global Christian mission of the twenty-first century if it turns a deaf ear to those it is still hurting? How can Western mission be transformed if it does not confront the ideas that engender intolerance and which not only have become part of the warp and woof of its culture, but are applauded?

This book, then, is about learning from Palestinian Christians who, with the rest of the Palestinian people in the West Bank and Gaza, are being victimized by Western mission that promotes their marginalization, and by an exaggerated Israeli nationalism that sidelines the ethical teachings of

4. Walls, *The Cross-Cultural Process*, 71.

Christ. Again, the individual Palestinian Christians who are highlighted are not above error; they are struggling to live out the teachings of Christ in the frailty of their humanness, as are all Christians. Yet, as in lives of important biblical figures, they have made decisions in the midst of turmoil that are remarkable in the degree to which they effectively illustrate the character of Christ, decisions which speak prophetically beyond their context. These decisions illuminate the way of Christ and are a reminder in the midst of daily routine that the way of servanthood in meekness may still be lived in this world. They point toward a renewal of mission by a return to humility that is willing to value others above oneself, as the Apostle Paul (hereafter Paul) exhorted (Phil 2:3), even if the other is a Palestinian, a Muslim, a woman, or whomever may be derided in one's culture.

The prophetic decisions of majority-world Christians also point toward a renewal of mission through servanthood, from a posture of weakness instead of from a privileged status. This is service not for the marginalized, or with the marginalized, but as the marginalized.

Lastly, concerning the importance of listening to Palestinian Christians, while I do not espouse a heightened sacredness of geography, the fact that the central act in God's redemptive mission, the crucifixion of Christ Jesus, occurred in the land that is today torn by bitterness and violence, highlights that the significance of the cross as the great act of reconciliation between God and humanity needs to be reaffirmed. Palestinian Christians are an example of people in the land who are seeking to make that reconciliation a reality.

Listening and learning from Palestinian Christians has been my journey, one that I've needed. They have helped me reground my theology of mission in Christ. Spiritually, they have helped me escape the fate of being one more victim of the Second Intifada and the ongoing violence in Israel and Palestine, as I could have been overcome by bitterness had it not been for the example of forgiveness and reconciliation in many of their lives.

The example of various Palestinian brothers and sisters is described from the perspective of my journey in Palestine. As a personal reflection, it is consequently oriented to and limited by my experience. I certainly could not have shared these reflections at the end of the Intifada in 2005. Our family's journey through the violence of the Intifada was a difficult one that did not leave us unscathed. Relocating our primary home to the United States in 2005 after almost twenty years overseas (although we maintain a residence in Bir Zeit and continue to serve as volunteers with the team there), we began the difficult journey of dealing with frayed emotions, painful memories, and, at times, my unfortunate reactions to those who had no idea what daily life in Palestine entails. We needed healing. But in spite of the hardship and fear we had experienced, I also sensed that we had been given an opportunity for spiritual renewal that should be shared with others.

The years since have allowed us to reflect on our experiences, sort through our emotions, and work through the theological implications we have drawn from them. Several of the important ideas that are developed in this book were first presented in conferences of missions scholars, which afforded me the opportunity to receive valuable feedback. This time has also allowed me to reflect more deeply with several Palestinian Christian leaders about their decisions to walk in the way of Christ.

One of the difficult aspects of trying to draw spiritual lessons from the lives of people caught in the vortex of violence in Israel and Palestine is that the issues involved in the conflict can overwhelm the discussion. Also, people bring such strong reactions to this topic that they might immediately reject the discussion if some issue is raised that contradicts their fervent convictions. Perhaps this has already happened for some readers in these first pages!

Acknowledging this difficulty, I would state that it is important to recognize the limitations of this discussion. To reiterate, the topic of this book is the renewal of Western mission spirituality so that it can find its place in global mission in the twenty-first century. Although this topic is discussed within the context of the conflict in Israel/Palestine, I do not attempt to analyze the complex causes of this conflict, or what the profile of a final peace agreement might be. When discussing the context of daily life, although the reality of violence will be clearly acknowledged, I make it clear that violence and the killing of the innocent is a reality in both communities.

While I do respond to the theology of Christians who uncritically support Israel's policies towards Palestinians, my response is primarily to ask Christians to consider the implications of the way of the cross for Israel and Palestine today. I do not formulate a comprehensive response to Dispensational Premillennialism. Accordingly, I do not attempt to develop a comprehensive theology of the Land, although I do indicate what I think the general contours of such a theology should include. As Mennonite scholar Martin Jeschke states, such contours should include that Israel still has a call to the land, but it is not a call to *possess* the land in the sense of exerting exclusive control over it.[5] I suggest with Jeschke that the call of Israel to the land pertains primarily to a manner of living in the land that seeks to make peace with its neighbors; in short, the call to the land is a call to a prophetic way of "possessing" the land that seeks peaceful coexistence rather than exclusive and exclusionary control. Jesus reiterates to Israel that inheriting the land is to be associated with humility: "Blessed are the meek, for they shall inherit the earth" (Matt 5:5, NKJV).

According to this perspective, Israel was elected by God to be a prophetic example of peacemaking in the world. In my opinion this call remains. It follows that the fact that the Palestinian people remain in the land is a gift to Israel, perhaps a final opportunity to fulfill its prophetic call. As I will discuss, many Israelis who are fervently seeking peace and justice are fulfilling that call today.

As children of Abraham through faith in Christ Jesus (Gal 3:7–8), all Christians inherit the same call to live in peace with their neighbors. It is important to note that Christians have failed in this as deeply as has Israel. Many Palestinian Christians have also failed in this call. This book seeks to learn from those who are trying to find their way back to the call of Abraham to live in peace, which was fulfilled on the cross by the true seed of Abraham, Christ Jesus. The lessons that Israel must learn, we in the Western church must also learn.

CLARIFICATION OF TERMS

In speaking of the need for renewal of the mission of Western Christianity, I am primarily referring to the evangelical community in the United States. I count myself a part of this community. I remain convinced of the integrity of scripture as the inspired Word of God, and the central tenets of historic orthodox Christianity that are foundational to evangelicalism. The central act in human history is the crucifixion and resurrection of Christ Jesus. Through the passion of Christ Jesus, God was speaking into our world in a way that no other philosopher, or religious or political leader, ever can. As a result of the cross, the good news of the forgiveness of God and of the gift of eternal life, may go out into the world.

As a result of the years my wife and I have spent working across Christian traditions, I do not carry a strong sectarian identity. Although raised in the Episcopal Church (a choir boy in the Washington Cathedral!) the

5. Jeschke, *Rethinking Holy Land*.

beginning of my convinced Christian walk was within Pentecostalism—complete with elaborate charts mapping out the events that are to unfold in the end of the age! Although I have mentioned that my wife and I began to explore new directions theologically during our years in the Philippines, I continue to affirm the conviction that God works with power in the world by the Spirit of God today. Though it is a far cry from the boisterous services we enjoyed for decades, when in the United States we are members of a small Mennonite congregation outside Philadelphia, ably led by a pastor who in her quiet way regularly encourages the congregation with her life-giving, conversational sermons.

But, how can one speak of Western mission needing renewal when this terminology necessarily includes hundreds of missionaries serving in very difficult places who are striving to serve their neighbors at great cost to themselves and their families? I certainly do not intend to cast aspersions on these missionaries. I am addressing broad trends in Western mission that have become part of its cultural milieu, acknowledging that such generality is inevitably imperfect.

As has been already stated, some of the issues that I discuss that are problematic in Western evangelical mission are also being replicated in majority world mission. Therefore, although this is primarily addressed to my own community in the United States, I hope that others outside of the West will also find it helpful, as ultimately it is a call to follow Christ more obediently.

To those who do not identify with Christianity, and to whom the idea of mission holds negative implications of efforts to force Western culture on others, or of intolerant Christians proclaiming the destruction of other world religions, I would hope that they might find in the lives of the Palestinian Christians whom I highlight examples of a completely different expression of Christianity and of its mission.

In speaking of "Western mission," I am referring to its various forms including long- and short-term missions; international media broadcasts; the array of professional evangelists, singers, and other speakers that fill the rosters of Christian conferences throughout the world, and so forth. "Western mission" includes efforts focused on evangelism and church planting, as well as efforts to respond to the brokenness of societies, including the neglect of the weak, pandemic illness, poverty, and the need for access to food and water. My understanding of what constitutes missions is that it is participation in the redemptive work of God in the world in the myriad forms in which that occurs.

Terms relating to Israel and Palestine are especially thorny and fluid, reflecting changes in Israeli and Palestinian societies and peoples shifting perspectives. The Palestinian National Authority, the internationally recognized government of the Palestinian people in the West Bank and Gaza, was formed as an outcome of the Oslo Accords in 1994. In 2013, the Palestinian National Authority achieved a certain degree of recognition as a sovereign state with its affirmation by the United Nations as an "observer state." Accordingly, it has changed its official name to the State of Palestine. Since its declaration of independence in 1988 almost 200 nations have recognized Palestine as a state. Yet, it does not control its own land or borders, so status as a sovereign state is still far from fully realized. Israeli organizations will often refer to the West Bank and Gaza as the "Palestinian Territories." Numerous international organizations refer to the same as "the Occupied Palestinian Territories," or the "OPT." Palestinians normally refer to the West Bank, including East Jerusalem, and Gaza as simply "Palestine." As I am primarily telling the story of the Palestinian community, throughout the book I use the term "Palestine."[6] The term "Palestinians" is inclusive of both its Muslim and Christian citizens. The term "Palestinian Christians," of course, refers to all Palestinians who identify themselves as Christians. Variations of these terms are occasionally used if it helps clarify the point being made.

In terms of the citizens of Israel, occasionally the term "Israeli Jew" is used rather than simply the designation "Israeli." This is important because 20 percent of the population of Israel is of Arab Palestinian descent. They were residents in the land for centuries before the formation of modern Israel in 1948. If ethnicity is important in a point being made then the term "Israeli" will be qualified, as in "the Israeli Jewish author . . ." However, generally, the use of the term "Israeli" will indicate citizens of Jewish identity.

---

6. The term "Palestine" is increasingly becoming normalized. The Internet search engine Google recently publicly announced it would use the term "Palestine" instead of "Palestinian Territories" across all of its products. See Associated Press, "Google lists Palestinian territories as 'Palestine.'"

THE BOOK'S STRUCTURE

In the first chapter, the recent dynamic global growth of Christianity is discussed. This growth is largely the result of the integrity of the witness of majority-world Christians, not unlike the witness of early Christians of the first through third centuries. In spite of the global growth of Christianity, which has resulted in the fact that the majority of the world's Christian population now resides in Asia, Africa, and South America, Western mission has not become obsolete. The extremity of global crises demands the partnership in mission of *all* members of the global Christian community.

Here is the dilemma. Contemporary Western Christianity has been deeply affected by the history of Christianity's alliance with agents of power, dating from the linking of the church with the authority of the Roman Empire by the Emperor Constantine. This linkage has produced a paradigm of Christianity, now referred to as Constantinian Christianity. In this paradigm Christianity is privileged in society by its alliance with the governing power. This alliance with secular power deformed Christian identity and the quality of its mission. The predominant model of church and state relations in Europe in the Middle Ages, it was subsequently imported to the Americas.

Majority-world Christians will no longer tolerate Western Christianity that assumes superiority in mission, or that leverages its resources to demote non-Western partners in mission. Yet majority-world Christians, often serving from the margins of privilege and influence, can reacquaint their Western brethren with the way of the cross. Learning from the least, as I have mentioned, should begin where Western mission continues to wound. Although such wounds can be found in many contexts, such listening may begin with the prophetic voices of Palestinian Christians.

The second chapter follows my family's introduction to Palestinian society and its history. It describes the difficulties of life under Israeli military occupation, and the effect this occupation has on people's lives. Israeli organizations (largely unknown to most Western Christians) that oppose the injustice of the Occupation are also discussed.

The third chapter describes how the struggles of living in a Palestinian village during the Intifada, and the challenge of making the message of God's grace and of the love of Christ Jesus real in a context of violence, led me to the ancient hymn quoted by Paul in Philippians 2:5–11. The effective stripping away of aspects of our Christian identity, and our emotional and spiritual support systems, by the environment of violence, made the self-emptying of Christ poignant to me. In the context of Christ's day he ministered to humanity through the ultimate weakness of his crucifixion. Here was a clue, even in the context of violence, that true servanthood that is extended from weakness can communicate the love of Christ. How, though, can this be lived out? The chapter describes the unusual decisions of a staff member, a convert from Islam, which exemplified such servanthood out of weakness, and how his actions helped to create an oasis of peace.

Violence and hatred in Israel and Palestine, like beasts that cannot be controlled, affect relations within both Israeli and Palestinian societies. The environment of tension has exacerbated tensions within Palestinian society between Muslims and Christians. In the fourth chapter I discuss the hurt Palestinian Christians have suffered historically and to the present at the hands of their Muslim neighbors. For Christians in the West such persecution of Christians by Muslims confirms their conclusions about Islam, that it is essentially a violent religion.

But Western mission cannot be effective if it is locked in conflict with Islam, which is also experiencing a global resurgence. For Western Christians to perpetuate such conflict undermines the integrity of their mission as agents of peace and reconciliation. How can Christianity turn a page in its historic hostility toward Islam? In spite of their history of marginalization since the rise of Islam, some Palestinian Christians are seeking to approach Islam with the attitude of learning from and serving Muslims. These Christians, who are a small minority in a Muslim majority society, are showing the way forward toward a new paradigm of Christian engagement with Islam.

Yet, the most bitter tensions in the Holy Land remain between Israelis and Palestinians. This tension is driven by their respective nationalisms, which neither side is willing to soften. This nationalistic conflict causes each side to view the other as less than human. How can reconciliation occur when the Other is regarded as bestial? Chapter five explores how Christ Jesus, in his embrace of humanity, did not empty himself of his national identity; rather, he redefined the character of the nation. The national purpose to which Israel was called would accept and protect the weak within its society, and extend empathy and relief to its neighbors. The chapter examines how a most unlikely Palestinian was willing to demonstrate the emptying of his national prerogatives to make peace with those he had only known previously as enemies.

The sixth chapter examines why Western evangelicals have been largely absent as voices for peace in Israel and Palestine. It explores the strongly held views that maintain that the restoration of Israel and its exclusive possession of the land is central to God's purposes in the end of the age. The popular movement known as Christian Zionism, which uncritically promotes this theology and which also supports a related Israeli nationalism, is also discussed. In response to this, the idea is explored that the call of Abraham, and thus of Israel today, to the land is for the purpose of reconciliation rather that exclusion. Accordingly, the efforts of Palestinian Christians to speak to Christian Zionism, as well as the efforts of some Palestinian Christians and Messianic Jews to build bridges of peace, are noted.

The seventh chapter continues to explore the implications of Christian Zionism for Western mission. Besides its identity as a political, theological and cultural movement, around which critique of Christian Zionism is customarily focused, it is also a missions movement. As such, it is evaluated by the standards of contemporary mission.

The eighth chapter reflects on the challenge of embracing the way of the cross today, of moving deeper into the vulnerability and servanthood of Jesus. It explores the importance of experience in this spiritual journey, especially the experience of interacting with other peoples—Palestinians, Israelis, Muslims, and Jews. Ways that Western Christians can interact with these communities both in Israel and Palestine, and in the United States, are suggested. The consequence of new perspectives is that leaders will face the challenge of journeying down unfamiliar roads.

The epilogue recalls a conversation with a Palestinian Christian leader who speaks widely in the West and seeks to answer whether in fact Western Christians are in fact "learning from the least."

A FINAL THOUGHT

Just as this book is a reflection on our spiritual journey, it is my hope that it will encourage spiritual discovery for others. With that in mind, I offer these two prayers written anonymously by a Palestinian Christian and an Israeli Messianic Jew.

> My daily prayer for the light of God to be revealed in me is expressed in Psalm 139:23-24: "Examine me, O God, and know my

mind; test me, and discover my thoughts. Find out if there is any evil in me and guide me in the everlasting way."[7]

Even though we are still seeing things through a cloudy mirror, may God help us to look at things the way he does.[8]

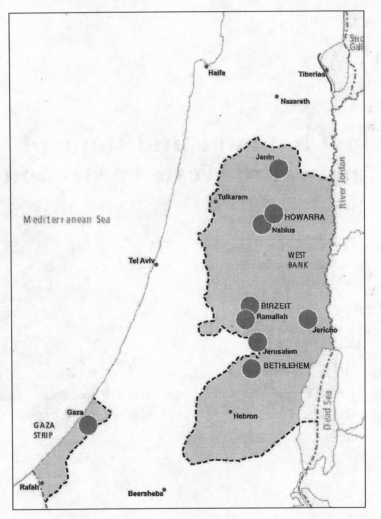

Partial map of Israel and the Palestinian Territories including the West Bank, East Jerusalem, and Gaza with locations of Palestinian Bible Society offices. (Courtesy of the Palestinian Bible Society)

7. *My Brother's Keeper,* Devotion for December 31.

8. Ibid., Devotion for December 20.

1

The Challenge and Hope of Renewal in Western Mission

He has done mighty deeds with His arm;
He has scattered those who were proud in the thoughts of their heart.
He has brought down rulers from their thrones,
And has exalted those who were humble.

LUKE 1:51–52, THE SONG OF MARY

Indeed the Christian faith which once "conquered the world" must also learn to conquer its own forms when they have become worldly. It can do so only when it breaks down the idols of the Christian West, and in a reforming and revolutionary way remembers the "crucified God."[1]

JÜRGEN MOLTMANN, THE CRUCIFIED GOD

A QUIET PROPHET

TWICE A WEEK SUBHA, a young Palestinian woman, makes the wearying journey on public transportation from Bir Zeit, a village in the hill

---

1. Moltmann, *The Crucified God*.

country north of Ramallah, to Jericho. Her trip takes her along winding West Bank roads and then down the highway that descends sharply from Jerusalem. Dun-colored barren hills rise on either side of the desert highway. Faint trails worn by foraging sheep and goats crisscross the hillsides, forming an intricate web. As Subha travels on this day, she passes Bedouin camps with their black tents, basic corrals, and portable water tanks. To the south, the hulking outlines of Israeli settlements sprawl like medieval walled cities misplaced in time. As the highway falls below sea level, the temperature rises.

The descent easing, the road emerges into the Jordan River valley. Just to the north is Jericho, the oldest inhabited city in the world. An Israeli military checkpoint stops traffic going into Jericho. Since the Palestinian uprising, or Intifada, that began in 2000 and finally exhausted itself in 2005, Jericho has had the feel of a boomtown gone bust. Tourists who once flocked to the city's sites—the excavations of the ancient city, the tree where legend has it that Zaacheus climbed to see Jesus, and to the purported cliff where Christ withstood the wiles of Satan—have been reduced to a trickle.

During the summer's cloudless skies the heat in the ancient city of Jericho is suffocating, *zay narr*—like fire—as Palestinians say in Arabic. The intensity of the desert sun empties the streets at midday. Dusty donkeys stand listlessly in what shade they can find, their tails swatting tormenting flies.

In this desert inferno Subha continues her journey on foot, a friend from Jericho with her. In spite of the summer's swelter, she is dressed as a typical Palestinian Muslim woman with a long-sleeved tunic and trousers. Since she is careful to observe her family's standards, a scarf, or *hijab,* is bound tightly around her head. Subha's appearance, though, is misleading; she is a follower of Jesus. Raised in a happy family in the bustling city of Nablus, she worked hard in high school and graduated from university. The normality of her life was overturned by an encounter with the gospel of Jesus.

For several days Subha had dreamt of climbing a ladder. With each higher rung she heard a voice that said she was going to meet new people who would teach her new things. Through a mutual friend she began an Internet chat with someone who began to converse with her about Jesus. Intrigued by the references to Jesus in the Qur'an, she wanted to know more. Her new friend encouraged her spiritual search, and in the months that followed, she began to radically reorient her life toward Jesus. She was moved by examples of Jesus's forgiveness in the Gospels. Her Palestinian government issued identity card, which can never be altered, classifies her as a Muslim. This social identity will always characterize her public life, but she is walking a different road.

When she arrives at a small home, a Palestinian mother with her kids tugging at her side opens the door and warmly welcomes Subha. The purpose of the visit is to encourage the mother and to listen to her concerns: her husband, who waited tables in a tourist restaurant, is out of work; they don't know how they will make it. Before Subha leaves, she prays for the mother.

New followers of Jesus often experience intense resistance from their families and villages in the Middle East. Subha's spiritual journey has been especially difficult. Four years ago she was traveling from Ramallah to Nablus in a Palestinian-marked public taxi. Sitting in the front seat of the vehicle, she was cradling her infant son in her arms when the windshield was suddenly shattered by a rock. Glass shards flew into her face, piercing her left eyelid and cheek. A militant Israeli settler had thrown the rock that would cause years of pain. Settlers are Israelis who reside in fortified housing colonies in West Bank territory that Palestinians claim as part of their future state.

As fiercely as Palestinians claim the land on which they have lived for centuries, many Israelis and their international sympathizers assert that the land is theirs by biblical mandate. While many of the several hundred thousand settlers who now live in the settlements on the West Bank are not fiercely political, there is a strain of militant settlers who intentionally attack Palestinian civilians (who have little recourse to Israeli authorities) in an effort to drive them from the land. As I write, a Palestinian family is recovering from having a fire bomb thrown into their taxi by settler youth.[2]

After two surgeries Subha still experiences pain from the glass splinters that cannot be removed and from permanent damage to the nerves around her eye. Specialists from London, whom she met in Amman, Jordan, warned her that further surgeries would risk the loss of her eye. All they could offer was a prescription for pain medication and the instruction that she must adjust to the pain.

In a land in which hatred of the Other—be it Israeli or Palestinian—scorches the soul as intensely as the Jericho heat, bitterness and vengeful intentions are the reflexive response to such attacks. Forgiveness and reconciliation, in their scarcity, are like strange fruit from a strange land. Yet,

2. Smith-Park, "Attacks on Arabs in Israel Prompt Soul-Searching."

for those who find it, forgiveness is a refuge, providing shelter from the destruction of the enmity of hate.

By the grace of God, Subha was able to hide herself in mercy's shelter, and finding that refuge, she is pointing others toward it. During a retreat in Bethlehem, she was able to meet with several Israelis. She told them about her injury. Saddened, they asked for forgiveness on behalf of their nation. Subha responded simply, yet profoundly, "We are all humans. We have all sinned. We all need forgiveness. So you do not need to ask for forgiveness. But since you have asked, be assured of my forgiveness."

This is the heart of the message and work of Jesus: reaching across chasms of misunderstanding and pain to bring reconciliation and forgiveness. It is this hope—that the wounds of old enmities between peoples may be healed, and that there is the possibility of peace in the midst of the brutality of conflict—that motivates Subha's journeys, through unpredictable military checkpoints and the suffocating heat in packed public transport, to encourage women in Jericho. She is a quiet prophet, a living witness of Jesus in the Holy Land.

UPENDING EMPIRE: THE WITNESS OF RADICAL SERVANTHOOD IN THE EARLY CHURCH

As an agent of the grace and life that is in Jesus, Subha is walking the path first blazed by followers of Jesus from the first century, who sought to take the transforming message of Jesus throughout the Roman Empire. Beginning with a handful of disciples in Jerusalem after the ascension of Christ, it is estimated that by the year 300 C.E., Christians comprised as much as 10 percent of the Roman Empire, or about five million people.[3] Members of the Christian community were found in all strata of society, including the aristocrats, the official court, the army, and among women, although those among the humbler people—slaves, laborers, and tradespeople—predominated.[4]

What characterized this phenomenal advancement was the extraordinary witness of the lives of ordinary disciples who, generally without power or prestige, moved the hearts of the citizens of the Roman Empire.

---

3. Neill, *A History of Christian Missions*, 39. Neill is careful to note that an estimate is unsure as accurate information is lacking, and the presence of Christianity was uneven in various provinces.

4. Harnack, *Mission and Expansion of Christianity*, vol. II, 31.

The historian of Christian mission, Stephen Neill, states that the mission of these early Christians was characterized by radical acts of charitable service: the opening of their homes to travelers; the rescuing of unwanted infants from the public garbage heaps where they were left to die; the care of orphans, widows, and prisoners; and the forming of burial clubs to provide an honorable grave for the impoverished. When the bubonic plague broke out in cities, most citizens would flee to the countryside to escape the pestilence. Christians, on the other hand, *traveled into the suffering cities* to care for the infected and to die by their side.[5]

The strongest acknowledgement of the profound effect of this sacrificial concern for others may be the rather pathetic complaint of the Emperor Julian (332–63 C.E.), who stated:

> Atheism [i.e., Christian faith] has been especially advanced through the loving service rendered to strangers, and through their care for the burial of the dead. It is a scandal that there is not a single Jew who is a beggar and that the godless Galileans care not only for their own poor but for ours as well; while those who belong to us look in vain for the help that we should render them.[6]

Now this is a criticism of which the church could be proud—that it cared for people so much it put an emperor to shame!

The first three centuries were also marked by faithfulness to Christ in the face of persecution. Citizens of the Roman Empire were required to recognize Caesar as the Lord of Lords by burning incense to him. Refusal to do so earned Christians the title of atheists! Polycarp (69–155 C.E.), who was reported to have been a disciple of the Apostle John, was the bishop of Smyrna. He refused to acknowledge Caesar as Lord. Seeking to avoid the guilt of burning an old man at the stake, the Roman centurion assigned to his execution entreated him to only make a small accommodation and then all could happily go home. Polycarp, tied to the stake, responded: "Eighty and six years I have served him. How then can I blaspheme my King and Savior? Bring forth what thou wilt." As the flames engulfed him it is said that he cried out praise to Jesus Christ. The account of the martyrdom of Polycarp became an important part of the writings of the Apostolic Fathers.[7] The martyrdom of good people such as Polycarp wounded the consciences of citizens of the

5. Harnack, *Mission and Expansion of Christianity,* vol. I, 153, quoted in Neill, 37.

6. Neill, *History of Christian Missions,* 38.

7. Bruce, *The Spreading Flame,* 174, as quoted in Tucker, *From Jerusalem to Irian Jaya,* 30–32.

Empire and drew so many to Christ that Tertullian (160–225 C.E.) said, "The blood of the martyrs is the seed of the church."[8]

THE DYNAMIC GROWTH OF THE GLOBAL CHRISTIAN MOVEMENT TODAY

In light of this radical service, and in spite of the early Church's weaknesses, it is no wonder that the followers of Jesus shook the Roman Empire! But we shouldn't waste time moaning about not living in the bygone era of *real* Christianity. Today the global Christian movement is profoundly vital. As in the first three centuries, so in our day, Christianity globally is experiencing unusual numerical growth. Cities and regions that for centuries stubbornly resisted the efforts of Western missionaries are now home to rapidly growing Christian communities. In 1970, there were about three million Chinese Christians; today the World Council of Churches estimates that there are 130 million.[9] There are more Christians today in China than in all the European nations combined. In Sub-Saharan Africa in 1910, Christians comprised about 9 percent of the population; today the Christian community has grown to 63 percent of the same population.[10] There are more Christians in Nigeria—eighty million—than in Germany, the historic seat of Protestantism!

The growth of the Christian movement in the non-Western world has been so significant that sometime in the later part of the twentieth century an unheralded, but profound, shift occurred: the numerical base of Christianity moved from the West to the non-Western world. Today more Christians are found *outside the West* than within it. Consider this: in 1900, less than 10 percent of all the Christians in the world were found *outside* of the West. By contrast, remarkably, by the year 2000 almost 70 percent of the world's Christians were non-Western,[11] therefore the term majority world Christians.

Certainly, the growth of world Christianity has been the outcome of the globalization of Christian mission. From the beginning of both European exploration and mission in the fifteenth century and of the modern Protestant mission era at the end of the eighteenth century, Christian

8. Bainton, *Early Christianity*, 26.

9. Samuel, "Church in China Experiencing Explosive Growth."

10. Pew Research Center, "Global Christianity."

11. Wright, "An Upside Down World."

mission has been a predominantly Western enterprise. As the catchphrase states, mission has historically been "from the West to the rest." Today, mission is increasingly a global movement of grassroots servant messengers. As the Peruvian mission leader Samuel Escobar asserts, mission is now from "everywhere to everywhere."[12] These majority world sisters and brothers are sending out mission servants from their churches in Bangkok, Seoul, and Lagos—and in Jerusalem, Ramallah, and Bethlehem. They are pointing to the reality of life in the way of Jesus with their unique voices. As in the case of Subha in Jericho, their efforts are appreciated by their neighbors, with whom they share the same disappointments and struggles of life on the bottom of the heap. Their acts of service, offered out of weakness instead of strength, from below instead of above, are liberating and enabling, rather than manipulative and debilitating.

As scripture is read and understood from the context of the reader, these new participants in global mission are bringing fresh perspectives to the reading of scripture. Not having been hamstrung by theology that is either molded by, or in reaction to Enlightenment rationalism, which robbed much of the church in the West of its confidence in scripture, they are able to more readily accept the miraculous works of Jesus, the reality of spiritual battle with demonic powers, and the presence of the Spirit of God with power in the church today. They can appreciate Jesus's exhortation to prayer, because prayer has often been their only hope for healing, for food on the table, for a future for their children, or for a roof over their heads. More importantly, as men and women who have often known the pain of deprivation, the fear of war, the ravages of illness without access to remedy, they read the Gospels of Jesus with empathy for the weak. They understand what it means to be among "the least," whom Jesus called his brothers (Matt 27:40).

Besides the effectiveness of their service resulting from the identification of majority world Christians with their neighbors, it is important to acknowledge that God specializes in showing himself mighty through the sister or brother who is without reputation, wealth, or education. As Paul wrote:

> For consider your calling, brethren, that there were not many wise according to the flesh, not many mighty, not many noble; but God has chosen the foolish things of the world to shame the wise, and God has chosen the weak things of the world to shame the things which are strong, and the base things of the world and the despised God has chosen, the things that are not, so that He may

12. Escobar, *New Global Mission*, 18.

nullify the things that are, so that no man may boast before God.
(1 Cor 1:26–29)

Paul's words perfectly describe a unique pastor who is a friend in northern India, and a faithful servant of the very poor in Manila.

BROTHER TONY

Augustus Anthony, or Brother Tony as he is known, was raised in deepest poverty in Lucknow, the capitol of the state of Uttar Pradesh in northern India. Tony and his mother and brothers and sisters were abandoned by their father when Tony was a child. Tony remembers that his mother had to sell all their furniture for food. They were reduced to living on a rooftop. Under the intense heat of the Indian summer, Tony's mother would hang a wet rag over them for shade. Several times an hour she would douse the rag so they could gain some faint relief from the blistering heat.

As a young man, Tony had a vision of Christ on the cross, who spoke to him and said, "I have done this for you. What will you do for me?" He began preaching in the streets and fields where workers were bent under their labor. Tony describes being laughed out of several churches when, as a shoeless teenager, he stated his intention to become a pastor. At the time in early 1982 that I first visited Tony in India he had become the pastor of a small Pentecostal church in an obscure suburb of Lucknow. There he started a small Bible college with about ten students, whom he mentored as his sons. Today, Tony oversees more than 500 daughter congregations that have been planted by his students. This is entirely an Indian-led movement that is sustained by the unshakeable confidence that an encounter with the love of Jesus will transform any life, and that servanthood is the way of Christ. I recall that when his church would cook huge vats of curry for large gatherings, it would be Tony who was sweating over the fires, stirring the delicious concoction. He taught the young men in his college that a leader unwilling to push a broom was unqualified to lead.

LOVE FOR THE FORGOTTEN

In Manila, the Philippines, where American missions have had a long and, at times, suffocating presence, Lyn, a Filipina and a registered nurse, was a member of an Evangelical Filipino congregation of which I had the joy of being a part. She had a concern for the desperately poor families that live along the railroad tracks that pass through the center of the city. Life along the tracks is a human drama. People conduct their business, bathe, and just relax on the active tracks, the *riles* (pronounced *reelays*) in Tagalog. When the trains come through, everyone scurries into their shanties, built just inches from the tracks.

Beginning with a Bible study in a shanty made of scavenged tin, plastic, cardboard, and bamboo, Lyn nurtured her disciples, many of whom could not read, into a vital congregation, which subsequently has established several more congregations.[13] One of the first to the come to the Lord was a young man and his wife, Anthony and Rose, who lived *under* their parent's shanty in a crawl space that was only a meter high. Most of Lyn's outreach workers have come out of the railroad track shanty community. Today, one of their outreach ministries meets in an abandoned sepulcher where it serves those who live in Manila's largest cemetery! Life flows from this fellowship into regular prison ministry, health clinics, and a pre-school for kids with a daily feeding program, and more. From its simple beginnings the congregation has become a fount of life. Lyn describes how they stress the Filipino value of *bayanihan*, or communal cooperation. She says, "Paul's exhortation to 'bear one another's burdens' might has well have been written about Filipinos. For example, the brothers and sisters will stay up late into the night praying together to console a bereaved member of the community."[14]

THE END OF WESTERN MISSION?

An obvious question arises: if Christianity has become a global movement, is mission from the West now obsolete? There have been several responses to this challenge. First, for churches that started down the path of pluralism decades ago, mission as evangelism—and, indeed, for some in this stream, mission of any kind—has been abandoned as colonial and irrelevant. From this pluralistic perspective, all religions provide a legitimate expression of spiritual longing for knowledge of God and for a way to eternity. If some confidence remains in Christianity, it is no longer the role of the West to

13. Ideas in this section about Manila were first presented in a paper by the author entitled "A Profile of Harvesters Christian Fellowship Tondo."

14. Sylvano, interview with Andrew Bush.

communicate its message. To such Christians, missionaries are an embarrassing colonial throwback.

Second, some majority-world Christians, reacting to the long dominant presence of Western missionaries, have argued that the best thing for the continued growth of the global Christian movement would be for Western missionaries to go home and for Western mission to impose a moratorium on its work in non-Western contexts. A Nigerian pastor, speaking to a class of mission students I was leading in America forcefully stated: "We don't need your missionaries. Our churches are growing faster than yours."

A third response is to act as if nothing has changed, that the urgency of the call overrides an informed response to the implications of the global shift of Christianity. Indeed, for many local congregations, the rise of the global church has yet to become a significant fact for consideration.

A more nuanced conclusion is needed. Majority-world mission leaders recognize that the deep brokenness of the world—brutal ethnic wars, pandemic illnesses, the hard yoke of poverty, human trafficking, the scarcity of fresh water for millions, environmental destruction, and the fact that still more than two billion people have not been introduced to the message of Jesus—demands the response of the global church working in a new global partnership, not in segregated factionalism. The idea that the Western church and its missionaries, but not their financial resources, should stay home merely perpetuates old forms of Western control that are part of the problem.

This new global mission will require major adjustments on the part of Western Christians. Old patterns of Western dominance will not be tolerated. The challenge for Western mission in all its expressions is to find a new way of walking alongside brothers and sisters in the majority world. Long in the driver's seat, Western mission must adopt a role that has never been a comfortable one, to be a servant alongside—and serving from below—national leaders such as Subha, Tony, and Lyn: to be recipients, as well as givers, of ministry. The great difficulty is that Western Christianity, and consequently its mission, has been molded by a long and deep Western cultural tradition of privilege, dominance, and triumph. Even when its intentions are the best, it often conducts itself with assumed privilege. In contrast to Subha's humility, consider another encounter in the Jordan River valley which illustrates this.

ANOTHER CHRISTIAN IN THE JORDAN VALLEY

It was a fun day for an evangelical congregation of Palestinian Christians from the Old City of Jerusalem. With lunches packed, the congregation crowded into a chartered bus and headed down the twisting roads through the desert toward Jericho. Their destination was a shaded spot by the side of the Jordan River, a few kilometers south of the Lake of Galilee, where several members of the congregation would be baptized.

Arriving at the river, those who would be submerged in the Jordan's waters put on bathing suits and long white robes. There were some convenient concrete steps built into the river banks. Benches and a small ledge next to the water's edge had been constructed to facilitate the many pilgrims who came to this spot to be baptized. The fifty or so members of the church gathered on the river bank, the baptismal candidates in the seats of honor. This was an important event. Palestinian Christians have been pouring out of Israel and Palestinian for decades, emigrating to other countries. They are dissuaded from building their future in this torn land by the never ending conflict with Israel and their increasing marginalization in a Muslim majority society. So, this baptism, with its dozen Palestinian Christians, represented no less than the hope for the future of Christianity in the land.

With prayers and songs of praise, one by one the believers made their way into the waters of the Jordan. As the celebration proceeded, a tour bus pulled up in a cloud of dust. A large group of Americans emerged. Their leader, a bearish man, red in the face and perspiring in the heat, walked briskly over to where the Palestinian baptism was underway. He scowled and said aloud in the general direction of the Palestinians seated on the shore, "What's going on here?" Nonplussed, those who heard him did not know how to respond. It seemed obvious what was going on. No one turned his way, so I volunteered that it was a baptism of Palestinian Christians. Turning, he stomped back to his bus and conferred with his group. They went over to another baptism spot by the river ten meters downstream. There were built in concrete steps to the river there also, but the location was not as thoroughly developed.

I noticed that he kept glancing our way with frustration. He had obviously intended to bring his group to our spot. Again he walked toward the Palestinian worshipers. To no one in particular and all in general, he muttered, "Our church paid for this, you know," pivoted, and stomped away. It was a stunningly ugly encounter. Thankfully, most had not noticed. I was left shaken.

Taking this man at face value, his church had funded the concrete steps and benches at this place in the river where perhaps Jesus himself had been baptized. For that effort he apparently had a sense of entitlement and a disregard for the most significant act in the Christian faith, which non-Western Christians were performing right in front of him.

It is unfair to hang too much significance on one loutish fellow's behavior, but it can stand as a metaphor for troubling historic trends in Western mission. This broad characterization certainly does not give credit to Western missionaries who serve selflessly and are beloved by their national coworkers. It does, however, symbolically highlight the fact that Western mission must adjust to new global realities.

These two portraits—of Subha, and of a misdirected American—contrast simplicity versus wealth and abundance, vulnerability versus strength and influence, and humility in contrast to arrogance. They speak not so much to the need for new mission strategies and structures—new "roles," new "partnership," etc.—though these are certainly relevant, but, rather, to the need for a new spirituality for mission. The wide gulf between an ethos of power that has characterized Western Christianity and much of its mission, and an ethos of lowliness and servanthood, is so vast that the formation of a deeper unity in the global church will require a profound spiritual renewal that can overcome historic trends.

THE DIVERGING ROADS OF WESTERN CHRISTIANITY

This discontinuity that exists between Western and majority world Christians is not a recent one in Christianity. Throughout church history, Christians have gravitated toward different spiritual paradigms: the emphasis of power, privilege, and force on one hand, and the meekness, simplicity and mercy of Christ on the other. Of course, there has been an intermingling of these paradigmatic trends in Christian history, including some acknowledgement on the part of triumphal Christianity of the prophetic voices on its margins; nevertheless, historic trends are obvious. The remarkable spirituality that characterized the early church would be challenged by an ethos of power, which would intrude into the church with the conversion of the Roman Emperor Constantine and his decision to make Christianity the official religion of the Empire. As a result, a major shift occurred in Christianity's understanding of what it should be in this world. From that time forward there would be diverging paths in the Christian world.

To understand how thoroughly this shift has affected Christianity, and even now affects the challenge Western Christianity faces in finding a way forward in global mission, it is helpful to briefly sketch a few high—or low—points in its development, beginning with the fourth century purported conversion of the Roman general who would be emperor, Constantine. Before the crucial Battle of the Milvian Bridge north of Rome in 312 C.E. that would consolidate his rule, tradition has it that Constantine had a dream in which he saw the image of the initial letters of Christ's name with the words, "In this sign conquer."[15] Constantine is said to have converted to Christianity at that time, though he wouldn't be baptized until his death approached in 337 C.E. In response to his vision, he had the symbol of the initial letters of Christ's name painted on the helmets and shields of his soldiers, who then proved victorious in battle.[16]

Constantine would consequently issue the Edict of Milan in 313 C.E., officially granting full freedom to Christianity, and restoring property to Christians that had been confiscated during the persecution of the emperor Diocletian. Constantine's conversion would lead to Trinitarian Christianity being declared the official religion of the Roman Empire in 380 C.E., by the Emperor Theodosius I.[17]

The radical transition from being a persecuted minority to an empowered faith that was endorsed by the power of the Roman Empire has been termed the "Constantinian shift." Mennonite scholar John Yoder writes, "The most impressive transitory change underlying our common experience, one that some thought was a permanent lunge forward in salvation history, was the so-called Constantinian shift."[18] From the fourth century onward, all Christian traditions—Orthodox, Roman Catholic, and Protestant—would become entangled with the machinations of civil governments and with the problem of alliance with power.[19]

Henceforth, it would be difficult for Christian mission to escape the influences of agents of power. Mission scholar Don McCurry states, "From that time forward, Christianity has been compromised with various levels

---

15. Walker, *A History of the Christian Church*, 101.

16. Ibid., 110.

17. Ibid., 117–18.

18. Yoder, "Is There Such a Thing as Being Ready for Another Millennium?," 65.

19. This is not to overlook that during the first three centuries there were developments in the Christian world that betrayed its foundational values, especially the rise of anti-Semitism.

of entanglement with empire, and plagued by those who have failed to distinguish the secular realm from the spiritual, who have used force to defend their faith, or promote it, as a banner under which to wage its unholy wars."[20]

The culture of Christianity shifted from the margins to the mainstream. Christianity became associated with ruling power, which inevitably led to an abandoning of its pacifist stance and a too easy acquiescence to the use of force by the state.[21] Christianity in too many ways became characterized by the power of Constantine instead of the powerlessness of the crucifixion of Christ. Such a "Constantinian Christianity" revels in being granted a favored place in society as a result of a mutually self-serving relationship with the governing powers. Such Christianity advances its mission by the use of the many levers of power at its disposal.

For those Christians in the fourth century who were experiencing a relief from persecution and confiscation of their property, this shift must have been understood as answered prayer. The implications of cultural trends are difficult to discern when one is in the midst of the shifting tides of history. Aligning itself with power would gradually obscure the spirituality that had caused the Christian movement to expand explosively in the first three centuries after Christ. But at the time, Christians praised God for their good fortune.

Metaphorically, the Church of the Nativity in Bethlehem, today in Palestinian West Bank, is a powerful symbol of the corruption of Christian spirituality. The first basilica was constructed from 327–333 C.E. under the direction of Helena, the mother of Constantine, over the cave that had traditionally been regarded as the site of the birth of Christ. After its destruction, it was rebuilt in 529 C.E. under the Roman Emperor Justinian, with massive pillars lining the nave. Erected to commemorate the most radical act of weakness, Christ's incarnation in the frailty of infancy, the church's architectural motif is a statement of imperial power.

In spite of this co-opting of Christianity by imperial power, there were unlikely voices on the margins—as there would be until the present, such as the most unlikely prophets of peace in the Middle East, Palestinian Christians—who sought to call Christianity back to its foundations in Christ.

20. McCurry, "Islam and Christian Militarism."

21. Roland Bainton observes that the pacifism of early Christianity was abandoned with this shift in orientation toward power. He states, "The accession of Constantine terminated the pacifist period in church history." See Bainton, *Christian Attitudes Toward War and Peace*, 85.

While Christianity was merging with power, some Christians were disappearing into the desert to "die" for Christ through radical self-denial while still in this life. Following the pioneering example of Anthony in the Egyptian desert in the end of the third century, thousands of men and women lived as hermits in the desert barrenness.

Devoting their lives to prayer, the Desert Fathers and Mothers' radical self-denial was an act of service to the wider church in its reminder of the simplicity of Christ. Their spirituality of quiet, solitary prayer was a stark contrast to the Christianity in Rome, the public worship of which was beginning to resemble Roman civil functions. That they were a voice on the margin, a witness that to many was incomprehensible, is expressed in the saying of Anthony: "A time is coming when men will go mad, and when they see someone who is not mad, they will attack him saying, 'You are mad; you are not like us.'"[22]

CHARLEMAGNE AND CELTIC MONKS

The ethos of Constantinian Christianity was vigorously reinforced and advanced through the Middle Ages. A few low points along this dismal journey include Charlemagne's joining of the sword and Christian mission, and the nadir of Christian history, the Crusades against Islamic rule in Jerusalem and the Holy Land.

Charles the Great, or Charlemagne (742–814 C.E.), one of the most influential people in the history of Christianity, was a Frankish (Germanic) king who was installed by Pope Leo III as the emperor of the Holy Roman Empire on Christmas day in 800 C.E. in the Old Saint Peter's Basilica in Rome, which had been built appropriately by Constantine.[23] He consolidated power and advanced Christianity with the sword, forcibly Christianizing the Saxons (Germanic tribes to the east of the Franks). It is said that in one day he slaughtered 4,500 Saxons.[24] Under the territory he governed, he sought to strengthen the cause of Christianity by advancing theological learning and putting order in the churches. Nevertheless, by forcing the Christianization of those who were defeated in war, an "association of the new religion with

---

22. *The Sayings of the Desert Fathers*, 6.
23. Noll, *Turning Points*, 118.
24. Neill, *A History of Christian Missions*, 68.

the conquering power that could only be dangerous" was formed.[25] Certainly, this reinforced the alliance of Christian mission with militarism.[26]

While Christianity was advancing by force in Europe, other strange Christians were building primitive retreats on the most remote islands off the coast of Ireland. Following the example of the Desert Fathers and Mothers, Celtic monasticism sought to follow Christ to the ends of the earth, and there devote itself to prayer. Celtic monasticism would grow into one of the most dynamic mission movements in history. A missional monasticism was developed in which groups of monks were sent out from an established monastery to new areas where they founded new communities. There they would farm alongside the local people, provide education, and call them to Christ. When their numbers increased, another group would be sent out to repeat the pattern, ultimately reaching the European mainland. Celtic Christianity has left a legacy of vibrant spirituality marked by a unique reverence for the created world, contemplative prayer, art, and the journey of faith.

THE CRUSADES AND FRANCIS OF ASSISI

First launched by Pope Urban II in 1095 to reclaim Jerusalem and the Holy Land from Muslim rule (as well as to reduce tensions between local princes in Europe and help the Eastern church in Constantinople), crusaders with the cross on their shields left a bloody path of destruction. In their fervency to advance their cause, they destroyed anything that was foreign to them or not part of their effort. They slaughtered European Jews, Orthodox Christians in the East, and Arab Christians in the Holy Land. The slaughter of Muslims in Jerusalem was most beastly. Tamim Ansary writes, "Upon securing the city, the Franj (crusaders) indulged in an orgy of bloodletting so drastic it made all the previous carnage seem mild. One crusader, writing about the triumph, described piling up heads, hands, and feet in the streets. (He called it a 'wonderful sight.') He spoke of crusaders riding through heathen blood up to their knees and bridle reins."[27]

---

25. Ibid.

26. As Noll states, "The Christendom of the European Middle Ages affected the practice of the Christian faith in every way. The 'medieval synthesis,' as it is sometimes called, harmonized (at least in theory) what we today regard as separate sacred and secular spheres of life." In Noll, *Turning Points*, 114.

27. Ansary, *Destiny Disrupted*, 140. Ansary cites Maalouf, *The Crusades Through*

In spite of their first victory, the crusading enterprise was ultimately defeated. Intended to defeat the Saracens, or Muslims, these wars were a disaster for Christianity, coarsening its ethical life, profoundly severing the relationship of Western and Eastern Christianity, and wounding its relationship with the Muslim world. Today many Muslims still use the Arabic term *salibiin*, "people of the cross," or crusaders, to describe Christians. Tragically, the cross of Christ is viewed by many Muslims through the perspective of this bloody debacle.

The Crusades were the ultimate perverse merging of worldly force and Christian spirituality. To motivate noblemen to fight in the crusading armies, a religious order, the Knights Templar, was formed. A crusader in this order would spend hours in spiritual reflection, like any monastic brother, and then either prepare for, or engage in, combat. He could, as it has been described, cut off his enemy's head and shout *hallelujah* at the same time! Joining the crusading army was also an act of penance. One's sins could be forgiven by going to battle.

During the twelfth century, when the collective European cultural consensus was that the only good Muslim was a dead one, another peculiar person came onto the scene, Francis of Assisi (1181–1226 C.E.), who stood in opposition to violent Christianity and insisted that this was *not* the way of Christ. A too rarely known fact of his life was that during this crusading era, he made it his life's goal to take the gospel of grace in Christ to the Muslim world. After two failed attempts he reached the military camp of the Sultan of the Muslim armies, where he brought the message of God's love and forgiveness. He wanted to be martyred to communicate Christ's love, but the Sultan, not wanting this good man's blood on his hands, sent him back to Europe.[28] The example of Francis continues to be relevant today, challenging the current of Islamophobia in the West and especially in Western Christianity. At the same time, his witness challenges the Western Christian crusader approach to the Holy Land today, which sanctions the taking of land by force, an example of Constantinian Christianity that is alive and well in Western Evangelical mission, and which will be discussed at length in chapter six.

Arab Eyes, 38–40.

28. For a fuller description of Francis of Assisi's ministry among Muslims in North Africa at the height of the Crusades, see Mallouhi, *Waging Peace on Islam*, 263–87.

CONQUISTADORS AND DE LAS CASAS

The ferociousness of the Crusades would be continued in the struggle to rid the Iberian Peninsula from Muslim rule, which was achieved in 1492. The European age of exploration and the colonial expansion of the *conquistadores* planted the cross in the New World and Asia, particularly the Philippines, with the same crusading zeal, leaving enslaved indigenous people and societies destroyed in their wake. The callousness of this expansion can be understood as a frantic attempt of European Christianity to out-flank Islam, which had dominated trade routes to Asia for seven centuries.

In the New World, one of the most odious practices of the colonizers was the *encomienda* system.[29] This was a policy that was utilized by the Spanish crown throughout the colonization of the Americas. It entrusted a certain number of indigenous people to the "care" of an *encomendero*, or colonist, in exchange for labor. This care was meant to include protection from other tribes and the instruction in the Roman Catholic faith. In practice it was systematized and brutal slavery.

Bartholomé de Las Casas (1484–1566) was himself an *encomendero* in Hispaniola, or Cuba, who participated in the oppression of the indigenous people. At the age of thirty, he experienced a spiritual conversion and entered the Roman Catholic priesthood. Even as a priest, however, he continued in the lifestyle of a privileged colonist. It was the preaching of the Dominican brothers, who were protesting the treatment of the indigenous people, which finally troubled his conscience. In 1514 he was deeply convicted by the condition of the victims of the *encomienda* system. He resolved to dedicate his life to working for justice for the indigenous people in the New World. Becoming a Dominican brother, he labored to overturn the *encomienda*. For Las Casas "the oppression of the Indian 'is contrary to the intention of Jesus Christ and the way of love with which he charged us in the gospel.'"[30] His treatise, *A Short Account of the Destruction of the Indies*, portrayed the brutal treatment of the indigenous people.[31] This is perhaps the first essay on behalf of the indigenous people in the New World, and an eloquent description of the effect on the latter of annihilating European am-

---

29 From the Spanish verb *encomendar,* to entrust.

30. Bartholomé de Las Casas, *Historia de las Indias*, as quoted in Gutierrez, *Las Casas*, 314.

31. Gutierrez, *Las Casas*, 194.

bition. Las Casas chose the way of protest against power. And he was heard. He was partially responsible for the New Laws of 1542 instituted by Charles V of Spain, which began to limit the *encomienda,* though they would be bitterly opposed by the colonialists, and partially overturned.[32] Returning to Spain, Las Casas continued his efforts for justice until his death at eighty-two years of age. Las Casas, in abandoning his privileged status as colonist and identifying with the outcast, the weak, and the despised, is one of the great voices for justice for the powerless in mission history. Further, Las Casas is an example of one who escaped the entrapment of his own cultural context, living out Paul's exhortation to "not be conformed to this world, but be transformed by the renewing of your mind, so that you may prove what the will of God is, that which is good and acceptable and perfect" (Rom 12:2). The path he blazed is a challenge still to Western Christianity, which often confuses alliances with agents of power with the true power of God that perfects itself in weakness.

PROTESTANT CONSTANTINIANISM
AND PROTESTING VOICES

Protestants have usually explained the warped militaristic and triumphal Christianity of Charlemagne, the Crusades, and the New World Spanish and Portuguese colonialism by arguing that, of course, it was corrupt, it was derived from an aberrant, unbiblical Christian faith. According to this reasoning, the nominally Christian Roman Catholic community drifted from the true way of Christ because it lacked both the energizing presence of Jesus through the Spirit and the correcting influence of a proper reading of scripture. However, Protestant Christians have had a huge blind spot concerning their own enthusiastic embrace of power and the consequent violent and oppressive outcome.

Most pertinent to this discussion of Western Christianity and the challenge it faces in finding a new way to walk with majority world sisters and brothers is the re-emerging of the Constantinian Christian paradigm in America, and the example of those brave souls who have tried to walk the way of the cross, going against the flow of the prevailing trends in Christendom.

The Puritan leader John Winthrop had a vision of America as the New Israel, a shining "city set upon a hill," with a call to show forth the light

32. Ibid., 316–17.

of truth to the nations. This image of a nation established by God with a divinely ordained destiny has become central to the narrative and identity of the Unites States.

There are great dangers in this national self-identity. The absolute certainty of divine purpose easily leads to the slippery slope of the use of force and the toleration of oppression if they seem to advance the cause of Christianity. Indeed, the Puritan colonies would quickly become intolerant and exclusive. Codifying the way of Christ to govern a community proved more difficult than those who first envisioned the possibility of a Christian nation had expected.

Native Americans would become the first victims of the colonists' ambitions to grasp more land, in spite of the fact that the rationale for the formation of several colonies was the evangelization of the indigenous people. The efforts of those such as John Eliot (1604–1690 C.E.) in Massachusetts, who labored for decades among the Algonquin people, and David Brainerd (1718–1747 C.E.) in New Jersey, sought to insure that Native Americans were justly treated and their land secured. Tragically, however, in a pattern that would be frequently repeated, advances of the Christian faith among Native Americans would be undermined by the theft of their land by the colonists and the actions of the United States government. Several hundred years later the political/theological idea of "manifest destiny" legitimized the Western expansion of the American colonies at the expense of the brutal genocide of the Native American people.[33] Remarkably, the same argument for the expansion of this "New Israel" in the New World are similar to those used by some evangelical Christians today to justify the expansionist policies of the modern State of Israel. The argument in both cases is that this is God's will—and both cases have wreaked havoc on a weaker indigenous people. As this book will argue, the renewal of Western mission will be to a large extent dependent on the degree to which it challenges this and other oppressive conceptions of God's will within its own circles.

From early American history, the economy of the colonies was undergirded by the forced labor of slaves. Perhaps as much as 15 percent of the more than 600,000 African slaves dragged in chains to America were

33. The term "manifest destiny," coined by journalist John L. Sullivan of *The New York Times*, thrilled the American imagination. As the historian Daniel Boorstin in *A History of the United* States, 247, observes: "It was an up-to-date, expanded 1800s-version of an old American refrain. The Puritan City of God, their 'City upon a hill,' was transformed into a continental Empire for Liberty. Both would be beacons for the world."

Muslim. That Muslim slaves were a factor in building the early American economy is a sobering fact, linking America to the Muslim world in a way that few are aware. Later, after the Emancipation Act of 1863, which freed all slaves, and the passing of the Thirteenth Amendment to the United States Constitution, which made slavery against the law, the tyranny of unjust Jim Crow laws that relegated African Americans to a second class status was justified with scripture by some Bible-believing Christians. (They referred to such texts as Genesis 9:25.)

During the civil rights movement, which strove to overturn the injustices of Jim Crow in the 1950s and 1960s, evangelical Christians were some of the *last* to support calls for justice. Nevertheless, there were courageous Christian voices in the South that were speaking up, calling for a new way of living together guided by the values of Christ. The Koinonia Farm was founded in 1942 in Sumter County, Georgia by two couples, Clarence and Florence Jordan and Martin and Mabel England. Their goal was to develop a "demonstration plot of the Kingdom of God," where whites and blacks could live and work together in a spirit of brotherhood.[34]

This was a direct challenge to Jim Crow-era Georgia. Even though Koinonia Farm suffered violent attacks by white supremacists, it maintained its witness of nonviolence and reconciliation. Clarence Jordan spoke widely in churches throughout the country during those years and is well known for writing *The Cotton Patch Gospel*, which presented scripture in the colloquial language of rural Georgia.[35] Koinonia Farm was a prophetic voice to a malformed Christian society in the American South.

Even with the passage of only a few decades it is convenient to assume that we know better today. But there is no evidence that we do. Many Christians are vexed by the ebbing presence of Christianity in the civil sphere: prayer eliminated from schools, statements of faith banned in high school graduation ceremonies, and Christmas nativity scenes removed from the lawns of courthouses.

What is actually being dismantled is the structure of Constantinian Christianity. American society is gradually withdrawing the *carte blanche* privileges that the Christian church has enjoyed. As Darrell Guder states in his important book *The Missional Church*, American Christianity is transitioning into a post-Constantinian era. He writes:

34. "Koinonia Partners."
35. Jordan, *The Cotton Patch Gospel*.

On the other hand, while modern missions have led to an expansion of world Christianity, Christianity in America has moved (or been moved) away from its position of dominance as it has experienced the loss not only of numbers but of power and influence within society.[36]

That this is judged as a loss testifies to the degree to which the merging of Christian faith and privileges of power is viewed as essential to being a Christian nation. The response to this loss has included a frantic attempt to find new methods and programs to generate more numbers, but Guder observes that, as with Western mission, the American church cannot move forward by trying new techniques, but only by a deep spiritual renewal.[37] Similarly, others see in the dismantling of Constantinian Christianity an opportunity for the Christian community to reacquaint itself with the core values of its faith and to become truly missional by walking in humility and service toward wider society.

TRIUMPHALISM AND ATTEMPTS TO RENEW WESTERN MISSION

How has this long history of Western Christianity's embrace of power and privilege affected Western Protestant Christian mission? After the entrance into global missions of Western Protestantism at the end of the eighteenth century, missions would be dominated by the primarily English-speaking West for the next two hundred years. The missionaries and the mission agencies they represented exercised inordinate control of the national churches, mission schools, and hospitals that they regarded as theirs. National leaders were frequently treated patronizingly by their Western mentors.

In the present, Samuel Escobar has argued against the overreaching of Western mission strategists who seek to map out a strategy for evangelization of the world. To impose upon the world a global strategy that was largely conceived in America seems presumptuous at best. He has referred to the use of Western corporate strategies to plan the mission of God as "managerial missions." Escobar maintains that the association of Western mission with some agent of power, in this case corporate structures, has been a trend throughout Western mission history.[38]

36. Guder, *Missional Church*, 1.

37. Ibid., 3.

38. Escobar, *New Global Mission*, 26.

Besides the influence of career or longer-term missionaries and their related agencies and institutions, Western influence in majority world Christian communities is extended through countless short-term missions trips, which can have a tourist-like quality, reducing majority world Christians to objects of curiosity, and subjecting them to the inordinate influence of highly produced Western praise and worship music, as well as an unending flow of American evangelists, conference speakers, and the like who present themselves as experts of the latest trend in church growth, evangelism, worship, or discipleship. For years I watched firsthand the demoralizing effect this wave of Western mission presence had on Filipino Christians in Manila, inevitably leaving them feeling inadequate and less confident to discover their own authenticity in Christ. The Korean American theologian and pastor Soong-Chan Rah argues that evangelicalism internationally and at home has been held in captivity to the Western church.[39]

Returning to the question of how Western mission can find its place in an era of globalized Christianity, it is obvious that overcoming its historic orientation toward power and primacy will require, as I have mentioned, something more than learning innovative mission strategies, or generating revised agendas. The roots of Western Christian triumphalism are deep. A proper renewal will require a spiritual reorientation of such vigor that it will have sufficient vitality to overcome the influence of long entrenched cultural norms. It will necessitate an immersion in the radical way of Christ Jesus. Essentially, it will demand a reacquaintance with the way of the cross.

Spirituality has been a neglected stepchild in missiology, a trend which fortunately has recently begun to be remedied. There has been some quiet acknowledgement and reflection on spirituality for mission in the background of mission studies, but the focus of discussion in evangelical mission during the last several decades has emphasized practical topics such as missional strategies to reach all "unreached" peoples, the role of culture and contextualization in mission, and the relationship of evangelism and social responsibility, among other things. There has been a certain technocratic slant in evangelical missiology. It apparently has been assumed that as missionaries worked through cultural and strategic issues, they would simply be good Christians, praying and reading the Bible.

The limited reflection on spirituality and mission has not probed sufficiently important questions that would provide an opportunity for renewal. More probing questions might include: What does it mean to be spiritual as an earthly human being? If, as Paul stated, God's power is completed in

39. Rah, *The Next Evangelicalism*, 22.

weakness, what does it mean to become weak? Is weakness intentionally chosen, or is it merely a circumstantial phenomenon? How can spirituality be emptied of an ethos of power? How can spirituality rise above the pervasive influence of culture? As we are not only ethnocentric, but also "spiritual-centric" people, how can we gain some perspective on our spiritual journeys? What are the essential aspects of a spirituality for mission?

LEARNING FROM THE LEAST
OF THESE WE HAVE WOUNDED

A renewed spirituality will necessitate a deeper encounter with Christ. However, when even our devotions and how we understand Christ are affected by pervasive cultural traditions, where shall we turn? Western mission can learn from the least, from those who have always been on the bottom of the heap, who have never triumphed in this world. We can learn from majority world Christians who intentionally have chosen the way of Christ in lowliness and service, instead of the way of worldly power. This journey could include listening to women who have escaped the Western driven sex trade in Bangkok, or hearing the testimonies of Chinese believers in their house churches in Guangzhou, or walking with rural evangelists in Malawi.

It is unhealthy to idolize majority world Christians. Their churches have many of the same problems as churches in Boston, Miami, or Los Angeles. Yet, their life on the margins holds potential for unique insights into the way of Christ, for a glimpse of the character of the Christian community before Constantine's deadly embrace.

And among those on the margins whose voices we must learn to hear and value, perhaps it is those who have been—and still are being—most deeply wounded by Western mission whom we must first seek out. At the head of this list could certainly be the Arab Christians of the Middle East, and especially Palestinian Christians who live in the West Bank and Gaza. Historically they were some of the first to experience the negative effect of the Roman Empire's embrace of Christianity, which alienated them from their non-Christian fellow citizens. They have suffered the brutality of the Crusades, and the imperiousness of modern Western mission that has been largely ignorant of the contribution of Arab Christians throughout Christian history. Further, they are being wounded by the contemporary Crusade-like theology of some Western Christians whose unqualified support of Israel is openly antagonistic to Palestinians, and the wider Arab and Muslim community.

The fact that Christians have injured the Palestinian people is easily discerned if we are willing to listen. I recall the words of Munir, a Palestinian Christian engineering student at Bir Zeit University on the West Bank. It was a cold February day; students were crowding into the university cafeteria. I was having coffee with Munir. He was worried about something, just fidgeting with his cup. The Intifada was raging, reducing Israel and Palestine to a war zone. During that time, conversations among students typically turned to the road closures, as they worried whether they would be able to travel to their homes. I expected this was on Munir's mind, but then he opened up: "Andrew, why do American Christians hate us?"

Mission cannot go much further wrong than to convey hate to an already suffering people! If the idea of learning from Palestinians is a shock, it is the kind of redemptive shock that Jesus intended in the parable of the Good Samaritan, one that jerks us into a startling perspective. A pastor who visited me on the West Bank for three days said of his brief experience of fellowship with Palestinian Christians and Muslims and their families that it had completely changed his life. Listening to the voices of Palestinian Christians about their journey is not meant to provide a comprehensive reflection on spirituality for mission. They are just one witness, although a most relevant one, providing a source for reflection on some of Western mission's weakest aspects.

Certainly, in considering the renewal of mission, it is reasonable to turn toward the land of the passion of the crucifixion of Christ. It was at the foot of the cross that the first confession of faith was heard, a harbinger of those who also would be drawn by the love of God revealed in the terrible suffering of Jesus. The callous Roman centurion cried, "Truly this man was the Son of God!" (Mark 15:39b).

It was in that land that the lives of Palestinian brothers and sisters would help me know the love of Jesus more deeply. And none too soon, as the currents of hatred that flow through the Holy Land threatened to drag me under their dark waters.

2

Surprised by Palestine

But in all things we commend ourselves as ministers of God: in much patience, in tribulations, in needs, in distresses, in stripes, in imprisonments,
in tumults, in labors, in sleeplessness, in fastings; by purity, by knowledge, by
longsuffering, by kindness, by the Holy Spirit, by sincere love, by the word of
truth, by the power of God, by the armor of righteousness on the right hand
and on the left, by honor and dishonor, by evil report and good report; as
deceivers, and yet true; as unknown, and yet well known; as dying, and behold
we live; as chastened, and yet not killed; as sorrowful, yet always rejoicing; as
poor, yet making many rich; as having nothing, and yet possessing all things.

THE APOSTLE PAUL, 2 CORINTHIANS 6:4–10[1]

OUR PALESTINIAN CHRISTIAN FRIEND

OUR JOURNEY TO PALESTINE began most unexpectedly on the other side
of Asia. My wife and I met Yacoub "Jack" Sara during a tropical November
in Manila, the Philippines, in 1994, where we were both studying theology. There was no way we could have foreseen that our acquaintance would
eventually lead our family down a path to harrowing nights of terror,

1. New King James Version Bible.

through deep loneliness, and ultimately to fresh spiritual awakenings. Jack is a Palestinian evangelical Christian, and because of our friendship, a Palestinian village would become our home.

"Palestinian" and "evangelical Christian" was a surprising collision of identities for us, just as Jack's story was a jolt to our stereotyped assumptions of who the "good guys" and the "bad guys" were in the conflict between Israel and Palestine. For almost fifteen years of ministry in Pentecostal/Charismatic churches I had been firmly situated in dispensational theology, the particular brand of which, drawing from Genesis 12:3, emphasized that those who opposed the modern State of Israel were cursed by God. How my eyes would be opened.

Jack was raised in a cramped three-room house near the eighth station of the cross in the Old City of Jerusalem. As a young Palestinian frustrated with the stifling military occupation of his community, Jack became caught up in the first Intifada during the years 1987–1993. This was a youth led resistance movement protesting the Israeli occupation of Palestinian communities. The first Intifada pitted youth against the fully armed Israeli army. This mismatch, and Israel's repressive response, caused Western media to begin to present Palestinian concerns favorably for the first time.

Jack occasionally joined our family for dinner. In our conversations he began to give us a glimpse of Palestinian life under occupation with his story:

> In my teen age years I became involved in active resistance against Israel's occupation of Palestinian land. During the years of the first Intifada I became involved in active resistance. From 1987 to 1991, before I was fourteen years old, I was arrested seven times. In those days you could be arrested and imprisoned for having pro-Intifada pamphlets. For having a Palestinian flag you could be imprisoned for six months, for throwing stones at soldiers, one year, for having a can of paint to write graffiti, three months.
>
> Once I was arrested with my friend Nader, who was my age. He was beaten severely by the soldiers. He was kicked, and beaten with the butt of rifles. He began to spit up blood. Even the soldiers were slightly alarmed at what they had done, so that time I got off easier. But I was beaten at other times with the soldiers' steel helmets. I still have lumps on my head from that.
>
> After these arrests, I made the decision to leave active resistance. First, my imprisonments were very hard on my mother. She had to go from one prison to another to find me. It was very hard for her to see me in prison. Also, I felt my life wasn't getting anywhere. I really liked to read. I wanted to learn. After leaving

activism, I was part of a band. I spent time playing at parties, and becoming involved in alcohol.

One day my neighbor who was a few years older than me was visiting with another Christian friend. I went over to visit, and they really poured out the gospel of Jesus to me. That afternoon I believed in Jesus. I was really touched by the compassion of Jesus, his love for me. I gave my life to Jesus, and my life totally changed. Some people were so shocked at how I had changed; they thought that I was brain damaged from the beatings![2]

After his conversion, Jack became active in a Palestinian led evangelical congregation in Jerusalem's Old City. Completing his college studies at Bethlehem Bible College, he traveled to Manila to study theology. Concluding his seminary studies, Jack returned to the same Old City congregation, which he then led for ten years. Today, Jack is the President of Bethlehem Bible College.

In our visits with Jack in Manila, what most sparked our interest was his portrayal of the hurts and hopes of the Palestinian people, and the scarcity of intentional Christian engagement with the predominantly Muslim population of over four million in the West Bank, Gaza, and East Jerusalem. Palestinian Christians, including Orthodox, Roman Catholic, and Protestant believers, comprise less than two percent of the population.

Against the worried advice of our families, we opted to invest our lives in the troubled land. In August of 1998 Karen and I, with our two youngest children, then twelve and sixteen years of age, made our new home in Ramallah on the West Bank, four houses down from Yasser Arafat's government compound, the *Muqata*, on Port Said Street. In the launching of a student ministry, Living Stones Student Center, with the Palestinian Bible Society (PBS) in the village of Bir Zeit north of Ramallah, and my wife's unique vantage point as a licensed midwife in the maternity department of the Red Crescent Hospital in Ramallah, we embarked on our discovery of the Palestinian people, their culture, history, hopes, and struggles. We began to experience with our Palestinian neighbors the dangers and anxieties of life under Israeli occupation.

What immediately became apparent was the wide chasm between the character of the Palestinian people as expressed in their national narrative and the harsh estimation of them, complete with distorted facts of their history, by many Christians in the United States. Speaking to a large

2. Jack Sara, interview by Andrew Bush. In this interview Sara reviewed the story of his personal journey that he first shared with us in 1993.

congregation in the U.S. during our first years of service on the West Bank, I was introduced as serving among the *Philistines*, with all the negative connotations of that epithet intended.

Unfortunately Constantinian Christianity will almost invariably accept the slanted narrative about marginalized persons that an oppressing power promotes. Thus, Christians accepted the view that Native Americans were pioneer-scalping "savages"; African American slaves were "like children," too simple to be educated; and, as one national televangelist stated, Palestinians are "all terrorists." Concerning attitudes toward Palestinians such as this, it can be argued that by sharing with Israel the narrative of their being God's special nation, Christians in the United States are prone to seamlessly affirm Israel's nationalism and its consequent derogatory perspective of Palestinians. To challenge the Constantinian Christian narrative of the marginalized, and learn from the latter, requires a radically changed perspective. One cannot learn from a belittled stereotype.

An important step in humanizing Palestinians is to become familiar with the fact of their historic presence in the land, their existence as a distinct people that predates Zionism, and the narrative of their national destruction in 1948.

HISTORIC PALESTINIAN PRESENCE IN THE LAND

From the carefully tended olive tree orchards on terraced hillsides around Ramallah, to the desert hills that slope down to the Jordan River to the east, and the desert of Gaza on the Mediterranean Sea to the west, and from Nablus and Jenin in the north to Jerusalem, Bethlehem, and Hebron in the south, the land is like a warm embrace to the people whose heritage is tied to centuries of its patient nurture. Painful is the memory of homes, farms, and orchards lost to Israel in 1948. The internationally acclaimed Palestinian poet, Mahmoud Darwish, in a speech to commemorate the fiftieth anniversary of the *Nakba*, the Destruction, spoke of the meaning of the land to Palestinian life:

> We who are born here on this divine land, we who are dedicated
> to the message of peace and freedom and the defense of human
> values, and of the strength of the olive tree, we who are yoked
> to the night of fifty years of occupation and dispersal, who are
> wounded from the heart's vein to the artery, we declare our pres-
> ence as a wound crying in the depths of time and space in spite

of the tempests which try to rend our roots from the very earth
to which we gave our name.[3]

To counter the inconvenient historicity of the Palestinian presence in the
land, the idea of Palestine as "a land without a people for a people without
a land" was promoted by Zionist apologists at the time of Israel's founding
as a modern state in 1948. According to this claim, Arabs immigrated to
the land as a response to the colonization of Israel by Jewish settlers and the
opportunities that this improvement of the land offered; there was not an
indigenous Palestinian population in the land.

Although this propagandistic myth is largely absent from contemporary Israeli society, it is still widely promoted among Western Christians.
For example, while I was recently enjoying Sunday dinner in a pastor's
home in a midwestern state, the conversation turned to Israel and Palestine.
Another guest stated emphatically that there were only 80,000 Palestinians
in the land in 1947; so how, he asked rhetorically, could Palestinians have
any claim to the land since there were more than one half million Jews in
the land at that time?

Similarly, the International Christian Zionist Center in Jerusalem states:

> Palestinian leaders claim that Israel is built on Arab land, when the
> truth is that eyewitnesses such as Mark Twain and Rev. Manning
> of England who visited the Holy Land in the last century wrote
> that the *land was barren and empty*. The population then was less
> that 5% of today's population.[4]

An empty land? Far from it. The land between the Mediterranean and the
Jordan River was home to a people with a developed society and deep historical roots. Colin Chapman, a British theologian and mission leader who
has lived in the Middle East for many years, states:

> The new histories that are being written are making it even clearer
> that the potential for conflict between the Zionists and the Pales-
> tinians Arabs was there from the beginning. The land to which
> the Jews returned from the 1880s onwards was not empty, and
> they knew it. But with the typical arrogance of Western colonial-
> ists they believed that they had a right to settle where they wished
> and that they would bring the benefits of Western civilization to
> a backward region. If they ever tried, they failed at almost every
> stage to come to terms with the people who were already there,

3. In the Press, "Mahmoud Darwish spoke in the name of the Palestinian people."
4. International Christian Zionist Center.

people who like the Jews in the biblical period had been rooted in the land for centuries and whose identity was bound up in this particular piece of land.[5]

In actual fact the Arab Palestinian population of Palestine under the British Mandate in 1947 was about 1,300,000, which comprised approximately two-thirds of the total population.[6] These Palestinians were not newcomers. Although, under the Ottoman Empire, the last pan-national Islamic empire based in Istanbul, there was not a census of individual nations, other sources indicate a steady population growth in Palestine as a result of high fertility rates, rather than immigration, from 411,000 in 1860 to more than one million in 1946.[7]

A compelling record of the historic presence of the Palestinian people in the land is also found in their architectural history. The architectural conservation organization, RIWAQ, has restored hundreds of Palestinian buildings, some still in active use, including stone watchtowers in the fields, elegant villas, the humble homes of average farmers, and the ornate "throne" architecture of regional governmental buildings, each of which underscores the historicity of Palestine society. RIWAQ, partially funded by the Ford Foundation, received the prestigious international Claus Award in 2011 for,

> significant achievements in preserving and reinvigorating sites of historical and architectural significance, for linking cultural heritage with community development and economic opportunities, for nourishing collective memory and strengthening Palestinian identity, and for its daring and pioneering work in a context marked by conflict and military occupation[8]

The old village of Bir Zeit is currently one of RIWAQ's projects. Two years ago, much of the original old village was neglected and going to ruin. Walking through the narrow streets today, the courtyards of centuries-old homes have been restored. The golden limestone walls are again gleaming under the sun. Moving inside one particular house, transitioning from the searing sun to the cool shadows of the interior, it takes more than a moment for one's eyes to adjust. Then, the graceful curves of the concave, arched

5. Chapman, *Whose Promised Land?*, 280.

6. Pappe, *The Ethnic Cleansing of Palestine*, 35.

7. McCarthy, "Palestine Population."

8. "Riwaq wins the Prince Claus Award."

ceilings are revealed. Rounded niches are built into the wall where the sleep mats were stored during the day. During Bir Zeit's summer Heritage Week, I spoke with an American Palestinian family who told me of visiting their grandfather who lived in this house. Some of the homes have still intact the old granaries that provided sustenance both for the family and for the animals that were sheltered below the main level.

Along a narrow steep road in the old village, the stones in a high wall are noticeably larger and more roughly cut at the base, indicating much older masonry. This wall encloses an ancient *khan,* or inn, from the ninth century C.E. Perhaps when Jesus traveled from Jerusalem to Samaria, he would have taken the route through the mountains and spent a night in this old village.

THE PALESTINIAN PEOPLE AS A NATION

As people residing in a land called Palestine since Roman rule, it should be no surprise that Palestinians have had a sense of ethnic or national identity for the last one hundred years. Certainly today Palestinian national identity is alive and well. Symbols of their identity emblazon all Palestinian villages and cities. The Palestinian flag, with its red triangle and black white and green stripes, flies from government buildings, is painted on walls, and worn on the yokes of university graduates. One Palestinian student stated emphatically to me, "Every Palestinian child is taught by their mother, 'You are a Palestinian.' This is a big part of our life."

Flying in the face of this vigorous national pride is the theme often heard among pro-Israeli Christians that the Palestinian people simply do not exist; they are an invention of Yasser Arafat to counter Israel's rightful claim to the land. Pandering to evangelicals, a recent candidate for the U.S. presidency, who touts his historical knowledge, referred to Palestinians as an "invented people."[9] This myth was part of Israel's early propaganda as a state. Golda Meir, the fourth prime minister of Israel, stated, "There was no such thing as Palestinians. When was there an independent Palestinian people with a Palestinian state? . . . They did not exist."[10]

---

9. Associated Press, "Palestinians angry over Gingrich's 'invented' people comment."

10. Cited from *The Sunday Times*, London, June 15, 1969, in Kimmerling and Migdal, *The Palestinian People*, xxvi—xxvii.

Sadly, these untruths are frequently asserted in American evangelical circles. For example James Hutchens, the President of The Jerusalem Connection International, states:

> First, let us clarify who the "Palestinians" really are. The notion of a distinct "Palestinian people" with a language, culture and religion of its own, is a creation of Yasser Arafat and nurtured by the surrounding Arab nations, after their ignominious defeat in the 1967 war with Israel. The so-called "Palestinian people" are, in reality, Arabs whose mother tongue is Arabic, whose religion is Islam, and whose culture is shared by most of the 22 surrounding Arab countries. There simply is no distinct Palestinian entity.[11]

Ironically, in recent decades, evangelical mission has made much of identifying all the ethnic groups in the world in order to determine the task remaining for global mission.[12] In absolute contradiction to this trend is the refusal by many of the same evangelical Christians to recognize the ethnicity/nationality of the Palestinians. In fact, Palestinians are the *only* people group in the world whose existence is argued *against* by these evangelical Christians, in spite of the fact that they have a national flag and an elected president and prime minister.

Being defined as non-existent, Palestinians are rendered invisible. This is a fate well known to African Americans. The central theme in the African American author Ralph Ellison's novel, *The Invisible Man,* written in 1953, is that African Americans are socially invisible to white society, since whites only see blacks as stereotypes.[13] Consequently, their individual identity, and, thus, their dignity and personal worth, is negated. When Palestinians are seen only as "Arabs," and terrorists to boot (although this collective pejorative term implies the existence of an ethnicity!), this same social myopia is at work. This is ethnic cleansing by bogus scholarship. As the popular theology that supports Israel's claim to possess all the of the Holy Land, often referred to as Christian Zionism, is missional, this marginalization by the negation of ethnicity indicates that aspects of colonialism, which in the past systematically suppressed indigenous people, is alive and well in modern Western mission.

---

11. Hutchens, "What about the Palestinians?"

12. The Joshua Project identifies more than 7,000 unreached people groups that include 2.9 billion people. See the Joshua Project.

13. Ellison, *The Invisible Man.*

Not only is this morally wrong, it is also factually false. A basic anthropological principle is that self-identity determines ethnicity. The authenticity of the Palestinian nation is found in these people's self-identity as "Palestinians." Palestinian identity, as distinct from their being joined with all other Arabic speaking people (which defines the term "Arab"), is emphatically asserted.[14] This is not a recent formulation for the purposes of political expediency. Eminent historian of the Arab peoples, Albert Hourani, states that Arab nationalism was developing during the final decades of the Ottoman dynasty.[15] After Turkey's defeat in World War I, which ended the Ottoman Empire, Arab nationalism challenged the Mandate authorities, resulting in the emergence of the new states of Syria, Lebanon, and Iraq. Rashid Khalidi of Columbia University, in *Palestinian Identity: The Construction of Modern National Consciousness*, the most thorough discussion of the origins of Palestinian nationalism, also argues that Palestinians had a developed sense of national identity by the early 1920s, but acknowledges that it was continually frustrated by the British Mandate, which governed the land that is presently Israel, Palestine, and Jordan.[16]

An interesting political poster recently caught my attention in Ben Gurion International Airport, Israel's main airport near Tel Aviv. Walking toward the departure gates down the long ramp into the central hub of Terminal Three, I passed an exhibition of patriotic posters commemorating every year in the history of the modern State of Israel and before. I had seen these posters numerous times before, but this time my eye paused on the poster for 1930. Rendered in the muscular labor movement aesthetic, the poster depicts a Jewish immigrant toiling on the land. Bold letters in Hebrew and English read, "Help him build Palestine!"

Inconvenient evidence such as this poster cannot be ignored by intellectually honest scholars. Israeli historians Baruch Kimmerling and Joel S. Migdal correct the myths of the founding of Israel in their *The Palestinian People*:

> One of the best known expressions of such a viewpoint [the denial of unique ethnicity and historicity] has been argued by Joan Peters'
> *From Time Immemorial: The Origins of the Arab-Jewish Conflict over Palestine*, a heavily documented and, apparently, serious work

14. See Abu El-Assal's autobiography *Caught in Between*, 80–81. Also, see Fasheh, "Reclaiming Our Identity and Redefining Ourselves," 129.

15. Hourani, *A History of the Arab Peoples*, 309.

16. Khalidi, *Palestinian Identity*, 187.

of scholarship. Its basic argument is that most of Palestine's Arab population was not indigenous. Rather, it consisted of migrants, attracted by opportunities offered by Jewish settlement, who came from separate streams and certainly did not (do not) constitute a people . . . But as numerous sober historians have shown, Peters' tendentiousness is not, in fact supported by the historical record, being based on materials taken out of context and on distorted evidence . . . We asserted then, and reaffirm in this book, that the origins of a self-conscious, relatively unified Palestinian people pre-date Zionism.[17]

More poignant in expressing a national identity are the words of a twelve-year old Palestinian girl, which she wrote during one of Living Stones Student Center's summer camps:

> Dear Friend:
>
> My name is Emaa. I have a big family consisting of ten members. I am living in Jibya village. It is a small village consisting of about 150 members near Ramallah.
>
> I would like to continue my studies but the situation is very bad. So I had to drop out of school. I am not a wealthy student. My family couldn't support me since the situation is very hard. Everyday a lot of people are killed. I was studying in the United Nations School in Bir Zeit.
>
> I wish to see the occupation far away from our land and our people.
>
> We are living in a small house consisting of three rooms. I am very tall. I have black hair and black eyes. I would like to be a police woman. I am now in 9th grade.
>
> I love Palestine very much. Yours truly, Emaa[18]

THE PALESTINIAN NARRATIVE OF 1948

For Israel, the 1948 Arab-Israeli war was the War of Independence. Palestinians refer to the same conflict as the *Nakba*, the Destruction. Destruction indeed. The Palestinian residents of almost 400 villages were driven out either by force, or by the terror of suffering the same fate that

---

17. Kimmerling and Migdal, *The Palestinian People*, xxvii—xxviii.

18. "Emaa" is a pseudonym. The remainder of her letter to an imaginary friend is quoted verbatim. Living Stones Student Center summer camp project, July 2003.

befell the village of Deir Yassin on April 9, 1948, when 107 Palestinians, many of them women and children, were massacred by extremists under the authority of the Hagana, Israel's military.[19] Israel used this destruction to strike fear in the hearts of Palestinians, most of whom were simple farmers. These emptied villages were then leveled. Tourists today traveling through Israel are usually not aware that many of the broken stone walls in the fields they pass are the remnants of Palestinian villages.

Within months, between 750,000 and 1,000,000 Palestinians fled to Gaza, the West Bank, and neighboring countries.[20] The displaced families fully expected to return to their homes in a few weeks when hostilities subsided. Israeli forces, however, closed the roads by force, preventing repatriation. Today, almost three million Palestinian refugees still live in UN funded refugee camps in Gaza, the West Bank, Lebanon, Jordan, Syria, and other countries. For many of these families, their most prized possessions are the title to their land and the key to the front door of their homes in Israel.

If the land was not empty, Zionists, however, tried their best to *empty* the land of its indigenous population in order to retrospectively make true their propaganda. This was not an unplanned result of the 1948 war. Israeli historian Ilan Pappe, in his text *The Ethnic Cleansing of Palestine,* describes the strategy that was in place even before 1948 to remove the Palestinian population from the land. He writes:

> From the founder of the Zionist movement, Theodor Herzl, to the main leaders of the Zionist enterprise in Palestine, cleansing the land was a valid option . . . The fact that the expellers were newcomers to the country, and part of a colonization project, relates the case of Palestine to the colonialist history of ethnic cleansing in North and South America.[21]

In spite of the fact that Israel is referred to as a modern democracy, the goal of ethnically cleansing the Palestinian population that remains within Israel proper is alive and well. Tzipporah Malkah "Tzipi" Livni, the leader of the Kadima political party from 2008–2012, stated in a speech to high school students that the Palestinians in Israel should probably move into the Palestinian state once it is formed:

19. Pappe, *Ethnic Cleansing of Palestine*, 90.

20. Kimmerling and Migdal, *The Palestinian People*, 156–59.

21. Pappe, *Ethnic Cleansing of Palestine*, 8.

> Once a Palestinian state is established, I can come to the Palestinian citizens, whom we call Israeli Arabs, and say to them, "you are citizens with equal rights, but the national solution for you is elsewhere."[22]

This is a remarkable statement, considering that the Palestinian or Arab Israelis account for one fifth of the population of Israel. Even more severe are some conservative members of the Israeli Knesset, or parliament, who continue to call for the "transfer" of Palestinians from not only Israel, but also from the West Bank. For those Palestinians who managed to escape the first purge in 1948, if these proposals become policy they might yet suffer the loss of their land.

LIVING IN A CONTEXT OF VIOLENCE

While listening to and learning about the Palestinian perspective concerning their nationality and legacy in the land, our family was exposed daily to the culture of violence that was the persistent context for life in the West Bank and Gaza. Especially during the Second Intifada, Palestinians suffered arbitrary and unprovoked violence—and inflicted the same on Israel.

October 12, 2000 is the day we were baptized into this maelstrom. Blood had been violently shed that morning. Two alleged Israeli undercover soldiers had been apprehended by Palestinian security forces directly in front of the hundred-year-old Friends Boys School, where our daughter was just beginning her morning classes. The captured Israelis were taken to a police station, just on the other side of an old stone wall from the school.

The Second Intifada had been ignited a few weeks earlier after Ariel Sharon, then the opposition leader in the Israeli Knesset made a provocative excursion onto the Temple Mount, known as the Noble Sanctuary to Muslims. During the first weeks of the Intifada, the Israeli military had responded forcibly to Palestinian demonstrations in Ramallah. Numerous Palestinians, including youth, were injured or killed during these first clashes.

That fateful October day, enraged at the deaths and the ongoing humiliation of the occupation, a furious mob of Palestinians stormed the station and beat the two Israeli soldiers to death. The images of this

22. Harretz Service and News Agency, "Livni: National aspirations of Israel's Arabs can be met by Palestinian homeland."

gruesome lynching were flashed on the international news channels before the day was over.

The reality of that day's horrors broke upon our family suddenly. Having just arrived the night before from overseas, I was sleeping off the jet lag when my wife, Karen, jolted me awake. Our daughter had called from school. She didn't know what was happening, but all the students had been taken to a classroom building down the hill from the front gates. She had heard rumors of two Israeli *jasuus,* or spies, who had been arrested in front of the school, their car torched. All the kids were being sent home. She needed someone to pick her up immediately.

The school was only a few blocks from our apartment. Karen had tried to take our VW to bring our daughter home, but Abu Mikhal, the head of the extended family with which we shared a building, wouldn't let her. It was not safe, he insisted. In the climate of violence that was gripping Ramallah, the Israeli license plates on our car would make it a target for Palestinian snipers. Someone would have to go on foot and bring our daughter home.

Walking toward the school, I passed the Muqata, Yasser Arafat's official compound, a half block away. Not even a cat was in the deserted streets. The strange quiet that had settled on this normally bustling Palestinian city was not one of peace, but of fear.

As I climbed the hill to the school, a Palestinian security vehicle sped by, then swerved down a side street, screeching to a stop. Heavily armed security forces piled out and disappeared among the houses. This was ominous. I felt exposed, the only person walking in the street.

I found our daughter with her friends, worry written across their faces. Quickly I tried to get more information, but no one knew much. We avoided passing the front of the school grounds on our way home, but we could see a car smoldering there. We made our way home.

That afternoon, families throughout Ramallah sheltered in their homes, dreading the reprisals of the Israeli military. Prime Minister Sharon warned on television broadcasts that Israel would take immediate action to respond to the deaths of the soldiers. For us, this was terrifying, uncharted territory. Being at ground zero of a military assault had been our worst fear in moving into the West Bank. Now it was about to break upon us.

As we waited with apprehension, there was a knock on the door. We opened it to find Imad, our coworker at Living Stones in Bir Zeit. What was he doing out on the streets at such a dangerous time? "I've come to bring you some bread," he said, handing me a plastic sack of warm pita bread. "I didn't think you might have any."

"But why bring it at such a perilous time?" I asked.

"This is normal for us. It's our life," he said with a shrug.

Imminent military attack. Paralyzing fear. Utter vulnerability. The roads blocked. Unable to move. How could this possibly be normal?

"It's our life." How many times I would hear those words in the next years of the Intifada. Standing in the rain on a cold January day at a checkpoint, "It's our life," someone might say.

In the middle of the night, when Israeli soldiers in full combat gear beat on the door of our Christian neighbor's house and insisted on waking their sleeping children to search the house, it was humiliating and infuriating to them. Acknowledging my shock, they said with bitterness, but with objectivity, "This is normal for us."

A TERRIBLE NORMAL

For visitors to the Holy Land who idealize Israel, Palestinian life under Israeli occupation, which they would find if they were to venture off their packaged tour route into the West Bank, would be a rude awakening. The realities of life under occupation is no surprise to the Israeli human rights organizations such as Peace Now, Israelis Against House Demolition, Rabbis for Human Rights, and Women in Black, which regularly publish reports of the unjust acts and policies of the Israeli Defense Forces (IDF) and the Israeli government.

These voices are virtually unknown to Western Christians. They record the destruction of dreams and lives: the demolition of homes, the confiscation of land and water resources legally held by families for centuries; the blockading of roads hindering commerce, kids from reaching their schools and the sick the from receiving needed medical care; and the imprisonment of youth and adults without due process. Their reports barely begin to describe the ongoing harsh treatment of Palestinians. Americans wouldn't tolerate living under such conditions for five days, let alone fifty years.

It is not possible, nor is it the purpose of this book, to develop a full discussion of the political and legal issues that surround the Israel/Palestine conflict. The purpose of describing the Palestinian context, however an unpleasant task it may be, is to highlight the significance of the decisions of several Palestinian Christians that were made in the midst of the conflict. To be oppressed under military occupation is a terrible fate, as we learned from our experiences, which would be regarded as light to most Palestinians who have lost sons and daughters, mothers and fathers, land and homes, access to decent employment, and more.

SURDA CHECKPOINT NEAR RAMALLAH: WINTER, 2001

From the *Manara*, the landmark circle in the center of Ramallah, the road north passes the *Muqata*, the compound that houses the offices of the Palestinian President and his security forces. Passing the outskirts of the city, the road falls off into a steep valley near Surda village. The north and south slopes of this valley are planted with olive trees. Buff-colored stone walls cross the fields, dividing property. The tall, dark green cedar trees provide a striking visual counterpoint to the red soil and silver and blue-green leaves of the olive trees. It is a picturesque sight, but Israel's harsh response to the second Palestinian Intifada overwhelmed and disfigured the beauty of this valley, turning it into a valley of tears.

For the thousands of Palestinians who had to travel from the northern West Bank to Ramallah, or to Jerusalem, Bethlehem, or Hebron in the south, the road through Surda was their only route. During the Intifada the main north-south route, Highway 60, was closed to most Palestinians. Highway 60 was effectively a highway for Israeli settlers.

At Surda valley's nadir, there was an Israeli military checkpoint. This checkpoint had morphed through the years of the Intifada from an Israeli military jeep in the road, to a full blockade with cement barriers guarded by the IDF. The closure made life hell for the Palestinian people. For months at a time no vehicles could pass this blockade. In the cold rains, when the roads were awash, and in the scorching sun, Palestinians old and young, students, the sick, regardless of their physical condition, had no choice but to walk from the top of one side of the valley to the other. Once I witnessed a frail old man wearing a hospital gown being pushed through the mud in a wheelchair. Bir Zeit University students, determined to attend their lectures, had to endure the gauntlet of Surda valley. As Sumaya, an engineering student explained to me, "Education is the one thing Israel cannot take from us."

At the Surda checkpoint we experienced the harassment and intimidation that is a regular part of Palestinian life. Three incidents convey some sense of the checkpoint.

Our thirteen-year-old daughter crossed the Israeli military checkpoint. Karen attempted to cross a short time later. Abruptly the Israeli soldier stood in her path, his weapon raised.

"The road is closed," he said. "You have to go back."

Alarmed that our daughter was by herself near this volatile checkpoint, Karen protested, "But my daughter is alone. When am I going to be able to reach my daughter."

"Not in one hundred years," the soldier replied.

What next? Turn back and walk out of the valley back toward Ramallah? Wait? But how long should she remain in this volatile place?

Our son was home with us in Bir Zeit for Christmas vacation from college. He is an avid photographer, a pursuit he had taken up as a student at the Anglican International School in Jerusalem. Hoping to go into Ramallah, we took our car and headed south toward Surda. The checkpoint was completely closed. No one could pass. We got out of the car on the northern edge of the valley to check out was happening. Our son innocently walked ten meters down the road toward the checkpoint to take some photos. Immediately he was spotted by an Israeli soldier, who demanded that he approach the checkpoint. At the checkpoint, the soldier took him behind a jeep and jammed his knee into our son's stomach. "Erase the photo," he was ordered. I tried to approach. What were they doing to my boy? A soldier lifted his rifle to his shoulder and ordered that I stay.

On a clear beautiful afternoon Karen, our daughter, and I were making our way home by public transportation from Ramallah. The public transport van stopped on the southern edge of the valley to let us all out. In a cheerful mood we sauntered down the road toward the checkpoint. Then two or three *shabab,* or young men, started throwing stones at the Israeli soldiers at the checkpoint. Wiser heads, persons who were just trying to get home, rebuked them and told them to stop, but the fires of the Intifada were raging and the *shabab* just became more aggressive. Within seconds the loud pop of tear gas guns could be heard and the air around us filled with the fog of the gas. In a panic, I started running *toward* the checkpoint. Karen, always more cool under fire, yelled for me to come back. Returning to relative safety of the public van, we wiped our eyes, trying to ease the burning. A Palestinian woman who had been in the taxi with us and was also caught in the gas, looked at us and said, "When you get out of this, tell people what we are going through."

———————◇———————

A moment of panic for both mother and daughter, unable to reach each other. A son roughed up; his dad powerless to come to his aid. A family caught in a cloud of tear gas. During the Intifada, we shared such experiences with all who were forced to traverse this dangerous checkpoint that would be a place of humiliation, suffering, and even of death for both Palestinians and Israelis. Sometimes, when we knew Surda was closed, we took the chance to bypass it.

A DANGEROUS CROSSING, WINTER 2002

"Surda's closed." Grim words. How were we going to get back to Bir Zeit? Taxis were taking people to a back road to the north edge of Ramallah. We would then have to walk across an open field, and pick up another ride in the Jalazone refugee camp.

The atmosphere was tense in the van. None of the eight passengers spoke as we headed toward the back route, the "closed" route that crossed an open field and then entered Jalazone refugee camp near the village of Jifna. What would be the price of trying to circumvent Israel's closure?

The taxi dropped us off two blocks from the open field we had to cross. Walking up the steep hill, our daughter was just ahead of me. We heard the grinding behind us of heavy machinery. We turned to see an Israeli tank moving slowly up the road toward us. What advice should I give our daughter in this circumstance? What to tell a daughter when you are being threatened by heavy military weapons was not something I had read in the Christian books about how to raise your kids.

"Don't look back. They won't shoot you in the back," was the best I could come up with.

The tank rumbled past us. We made it across the fields and home that day. But we soon would learn how incorrect my advice had been. A few weeks later, a ninety-five-year-old great grandmother, Fatima Hussein Muhammad, was in a clearly marked taxi that was crossing the same field on the makeshift road. Sitting in the back seat of the taxi, she was struck and killed by an Israeli soldier who fired on the vehicle.[23]

23. "Palestinians: IDF kills woman, 95."

BIR ZEIT, SPRING 2003

On a sunny day in early spring I was enjoying the walk through Bir Zeit to Living Stones. The fruit tree blossoms, wild flowers, and green grass would soon fade in the May heat, but in February they made a perfect spring day. Climbing a steep road, I walked down the narrow street toward the gate of Our Lady of Guadalupe Roman Catholic Church. The lower classes of the Church's K-12 school were dismissing, and happy packs of second and third grade kids were leaving the church compound. As I approached the school, an Israeli jeep passed me, slowing to make the sharp turn. Then . . . chaos. I heard the children's terrified screams. Acrid smoke and gas burned my lungs and eyes. As the jeep sped off, I realized what had happened. Without any provocation, an Israeli soldier had fired a tear gas canister toward the children. The kids ran screaming back toward the school. Shaken, I described what had happened to one of the staff at Living Stones. He explained that this is the real goal of the occupation, not merely the external control of movement, but ultimately, the internalizing of a mindset of fear and defeat. In short, the formation of a controllable people, a broken people, who ultimately will yield to Israel's demands.

I saw firsthand the effectiveness of this attempt to mold a people with violence. During one of Living Stones' summer camps in the village of Atara, while the third- through seventh-grade campers were playing in the school yard, an Israeli jeep drove by. At the mere sight of the jeep, the kids fled from their playing and ran screaming to the shelter of the school building.

One student describes his life in this way:

> *Dear Friend:*
>
> I don't know what I will say to you about my life. It is full of pains, destruction and killing. When I get up in the morning I see everything is sad. Then I go to school to face the army of occupation walking in our village. Some days we couldn't get to school due to this bad army. They close the entrance of our village. If anybody wants to go out, he has to walk between the trees on foot. When I go back to my home, sadly I see the people who are killed by the army of occupation. We are looking for the free world to say stop the killing, but there is no response.
>
> This is my life. Obed

Another student, Bushar, writes:

It is kind of funny. You see my mom and dad brought me here from the States because there were too many guns in the States. There is just one thing that is different. Where I used to live we just really heard 9mm fire, but over here M16s, AK47s, 250s and 500s, and bombing. It is sad because when I hear a gun I can tell you what kind of gun it is.[24]

How does one measure the human cost of the tragedy of generations of kids raised under the specter of perpetual violence? What is the ultimate effect of this violence to the soul? A culture of violence breeds violence.

This account of the harshness of the treatment of Palestinian society could easily be discounted as hopelessly pro-Palestinian, except for the many important cautionary voices that are raised in Israel. Israeli artists, writers, academics, and journalists have raised the alarm that the human rights violations committed against innocent Palestinians are destroying Israel's national character and undermining it as a democracy.[25] The prominent Israeli journalist Gershom Gorenberg in his recent book, *The Unmaking of Israel*, writes:

> Yet it has proven impossible to maintain a regime in occupied territories in which Palestinians and Jews live under separate laws or under no laws at all, without undermining law and democracy within Israel. By acting like a movement rather than a democratic state beyond the Green Line,[26] Israel has become less of a state in its own territory.[27]

The most remarkable actions have been taken by those who have seen first-hand the suffering of the Palestinians—active duty Israeli Defense Forces (IDF) soldiers. Courage to Refuse is an organization of IDF soldiers who, recognizing the oppressiveness of their actions against civilians, are refusing to serve in Palestine. In their "Combatants Letter of 2002," a foundational document for the organization, they state:

24. The students' essays were part of a summer camp activity of Living Stones Student Center, Bir Zeit.

25. For a collection of essays of these other voices see Carey and Shanin, eds., *The Other Israel*.

26 The "Green Line" is the 1949 armistice line between Israel and its neighbors: Syria, Jordan, Lebanon, and Egypt. It created the border for the Palestinian territories, including East Jerusalem, the West Bank, and Gaza. As it defined the border before the occupation of the West Bank, east Jerusalem, and Gaza it is also referred to as the "1967 border." It is the border that Palestinians argue should define a sovereign state.

27. Gorenberg, *The Unmaking of Israel*, 220.

- We, reserve combat officers and soldiers of the Israel Defense Forces, who were raised upon the principles of Zionism, self-sacrifice and giving to the people of Israel and to the State of Israel, who have always served in the front lines, and who were the first to carry out any mission in order to protect the State of Israel and strengthen it,

- We, combat officers and soldiers who have served the State of Israel for long weeks every year, in spite of the dear cost to our personal lives, have been on reserve duty in the Occupied Territories, and were issued commands and directives that had nothing to do with the security of our country, and that had the sole purpose of perpetuating our control over the Palestinian people,

- We, whose eyes have seen the bloody toll this Occupation exacts from both sides,

- We, who sensed how the commands issued to us in the Occupied Territories destroy all the values that we were raised upon,

- We, who understand now that the price of Occupation is the loss of IDF's human character and the corruption of the entire Israeli society,

- We, who know that the Territories are not a part of Israel, and that all settlements are bound to be evacuated,

- We hereby declare that we shall not continue to fight this War of the Settlements.

- We shall not continue to fight beyond the 1967 borders in order to dominate, expel, starve and humiliate an entire people.

- We hereby declare that we shall continue serving the Israel Defense Force in any mission that serves Israel's defense.

- *The missions of occupation and oppression do not serve this purpose—and we shall take no part in them.*[28]

This stand, taken by active duty soldiers loyal to Israel, should challenge the simplistic perception of many Western Christians that all that Israel does is righteous and that the Palestinians are only evil.

28. Courage to Refuse, "Combatant's Letter."

HOPE AGAINST HOPE

In spite of this inhumane environment, we found the Palestinian character to be incredibly resilient. Palestinians are ardent in their pursuit of education, and in their hope that someday Palestine will indeed achieve freedom and statehood. In the village of Bir Zeit near the municipality building is *Al Majida wa Sili* School for Girls public high school. As the teenage girls change classrooms during the school day, they bounce along, chatting and laughing. Except for their head scarves, they resemble American teenagers, full of fun and vitality. I became acquainted with the school when Living Stones conducted a program of extra-curriculum activities such as drama and computer skills, which the school couldn't afford to offer.

On the high wall that encloses the playground, there is a striking mural. It depicts a teenage girl flying a kite. As the string ascends, it spells "Palestine" in graceful loops. The kite, painted in red, green, and black, the colors of the Palestinian flag, flies high in a clear blue sky. It is a powerful image of the pride these girls have in their nation, and their hopes that the day will come in which their nation will soar free as a sovereign state.

Far from the desire to "drive Israel into the sea," the hope that we heard was that someday they would neither be oppressed, or be oppressors, but would find peace with Israel, and a normal life. Hadeel, a school administrator, said it this way: "We just want peace, and to live a normal life, to be able to come and go like people in other countries." As Obed, a high school student, writes: "Basically when this all stops and we make peace again, that would be great."

To value as instructive the voices and lives of the Palestinian people necessitates that hateful attitudes that demean their ethnicity and national suffering be confronted within the Western Christian community. The failure to do so not only perpetuates a corrosive influence in Western mission and encourages the further corruption of Israel, it puts more pressure on Palestinians Christians, hindering their life and witness in Palestine. It also frustrates Christian overtures to the Muslim community internationally. It confirms to Muslims that their association of Christianity with pro-Israeli, anti-Palestinian, Islamophobic prejudices is correct.

The Intifada inflicted terrible physical and psychological pain on Palestinian society. The Occupation grinds on, robbing Palestinians of normalcy in their lives and unmaking Israel has a democratic and just state. It was in this terrible context that we learned from our Palestinian brothers and sisters the way of Christ. They led us through the example of their lives on a journey toward the cross.

3

The Way of Weakness
in a Context of Violence

And He has said to me, "My grace is sufficient for you, for power is perfected in weakness." Most gladly, therefore, I will rather boast about my weaknesses, so that the power of Christ may dwell in me. Therefore I am well content with weaknesses, with insults, with distresses, with persecutions, with difficulties, for Christ's sake; for when I am weak, then I am strong.

THE APOSTLE PAUL, 2 CORINTHIANS 12:9–10

Weakness is an authentic characteristic of the apostolic ministry. Without the weakness which his opponents deride, there can be no real apostolic ministry and no true proclamation of Christ. The church is not made up of spiritual giants; only broken men can lead others to the cross. It is on men like Peter that Jesus builds His church.[1]

DAVID J. BOSCH, A SPIRITUALITY OF THE ROAD

1. Bosch, A Spirituality of the Road, 77.

REDUCED TO JESUS

COULD ANY GOOD THING come out of the Intifada? This uprising of the Palestinian community against the Occupation was fueled by the frustration of the daily spectacle of the land intended for a future Palestinian state being seized for Israeli settlements. Every step toward peace paradoxically generated a new wave of Israeli settlement outposts cropping up on the hilltops in the West Bank.[2] Palestinian resistance—nonviolent demonstrations against road closures and settlement expansion, stone throwing youth, and armed Palestinian militants—was met with the overwhelming force of the Israeli military. The immediate result of the Intifada was that the Occupation became more severe: more roads were closed; access to Israel for day workers was greatly restricted; Palestinians controlled less land; moderates in Israel were pushed to the political right; and the possibility of a final peace settlement was severely diminished.

The pain and destruction of this upheaval was terrible. The wounds it left on Palestinian society are still healing. Some families will never mend. It was in the extremity of this conflict, though, that my wife and I discovered ourselves on a spiritual journey, one that we had not intended, but one that could not be ignored. As children of the privileged West, we were accustomed to security, a sense of control, and freedom of movement—all of which were stripped away in the Intifada. Through the violence, we were reduced to the foundation of our hope and faith. The violence of that October day in 2000, which I have described, when we were baptized into the awful normality of Palestinian life, became pivotal in our lives.

Waiting in the dark that day, the electricity cut off in the neighborhood, our building shaken from terrible explosions, left us shocked and frightened. Our friend Jack Sara braved the violence and the risk of the extremely volatile checkpoints in the night's darkness to drive into Ramallah from Jerusalem to help us evacuate. We returned to the U.S. to weigh our options[3] and were surprised when Labib Madanat, the General

2. In fact Israeli officials publically urged settlers to seize more land as peace negotiations proceeded. Gershom Gorenberg states that following the Wye River negotiations in October 1998, led by U.S. President Bill Clinton and including Palestinian Authority President Yasser Arafat and Israeli Prime Minister Benyamin Netanyahu, Israeli Foreign Minister Ariel Sharon on Israel Radio urged settlers: "Everyone there should move, should run, should grab more hills, expand the territory. Everything that is grabbed will be in our hands. Everything we don't grab will be in there hands." See Gorenberg, *The Unmaking of Israel*, 125–26.

3. My brother and his wife were heroes to take us into their Boulder, Colorado home

Secretary of the Palestinian Bible Society from 1993–2007, and now the Coordinator of the Palestinian and Israeli Bible Societies, advised us that the Intifada would probably grind on for several years. He gave us our choices in stark terms: we could either abandon our work with Living Stones, which in its first two years was off to a promising start, or return to the West Bank and learn to survive with our Palestinian neighbors in the violence of the Intifada.

Hoping that the conflict would ease as it seemed too brutal to last much longer, we opted to return to Palestine in January 2001, three months after our evacuation. We would soon discover that we had entirely misjudged the forces that fueled the conflict. The violence not only did not decrease, but rather surged, dashing our naïve wishful thinking. Ramallah became a full blown war zone. Foreigners disappeared. Palestinian American families returned to the United States. We were part of a handful of foreigners crazy enough to stay. We did conclude, however, that for safety's sake it was not wise to continue to reside so close to Arafat's compound, ground zero in the Intifada. Indeed, as it so happened, during the next four years the house where we had been living would be occupied several times, as a battle station, by Israeli soldiers. In addition, since Living Stones' main hours of operation were in the evening, if we stayed in Ramallah, I would have to drive home from Bir Zeit at night. Night driving was a death wish. Either Israeli soldiers or Palestinian militants might fire on a strange car at night.

We could transfer to Bir Zeit, a few kilometers to the north of Ramallah, where Living Stones was located. My fear in this was that we would be moving deeper into the West Bank, further from evacuation routes to Jerusalem. Karen and I were also concerned that if we lived in Bir Zeit our daughter would have a longer commute to the Friends School every day. What if roads closed unexpectedly and we were cut off both from ways to escape and from our daughter? Our Palestinian friends assured us that this would never happen. Even during the first Intifada in the 1980s, they emphasized, the roads had never been completely blocked.

---

on a moment's notice! It was a disappointment to be out of Palestine, but it so happened that my father passed away while I was in the U.S. I was grateful to have seen him on the last day of his life. Early in his career in the 1950s, decades before other Christians were concerned for justice for Palestinians in the Holy Land, he had written an article about Israel and the Palestine in which he called for Christians to be more even-handed in their opinions about Palestinians.

Finally, trying to put all fear aside, we transferred from Ramallah to Bir Zeit in February 2001. On our third day in our fifth floor apartment in Bir Zeit, we awoke to find the village eerily quiet. No cars were moving in the streets. The Israeli military had bulldozed a deep trench across the road between Bir Zeit and Ramallah in the valley next to Surda village. There the infamous Surda checkpoint, which I have described, was established. During the following weeks, one by one, secondary routes were also closed. For Bir Zeit and surrounding villages travel to Ramallah and Jerusalem became a gauntlet of closures threatened by unpredictable violence.

DEEPENING ISOLATION

We began a very isolated life in our village of Bir Zeit. With passage out of Bir Zeit controlled by the IDF, or too dangerous to travel, we stayed in our village except to take our daughter to school in Ramallah, or to travel to church in Jerusalem when we could. We never felt safe, even in our own village, as clashes between militants and the IDF escalated. Innocent Palestinian civilians were frequently killed in the Ramallah region.

We felt no less vulnerable in our apartment. In 2003, Israeli soldiers entered our apartment building in full combat gear at 3:00 a.m. As they searched the building they reached our apartment on the fifth floor. Awakened by their banging on the door, I rushed to open it, but couldn't find the key. If the door wasn't opened immediately, the word was that the soldiers would blow it open. Finally, locating the key, I was gripped with fear. Should I put the key in the door? What if they took explosive action just as my hand was at the lock? I yelled out to wait; I would open the door. Slowly turning the key, I eased it open, still in my night clothes. The soldiers, after checking my identification, ordered me outside so they could search my car. There I had to sit on the curb with the other men from the building. Confirming that whomever or whatever they sought was not in the building, the soldiers allowed us back into our apartments. Thankfully, during this terrifying encounter our daughter was no longer with us, as she had been accepted into a welcoming and generous Quaker boarding school in Pennsylvania.

Traveling into Jerusalem occasionally was vital to try to maintain some perspective. Jerusalem was also wracked by militants' bombings and clashes, but it felt better than the volatility of the West Bank. Driving Highway 60 to Jerusalem, however, was like playing roulette, with life or death as the stakes. Palestinian snipers were firing on cars with yellow Israeli license plates, just like ours. The valley where Highway 60 passed near the Israeli settlement of Ofra was particularly dangerous. Several Israeli settlers had been shot to death there. In order to get to church in Jerusalem, we placed a black and white checked *kaffiyeh*, a typical Palestinian scarf, on the dashboard, a signal—hopefully—to Palestinians that we were not Israeli settlers.

The risk of passing through these roads isolated us from the spiritual support of our colleagues in the main office of the Palestinian Bible Society in Jerusalem. There were no Protestant churches in Bir Zeit. Christian visitors from abroad who were brave enough to venture into the West Bank, normally just a trickle, ceased for several years altogether. Our spiritual companionship was found in the Living Stones' staff, and friends in the Roman Catholic and Orthodox congregations in town.

Besides the spiritual isolation we were experiencing, we were struggling with the emotional distance that was growing between us and our friends, and in some cases family, in the United States. The tragedy of September 11, 2001 was opening a widening gulf of perception. For example, in the immediate aftermath of 9/11, Americans were shown images of Palestinian children dancing in their refugee camps (after having been given candy by callous authorities). On the other hand in Bir Zeit we experienced something completely different. On the night of 9/11 Muslim students came into Living Stones to extend their heartfelt condolences to us for the suffering of our country.

As Americans were experiencing a wave of Islamophobia, in our isolation we were drawn closer to our Muslim neighbors. They were willing to extend friendship to us as Americans in spite of the political distance between Ramallah and Washington. They offered some solace when the U.S. Consulate announced it could not reach its citizens on the West Bank in an emergency. Every day was an emergency. After a rare winter snow closed the roads, propane gas deliveries to the village were blocked, and in the cold our propane fueled heaters were running low. A Muslim neighbor with a heavy truck surprised us by braving the weather to bring us propane tanks.

Physically and emotionally isolated, stripped of the spiritual support we needed, as the months, and then years, passed we realized that our evangelical identity was slipping away. It was not that we were less convinced of the importance of the biblical message of Christ and of the need to communicate that to others, but, rather, in the extremity of our situation, sectarian designations seemed irrelevant. We were drawn increasingly to the essence of Christian faith, which is Jesus, and to a non-sectarian identification as "merely Christians."

At first, as we sensed this stripping away of superfluous religiosity, we had difficulty discerning what was happening to us. Were we becoming lukewarm? Were we falling away from our faith? These uncertainties gnawed at us; nevertheless, at the same time, we sensed we were diving deeper, finding richer depths of God's grace.

Our Palestinian colleagues who had introduced us to the "normal" Palestinian life, and whose lives had long been reduced to essentials, would help us understand this journey by their example. Ultimately, it was a journey to the cross. We would need their help along the way if we were not going to be dragged under by the rip tides of hatred.

It might seem obvious that living in the Holy Land, a person could become more alert to the centrality of Jesus. The prospects of renewed piety have drawn pilgrims through the centuries to Jerusalem and Galilee. But in fact, today, external religiosity and commercialism so cloak the sites of Christian pilgrimage that travel to the land can become a huge letdown for the pilgrim. The stones of religious sites can only do so much to provoke a revived spirituality. Rather, it is the *living* stones of the land, the sisters and brothers who, committed to remaining in the land, are signposts along the way, pointing to the way of Christ in the context of life's struggles.

THE CHALLENGE FOR LIVING STONES

As my wife and I were experiencing this intense spiritual journey, we were at the same time trying to understand how Christian ministry could be relevant in a place where people were struggling with dangers every day. When people were just hanging on, when the conflict was fomenting bitterness and dragging people down with discouragement, how could the biblical message of Jesus and the reality of his love be understood as something more than the usual spiritual talk that inundates the Holy Land?

Furthermore, whereas brutal conflict was pitting Israel and Palestine against each other, the Palestinian community itself was far from undivided. Downplayed for the sake of national unity, there were often, as one Palestinian Christian leader observed, sharp prejudices between Palestinian Christians and their Muslims neighbors.[4] Once I asked one of the leaders of

4. Khoury, "Living Together," 215.

the Christian students at Bir Zeit University why he chose to wear his gold cross *outside* his shirt. His reply: "Because we hate Muslims."

We wanted Living Stones to serve the whole student community, both Christian and Muslim. Especially we wanted the center to be a refuge for the Christian students who are a small minority at the university. However, the reality was that the majority of the students visiting Living Stones every night were Muslim. Even Muslim women wearing *hijab*, or head coverings, were studying in Living Stones, judging the center—which prohibited smoking—to be a safe place that would not sully their reputations. Ironically, we heard village gossip that Christians did not want to use the place because so many Muslims were there.

How could we encourage the Christian Palestinians to not only overcome their prejudices toward their Muslim neighbors, but also to accept that the grace of God extended to humanity through the crucifixion of Christ affirmed the value of all humanity—even Israelis?

The challenge did not stop there. There are also rifts between the traditions within the Christian community. Not surprisingly, there is a significant fault line between Protestants and the historic pillars of Palestinian Christianity, the Roman Catholic and Orthodox churches. Long held grudges aggravate relations between these historic traditions. Palestinian Christian ministries tend to define themselves by their particular sectarian alliances. Living Stones could easily have become caught in a tug-of-war between different churches that wanted to claim it as their own, reducing it to their own denomination's club house. This would frustrate ministry to the whole Christian community, which is the intent of the Palestinian Bible Society, with which Living Stones is associated. What could we do to negotiate all these divisions and tensions?

THE RADICAL SELF-EMPTYING OF JESUS

Isolated in Bir Zeit, with scant sense of physical security and the small comfort of religious identity stripped from us, and with the question of how to negotiate competing religious communities in front of us, I was repeatedly drawn to the account of another One who intentionally yielded to a stripping away of every vestige of security. Paul exhorted the believers in Philippi to remember the words of an early hymn[5] in Philippians 2:5–11,

5. It is widely acknowledged that Paul is quoting an early hymn in these verses, but one that might have been written by those influenced by Pauline teaching. See

encouraging them to follow the example of Christ's radical self-humbling in their attitude and behavior toward each other:

> Have this attitude in yourselves which was also in Christ Jesus,
> who, although He existed in the form of God, did not regard equality with God a thing to be grasped,
> but emptied Himself,
> taking the form of a bond-servant,
> and being made in the likeness of men.
> Being found in appearance as a man,
> He humbled Himself by becoming obedient to the point of death, even death on a cross.
> For this reason also, God highly exalted Him, and bestowed on Him the name which is above every name,
> so that at the name of Jesus knee will bow, of those who are in heaven and on earth and under the earth,
> and that every tongue will confess that Jesus Christ is Lord, to the glory of God the Father.

Paul exhorted the brothers and sisters in Philippi to "have the same attitude" toward each other as Jesus had toward humanity. That attitude was made known by the fact that he "emptied Himself," yielding the prerogatives of divinity and the glory of his place with the Father so that he could enter into the pains and limitations of the human experience.

Palestine under the control of the armies of the Roman Empire and its law was seething with the intensity of resentment and currents of revolutionary zeal, a context very similar to that which was fueling the Intifada. His disciples looked to him to usher in the messianic kingdom, to overthrow the Roman rule. The Jewish community wanted to see power unleashed.

Yet, Jesus taught that his way was to turn the other cheek to those who struck you, to carry the packs of the Roman soldiers for two miles when they demanded you to carry them for one mile. He said whoever would be the greatest should become the servant of all. This strange way to live in the face of an oppressing power, which he taught his disciples and Israel to follow, was ultimately expressed in Jesus's willingness to yield to the Father's will, and to surrender to the utter weakness and vulnerability of a brutal Roman execution.

If this was how the life of God could be planted in the context of the hard Roman rule, and the intense nationalism of Jesus's day that opposed

Murphy-O'Connor's discussion in his *Paul: A Critical Life*, 225–26.

it, perhaps there was hope through radical servanthood lived out in vulnerability. Perhaps the healing balm of Jesus could also bring relief in spite of the hatred, despair, and death in modern Israel and Palestine.

Perhaps this could be so. The strife of the Intifada, however, wounded deeply. The borders that were drawn on maps and by prejudice in the Holy Land divided the "blessed" from the "cursed," depending on one's perspective. In the Intifada those who were Other were belittled to the point of dehumanization by both peoples. There were legitimate political and security issues under contention, but each community sought to advance its cause with withering violence.

What hope did the way of the cross hold for Israel and Palestine torn by conflict? To answer this it is helpful to probe more deeply into how Jesus's emptying on the cross responded to the forces that were ripping at Jerusalem's society in his day.

JESUS'S EMPTYING TO EMBRACE HUMANNESS

The Gospel of John renders the Incarnation as something of a spiritual event, occurring mystically as spirit is transformed into physicality: "The Word became flesh, and dwelt among us," it says (John 1:14). Paul, on the other hand, emphasizes the intentionality of Jesus's incarnation. To take on the mantle of flesh, Jesus willingly *emptied* himself. There has been much theological ink spilled over the implications of the word *kenosis,* or emptied. It is certain that Jesus did not empty himself of his divine nature; he did not become less divine; he could not. Rather, he relinquished the prerogatives, the privileges, of his divine identity: his place in the glory of eternity with God the Father, his privileged authority of the Creator over creation, his existence free from the pains and limitations of this world, and the full exercise of his omnipresence, omnipotence, and omniscience.

As a result of his self-emptying, instead of enjoying the prerogatives of glory, he accepted the limitations of the human experience. Jesus emptied himself not to become a lesser spiritual being, a super angel of sorts, or a superman, for that matter; Paul emphasizes Jesus's "being made in the likeness of men" and "being found in appearance as a man" (Phil 2:7–8). Jesus resisted the satanic temptation to exercise his divine authority illegitimately by turning stones into bread to satisfy his hunger, or by casting himself down to be lifted up as a superstar. His miracles were performed in obedience to God (John 5:19) as a person of faith, like other people through whom God may work (John 14:12, Acts 3:1–8, 5:12–16).

The emptying of Jesus did not stop with the Incarnation. As one who "was teaching them as one having authority" (Matt 7:29), and whom the people were beginning to follow, he could have enjoyed prestige and acclaim; rather, he divested himself further, and "took the form of a bond-servant" (Phil 2:7). He was a servant to those who came to him for prayer. He served his disciples by patiently instructing them, by washing their feet, by cooking for them. He served social outcasts by listening to their needs and extending healing and forgiveness. To the blind man in Gaza who called after him, Jesus responded as a servant, "What do you want me to do for you?" (Luke 8:41). He served the religious leaders by pointing prophetically to the superficiality of their spirituality, the hungry by feeding them, and the demoniacs by delivering them from torment. Jesus said, "For even the Son of Man did not come to be served, but to serve, and to give His life a ransom for many" (Mark 10:45). The servanthood of Christ Jesus was full of empathy, as the writer of Hebrews stated: "For we do not have a high priest who cannot sympathize with our weaknesses, but One who has been tempted in all things as we are, yet without sin" (Heb 4:15).

Jesus emptied himself even further that he might serve all of humanity. He allowed the stripping away of all prestige, all reputation, and all claims to power to suffer death. Paul interrupts the cadence of the hymn to describe the horror of the manner of the death: "even death on a cross."[6] As it was the cross of the occupying Roman Empire, Jesus also emptied himself of militant nationalism, redefining it as will be discussed in Chapter Five. In his crucifixion, Jesus served humanity by suffering vicariously on their behalf. As Isaiah prophesied centuries before the day Jesus shouldered his cross to Golgotha:

> Surely our griefs He Himself bore,
> and our sorrows He carried;

6. Murphy-O'Connor states, "No one who goes to the trouble of creating such a perfect arrangement will destroy it. Hence, the extra words which appear in the letter, namely, "death on a cross" (v. 8c) . . . must have been added by a hand other than that of the original composer. Whose was it? The insistence on highlighting the brutal modality of Christ's death points to Paul. Paul, therefore, not only quotes a hymn, but adapts it to his own theological perspective. Originally the hymn must have been the inspired composition of a charismatic believer (1 Cor. 14:26; Col. 3:6), which Paul saw as reflecting to a great extent his vision of Christ. He accepted what it said, but made explicit what he felt was lacking." In *Paul*, 225–26.

> Yet we ourselves esteemed Him stricken,
> smitten of God, and afflicted.
> But He was pierced through for our transgressions,
> He was crushed for our iniquities;
> the chastening for our well-being fell upon Him,
> and by His scourging we are healed.
> All of us like sheep have gone astray,
> each of us has turned to his own way;
> But the LORD has caused the iniquity of us all
> to fall on Him. (Isa 53:4–6)

In Jesus's emptying of himself to become human, he affirmed the value of all of humanity. His humanity was an expression of God's love for all people. The ultimate expression of his embrace of humanity was in his willingness to walk through the pains of death in the crucifixion. It is at the cross, therefore, that God's love is fully manifest, as Paul states:

> For while we were still helpless, at the right time Christ died for the ungodly. For one will hardly die for a righteous man; though perhaps for the good man someone would dare even to die. But God demonstrates His own love toward us, in that while we were yet sinners, Christ died for us. (Rom 5:6–8)

By Jesus's sharing in our humanity, he invites us to move toward himself, to fellowship with him: "Come unto to me" (Matt 11:28). This invitation has special importance to those who, marginalized and forgotten in society, have not received any invitations. By Jesus's death on the cross, his experience of utter social shame and disgrace, he identifies with the discarded and despised, and invites them to the fullness of his life. Jürgen Moltmann describes this in *The Crucified God*:

> Following Philippians 2, a Christian theology speaks of the final and complete self-humiliation of God in man and in the person of Jesus. Here God in the person of the Son enters into the limited, finite situation of man. Not only does he enter into it, descend into it, but he also accepts it, and embraces the whole of human existence in his being. He does not become spirit so that man must first soar into the realm of the spirit in order to participate in God. He does not merely become the covenant partner of an elect people so that men must belong to this people through the circumcision and obedience to the covenant in order to enter into his fellowship, He lowers Himself and accepts the whole of mankind without limits

and conditions, so that each man may participate in him with the whole of his life.[7]

Through his affirmation of the value of humanity by emptying himself and sharing in our humanity to the point of death, Jesus established a foundation for reconciliation between peoples; as Subha, the young Palestinian woman injured by an Israeli settler stated to Israeli acquaintances who sought her forgiveness, "We are all humans. We all need forgiveness. You needn't ask for forgiveness." Through the affirmation of shared humanity, and the acknowledgement of our frailty, a way for reconciliation is made between the marginalized and the privileged, between the powerful and the weak, between genders, between the oppressed and the oppressor, and across the divide of culture.

Just as Jesus laid aside the prerogatives of glory, so reconciliation that recognizes a shared humanity requires the risk of laying aside the prerogatives of the identity one may rely on, such as "victim" or "oppressed" in the case of the Palestinian, or "rightful inheritor" in the case of the Israeli. ("All my life I have served you," said the aggrieved older brother of the prodigal son to his father. What if he had given *his* cloak to his wayward brother?)

This emptying does not negate the need for justice; rather, it creates a space for divine presence and the healing that can then occur. Justice that flows from empathy and reconciliation will have a very different quality than that which is compelled. For the Palestinians to see the Israelis with empathy, acknowledging their centuries of oppression in the Diaspora, and for Israelis to affirm the dignity of the Palestinians as a people and their own need for a land, would open the way for a true resolution of the conflict.

Is this impossibly wishful thinking? No. There is hope in the cross of Jesus. In the resurrection there is the promise that the love of God will triumph over hatred and destruction. Jesus was glorified *because of* his complete self-humiliation, his emptying of the prerogatives of retribution that were expressed in his forgiveness on the cross of his enemies. As the hymn Paul quotes states:

> For this reason also, God highly exalted Him, and bestowed on Him the name which is above every name,
> so that at the name of Jesus every knee will bow, of those who are in heaven and on earth and under the earth,
> and that every tongue will confess that Jesus Christ is Lord, to the glory of God the Father. (Phil 2:9–11)

7. Moltmann, *Crucified God*, 276.

All of humanity will bow in recognition of Jesus's name, not from the pressure of a conquering warlord, but in recognition of the victory of love and forgiveness over hatred. The confession that "Jesus Christ is Lord" is the essential confession of the Christian faith. The extent to which all of humanity will recognize the Lordship of Christ and enjoy his salvation is not clear in this hymn of praise, which is not meant to be a soteriological[8] treatise. The thrust is that universal homage will be paid to Jesus because he humbled himself unto death on a cross, and is now exalted. Similarly, the Apostle John's revelation attests to the fact that the one who now reigns on the throne is "a Lamb as though it had been slain" (Rev 5:6). The Lamb, as the one who poured himself out in love, is triumphant.

Laying aside that which one grasps to use as leverage against the other, makes possible the opportunity for both "sides" to praise God for the grace that restored their human kindness toward each other, a great gift in the brief earthly journey. As the Apostle James wrote, "Let the lowly brother glory in his exaltation, but the rich in his humiliation, because as the flower of the field he will pass away" (Jas 1:9–10).

The recognition of our shared humanity, and the empathy for the Other that it may engender, is facilitated by the personal experience of God's love in Christ Jesus and of the life that he gives. It was such an encounter that transformed Paul from oppressor to beloved brother. He wrote:

> For the love of Christ controls us, having concluded this, that one died for all, therefore all died; and He died for all, so that they who live might no longer live for themselves, but for Him who died and rose again on their behalf (2 Cor 5:14–15).

As the impact of the love of Jesus creates the potential for reconciliation, so the work of reconciliation provides wider vistas of the panorama of God's love for all mankind—its breadth, length, depth and height, as Paul wrote (Eph 3:18). Instead of the cycle of violence that feeds on attack and retribution, such an experience of Christ's love may produce a different cycle, one of forgiveness, reconciliation, and peace.

8. Soteriology is the study of Christian doctrines of salvation. It seeks to answer who will participate in God's salvation. What does this salvation entail? How does one become a participant in it, etc.?

HUMANNESS AND SPIRITUALITY

Paul exhorted, "Have this attitude in yourselves which was also in Christ Jesus" (Phil 2:5). As I reflected on this passage in the turmoil of the Intifada, it suggested that to make a difference in the context of violence in Palestine and Israel would require spirituality that incorporated vulnerable servanthood extending from an empathetically shared human experience.

As I considered this, I was struck that humanness had never been stressed as a quality of spirituality within the circles of fellowship I had encountered in my spiritual journey. On the contrary, in the Pentecostal movement with its emphasis on the power of the Spirit, there was an inference that humanness was contradictory to being spiritual. To be spiritual meant that one should be *less* of this world and its humanness. True spirituality afforded a way of escaping our humanness. The promulgators of the prosperity gospel argued that to live without suffering in total health and prosperity is the normal Christian life. The Spiritual Warfare movement created a dualistic perspective of the world in which the physical world was subservient to what occurs in the spiritual realm.

Is this what it means to be spiritual? On the contrary, Jesus's incarnation and servanthood indicate that true spirituality does not call us to negate our humanness, but rather to become more human, to press deeper into life in this world with its failures and struggles. Only when we embrace our humanness can we serve our neighbors with compassion. Servanthood that is extended from a spirituality of superiority that is above the failures of others is arrogant. Jesus, in forbidding his disciples to take an extra cloak or money, sent them on their first mission in vulnerability (Matt 10:9–10).

The idea of embracing vulnerability, serving out of weakness, had been ignored in the spirituality which I had known. It has little place in the tradition of Constantinian Christianity. Serving out of weakness was also a strange idea in the environment of violence in which force was being brought to bear to establish national supremacy, be that by Palestine or Israel. Yet, as the cross made a way for life to be received in the Jerusalem of Jesus's day—the Roman centurion at the foot of the cross uttered the first exclamation of faith, "Truly this man was the Son of God!" (Mark 15:39)—so, it could make a way for life in Israel and Palestine. But how could this be lived out? How could the way of the cross be translated into ministry plans?

FALTERING STEPS

With the Living Stones team, we considered whether Christ's empathetic servanthood could become the central value of the student center's ministry. Was this merely idealistic? Was there a practical way to act on the example of Jesus's self-emptying of the prerogatives of his identity as the Son of God; his embracing of the human experience; his self-humbling to servanthood, even to the extent of serving humanity through his death on the cross?

After reflecting on these questions, we decided to empty Living Stones, so to speak, of the prerogatives of religious identity by avoiding overt, gratuitous displays of Christian symbols that would be offensive to Muslims, and that might aggravate tensions between the Christian communities. We were careful with the music we played and with the art we placed on the walls. Most importantly, we sought to develop an attitude of acceptance and servanthood both toward those who came into Living Stones, as well in our programs conducted in the various churches and Muslim villages around Bir Zeit. We wanted to see those we served as *people* rather than as representatives of religious groups, that is as "Muslims" or "Christians," "Catholics" or "evangelicals."

With these values in mind, members of the Living Stones staff conducted programs for youth in the local Roman Catholic and Orthodox churches, and in the public schools whose student bodies are predominantly Muslim. During the summers, we initiated Life Camps for youth in Bir Zeit and surrounding villages. The association of Living Stones to the Bible Society was never obfuscated. Still, this approach was puzzling to some. Evangelical friends wondered if we had become a Muslim center. They couldn't understand ministry if it didn't display the trademarks of evangelicalism: verbal proclamation of the gospel and an expectation of conversion to a (Palestinian) Christian lifestyle. Local Christians in Bir Zeit were perplexed to see Muslim women with head coverings visiting Living Stones. Our openness to Muslims violated their sense that Christian ministries should be exclusively for Christians. At the same time, we were written off by some members of the ecumenical churches as being Protestant evangelicals.

For several years we felt we were hanging in space, mistrusted by the churches as well as Muslims in the village. Our approach would not have been possible without the open-minded national leadership of the Palestinian Bible Society, which was also searching for innovative ways of walking the tightrope between competing religious sensibilities, to bring the life and hope of Jesus into Palestinian society.

Our unorthodox approach caused some to draw the conclusion that we must be Israeli spies! Nevertheless, a fragile, but real, space was being created to serve Christians and Muslims simultaneously. Establishing a positive social space was important. During the years of the Intifada, Living Stones became a refuge. It gave the students an opportunity for a few hours of normality to play games, watch a movie, or surf the web. This in itself was a success, but Palestine needed more than this; it needed a spiritual refuge from the forces of hatred and violence, a place where the tensions that divided the communities in Palestine could be laid aside. It needed the refuge that is found in the radical love of Christ Jesus, ultimately revealed in the cross.

How could that love be revealed with such dynamism that it could break through the destructive forces at work in the conflict? Darker days lay ahead, but through them our Palestinian sisters and brothers would show the way toward this revelation, living out Paul's exhortation to have the attitude of Christ who humbled himself to the servanthood of the cross.

AHMAD

One of my most precious possessions is a photograph of the former President of the Palestinian National Authority, Yasser Arafat, wearing his trademark black and white *kaffiyeh,* inspecting his personal guard in 1997. This guard was part of the internationally approved security forces allowed in the Palestinian Authority. If Christians in the West happened to glance at this image in the media, how likely would it be that they might consider Arafat and his military guard as a probable place for the revelation of God's love? Yet, one of the men in this motley tableau would lead me deeper into the way of the cross.

In the photograph there is a young man, wearing a red beret in the front row of the guard, who bears an uncanny resemblance to a young Sylvester Stallone. Standing intently at attention he appears wholly absorbed in his duties. Yet, beneath this military bearing was a searching soul. His name is Ahmad.

Ahmad had been raised in Kuwait by Palestinian parents. His father was a successful businessman who lost everything when Saddam Hussein invaded Kuwait in 1990. Ahmad's mother and father moved to a village near Jenin in the northern area of the West Bank. Ahmad dropped out of high school and found work in a factory that manufactured metal frames for windows.[9] After several years he opted to enlist in the Palestinian security forces, where he made his way into Arafat's guard.

After his move to Palestine, Ahmad developed an unusual interest for a young Muslim man: he wanted to know more about Jesus. When asked what sparked this interest, he has a hard time putting his finger on it. At least in part, Ahmad explains, it arose from the references to Jesus in the Qur'an, which he had known since his childhood. He did not know any Christians.

Surreptitiously, he began to listen to gospel radio broadcasts in Arabic from Monaco. Standing guard outside Arafat's compound, he kept a small radio in his pocket to listen to the broadcasts. Once Ahmad's uncle caught him, and beat and threatened him. But his interest was too strong to stop. Ahmad had never been held in much esteem by those around him. He had not excelled in academics like his brothers and sisters. In Jesus's words of grace and promise, he found One who looked at his heart, not at his meager accomplishments.

Ahmad wanted to read a Bible, but it would not be easy acquiring one. Ahmad says:

> I went to the Roman Catholic Church in a nearby town to request one. But the *abuna* (priest) was very nervous. He didn't want to give me one. So eventually I wrote to an organization in Cyprus that I had heard of on the radio. They sent one to me. I lived in a small town and all the mail was received in a shop there. The shop owner was curious to see such a big package come for me. Not many packages reached our village. So he opened it to see what it was, and saw the Bible. He went and told my uncle I had received a Bible. My father had passed away by this time. My uncle was very upset with me, and threw the Bible in the garbage.
>
> After some more months passed I wrote to a Monaco radio station. I had opened a mail box in a larger city. There I finally received my first Bible. I enjoyed reading the Bible. I kept it under my pillow when I slept in the army barracks. The verse that drove the gospel home was, "It is not what enters into the mouth that defiles the man, but what proceeds out of the heart, this defiles the man" (Matt 15:11). I wanted to know the God who just looked at my heart.

9. Ahmad would eventually gain his high school diploma, a B.A. in Business Administration and, just as I was completing this writing, an M.A. in Regional Studies with an emphasis on Israeli Studies.

The Christian radio station inquired whether he would like to meet a Palestinian Christian. After considering for several weeks the risks of taking this next step, Ahmad assented. In 1997 Ahmad met Labib Madanat, a Palestinian Bible Society representative whom I have already mentioned. Over four months as they met Labib told Ahmad of the love of Jesus and of his death for him on the cross. He explained the price Ahmad would pay, the road of suffering he would have to walk, if he committed his life to Jesus. Ahmad listened, considered the cost, but could not deny his longing to yield to the love that was drawing him. Ahmad turned his life toward Jesus.

Muslim background believers, or MBBs, have a very tough road to walk. Islam does not permit the exploration of claims of truth by other religions other than as an academic pursuit. To "change religion" is to betray family, and faith, and to face the judgment of God, as the possibility of return is forbidden. It is to betray Muhammad, and to turn one's back on Allah. (The idea that those who leave Islam must be killed is not an explicit Qur'anic teaching.) Freedom of religion in Islam means that if you are a Christian or Jew you are free to remain one. The Qur'an does not justify compulsion in turning others to Islam, although historically compulsion has certainly been brought to bear on non-Muslims. That freedom to choose one's faith, however, does not extend to those already within the fold of Islam.

In Palestine, as in other Muslim majority countries, there is no place in society for converts to Christianity from Islam. In Palestinian society, if a Christian converts to Islam, a tragic occurrence in the view of the Christian community, she/he may change their government identification card's religious category to "Muslim." On the other hand, if a Muslim converts to Christianity, they may not similarly change their civil religious identity. In the eyes of all public institutions they are forever Muslim. If their children are in public school, they must attend the mandatory Islamic religion class, instead of the class for Christian students. If stopped by the IDF at a checkpoint, they will receive the harsher treatment that is at times reserved for Muslims.

While this is difficult, even more burdensome is the spiritual no-man's land in which the Muslim convert to Christianity finds herself. While there has been some recent breakthroughs, both ecumenical and evangelical Palestinian churches are cool to Muslim converts becoming regular attendees. There are several reasons for this. First, the Muslim community resents churches that share the gospel with Muslims, so churches are wary of retribution for welcoming those who are known as Muslims. Also, Christians, confusing faith with ethnicity, often argue that Muslims cannot become Christians; a leopard cannot change its spots. On a deeper level there is lingering ethnic resentment by Christians of Muslims for the persecution they have suffered through the centuries.

At the same time, Muslim converts to Christianity are wary of becoming identified as "Christians," an identity they similarly confuse with the culture of the Christian community. Muslims also have been raised with cultural prejudices: Christians eat pork; all the liquor stores in Palestine are owned by Christians; Christian women do not dress appropriately, etc. In short, Christians are viewed as a corrupt people. Consequently, if they are pressed, MBBs frequently prefer to refer to themselves as "believers in Jesus" rather than as "Christians." Such a self-identification is also necessary to avoid intense persecution. As Ahmad explains, his outward life still looks very much the same as before, but inwardly is where the change has occurred. As he states simply, "I am a believer."

The hardship an MBB faces, and an explanation for the Christian community's difficulty in understanding them, is that they are, in the important distinction made by mission historian Andrew Walls, converts rather than proselytes. They are not so much joining a new religious sect (a proselyte), as allowing Christ into their world and allowing him to reorient and redefine it. Walls states:

> Converts face a much riskier life. Converts have to be constantly, relentlessly turning their ways of thinking, their education and training, their ways of working and doing things, toward Christ. They must think Christ into the patterns of thought they have inherited, into their networks of relationship and their processes for making decisions. And new issues, cultural or intellectual, where it is necessary to make a Christian choice, are arising all the time and with no exact parallels in the past. Proselytes may walk by sight; converts have to walk by faith.[10]

The rationales for the Christian community's aloofness towards MBBs nevertheless do not ease the pain of feeling unwelcome. Ahmad and another MBB recounted the night they went into Ramallah to attend a Christmas Eve celebration and dinner at a Protestant church. The pastor met them at the door and explained that the church had only planned on so many attending, so, he was sorry to say, they could not be included. In Palestinian

10. Walls, "Converts or Proselytes?," 2–6.

culture, which places a high value on hospitality, this was more than inhospitable: it was an intense, painful insult.

Shortly after I was assigned to the Living Stones project in 1998, Ahmad joined me as my coworker. He spoke very little English, and my Arabic was feeble. By the beginning of the Intifada in 2000, Ahmad had endured the spiritual isolation of an MBB for several years. Our fellowship together was his primary source of spiritual input. I would try to help him understand the Bible; Ahmad guided me in Palestinian culture, patiently bailing me out when I committed a cultural *faux pas*.

Ahmad was as stubborn as me, and occasionally we would butt heads, finding ourselves in good shouting matches! There was, though, a tenderness I admired in Ahmad. He had felt the sting of being an outcast as a high school dropout and as a outsider in his family's village. Although his parents were Palestinian, when Ahmad moved from Kuwait he was labeled an *ajnabi,* a foreigner. He felt a deep compassion for the boys in our summer camps who were from poor families, and marked as troublemakers in their villages. When these boys would get rambunctious, Ahmad would take them aside and talk with them patiently, helping them calm down and cooperate with the program.

Ahmad wasn't oriented toward doctrine or theology in his Christian journey, and often it was difficult to gauge progress in his spiritual life. He had no idea of Christian lingo and the God talk of the ostensibly spiritual. He couldn't fake it if he tried. Since Ahmad was undereducated, untaught biblically, and a chain-smoking believer, in our first years of work together I considered Ahmad to be on shaky spiritual ground.

How wrong Ahmad would prove me to be.

Ahmad played an increasingly important role in Living Stones. People could not understand what this "Muslim" was doing helping to lead a Bible Society center. In the courage of his convictions he created a unique, living bridge between the Muslim and Christian students. Together we explored the way to make Living Stones an authentic spiritual center. But, in spite of some success, our progress seemed superficial. We were providing an important social service, but how could our efforts open the doors for an authentic encounter with Christ? We were still searching for a way to make the gospel of Jesus relevant in the conflict. For this to be realized, a deeper revelation of the cross would be needed. But how?

On October 28, 2005, just past midnight, an alarm in Living Stones blared, shattering the silence on the village streets. The closest neighbor to the center phoned Ahmad in Ramallah that there was a problem and asked him to please come turn off the alarm. Ahmad threw on some clothes and sped to Bir Zeit. What he found was ugly and disturbing. Across the stone façade of Living Stones someone had spray-painted in large red letters: "Believe in the Prophet Muhammad. Get out of this country." The front window was shattered. Smoke was billowing out through the broken panes. The lower floor windows were smashed. A second Molotov cocktail had been thrown into the office. The computers and desks were smoldering, completely destroyed.

As the village began to awaken and move through the streets, people were shocked to see the graffiti on the building and hear the news of the fire-bombing. In recent memory, the village had not known of an attack on Christian buildings by those who appeared to be Muslim fanatics. The wheels of gossip began to spin: What had we done to anger Muslims so? Were we indeed Israeli spies? Were we a Zionist organization?

Ahmad was shaken, but determined. As I was in the U.S. at the time, he contacted me immediately with the bad news. A wave of fear swept over me. What had we done wrong? We were relating well to the Muslim community. It seemed that all of our efforts to build relationships during the last five years had been futile.

What should we do? My advice was that Ahmad close Living Stones for a few weeks—or even months—in order to clean the place and to let the tensions ease. No, he argued, if we closed the center, our attackers would know that they could push us back.

Within hours, Ahmad had painted over the threatening graffiti. He swept up the broken glass, mopped and wiped off the smoke-smeared counter where students take their coffee. Then he did something strange. Ahmad went to the village sweet shop and bought a big box of candies. These are sweets that are normally shared with friends at a time of success and celebration, such as when a daughter or son graduates from high school. When Living Stones opened in the evening, Ahmad stood in front of the building, just a few feet away from where the ugly graffiti had been written. As villagers strolled by enjoying the evening air, Ahmad offered them the sweets from a large tray.

The next day I queried Ahmad, what was he thinking with this gesture? He answered simply: "I hope the people who threw the fire took some of the sweets. They gave us fire; we will give them sweets."

I was stunned by his reply. Here was the attitude of Christ that Paul exhorted. Ahmad had emptied himself of the prerogative of anger and ret-ribution. All the staff had been threatened by the attack, but none more so than Ahmad, as the only MBB leading a ministry on the West Bank. Never-theless, he embraced servanthood, and this was servanthood that extended out of weakness and vulnerability. What did Ahmad serve that evening? He served forgiveness, and, as he did so, he celebrated the love of Jesus.

In a culture that condones revenge to protect honor, this act of for-giveness was prophetic, and it began to break down walls of mistrust. A few days later the highest Islamic cleric in Ramallah stopped by the center. He wanted to inquire what we were doing. "We are trying to serve all people," Ahmad answered. The following Friday the shaykh of the local mosque in his Friday sermon, which is broadcast from loud speakers to the whole village, declared that no one was to touch Living Stones.

Living Stones enjoyed several months of peace, but the calm would be broken again by two more attacks, less severe than the first, but still dispir-iting and jarring. Finally, Palestinian security forces made an arrest. The attacks had been led by a university student and a few of his cronies who were enraged that a Christian ministry was making the gospel available to Muslims. After his arrest, the student was held in Ramallah, awaiting a decision on how he would be judged.

What to do with the militant student attackers? As many problems in Palestinian culture are still settled by negotiations between clans, rather than in courts, the head of the radical student's family approached Ahmad and asked what demands he was going to make. My enlightened spiritual advice at that time was that someone who repeatedly had committed arson should be incarcerated for a long stretch. Ahmad had a different idea. He said to the clan leader: "He has nothing. I have the Spirit of God. Do not do anything to the boy, only promise he will never hit us again." From that day five years ago, there has not been another attack.

Again, Ahmad's act of forgiveness, of emptying himself of the pre-rogative of judgment, had a real spiritual impact. Sometime afterward, the leaders of the town were invited to participate in Living Stones' dedication of a new garden terrace that we had built behind our building. The shaykh of the mosque also attended. After the local clergy prayed a blessing, the evening's program was going to proceed, when a hand was raised. The Muslim shaykh wanted to say something. A burly man with a big beard, he made his way to the front. As he came forward I was apprehensive. What in the world would he say? Would he disrupt what was a happy celebration?

Taking the microphone, the shaykh began his comments with the ubiquitous Islamic invocation: "*Bism Allah al Rahman al Rahim*," "In the Name of the God, the Merciful, the Compassionate." Then his voiced boomed, "We want to bless Living Stones. We thank God for what Living Stones is doing for our youth. We want to support you."

Here in one night we saw the fruit of ten years of work. The religious communities—the evangelical community, the ecumenical churches, and even the Islamic leaders—which had eyed us with such suspicion were now by our side. Against all odds, in a context more often characterized by enmity and suspicion, relations of peace and trust had been formed. This peace was gained by trying to walk in the way of Christ in his self-emptying unto servanthood out of weakness, and such a servanthood which offered forgiveness in the face of threat. In short, this peace was gained through the way of the cross. And the way of the cross was made real to us by a Palestinian Muslim who had found his way to Jesus.

4

Partnering with the Enemy

When the days were approaching for His ascension, He was determined to go to Jerusalem; and He sent messengers on ahead of Him, and they went and entered a village of the Samaritans to make arrangements for Him. But they did not receive Him, because He was traveling toward Jerusalem. When His disciples James and John saw this, they said, "Lord, do You want us to command fire to come down from heaven and consume them?" But He turned and rebuked them, and said, "You do not know what kind of spirit you are of; for the Son of Man did not come to destroy men's lives, but to save them." And they went on to another village.

LUKE 9:51–56

AHMAD'S EXAMPLE OF RADICAL servanthood and humility helped build bridges of peace. It created space for friendships to flourish, for trust to be strengthened. Nevertheless, this moment of reconciliation we experienced in Living Stones, a brief oasis of peace, did not lessen the reality of the persistent, tough tensions that continue to wrack Palestinian society. Palestine and Israel are no place for dreamy spiritual romanticism. Good intentions are easily disregarded, a blind eye turned to gestures of reconciliation. There are hard forces at work, driven by determined people who seek the supremacy of their communities at any cost. In this maelstrom of fevered political and religious passion, human life becomes dispensable, as the Christians of Gaza know well.

RAMI

Rami Ayyad was a quiet and gentle man with a strong frame and warm personality. Always willing to help, his friends say that he could often be found extending a helping hand with projects around the Gaza Baptist Church, where he was a prominent member. Rami had grown up in Gaza City in the Gaza Strip. This dusty and densely populated swath of desert along the Mediterranean Sea, bordered by Egypt on the south and Israel on the north and east, is part of Palestine. With a population of 1.4 million people, of which only about 1,500 are Christians, Gaza is one of the most densely populated and impoverished communities in the world.

Christians in the West, wary of the increasing, yet still comparatively small Muslim presence in their societies, should try to imagine what life is like growing up in Gaza as a member of its tiny Christian community. How would they relate to their Muslim neighbors in a situation in which Christians are not wielding power? Rami's response was to press deeper into Christ, seeking ways to serve the most impoverished of his Muslim neighbors in the refugee camps of Gaza.

Rami was the manager of the Palestinian Bible Society's center in Gaza City, the Teacher's Bookshop, and Gaza's only Christian bookstore. The Teachers Bookshop had first opened with joy and high expectations in 1998. It offered the Bible and Christian literature, but it also was a center for educational resources, professional training courses, and relief distribution in the crowded refugee camps where Palestinian families have eked out meager livings since being expelled from their villages in 1948.

With the rise of Islamic militancy in Gaza, the Teacher's Bookshop experienced several attacks. On February 3, 2006, militants detonated two pipe bombs, destroying the bookstore's doors. The assault was accompanied by a communiqué demanding the shop close immediately.[1] The team assessed the risks, but felt they should not close.

On April 15, 2007 a more serious attack occurred. A bomb destroyed much of the shop's downstairs storefront.[2] The bookshop's guard was severely beaten by masked assailants who entered the building to plant the explosives.[3] Following this attack, the bookstore began to operate more carefully, keeping closed the front doors, which opened onto a busy main

1. Alford, "Christian Bookstore Manager Martyred in Gaza City."
2. Ibid.
3. "Palestinian Bible Society Building Bombed in Latest Gaza Incident."

street. The Palestinian Authority's security forces did not know who was staging these assaults.

In the evening of October 6, 2007, after locking the doors to the Teacher's Bookshop, Rami was forced into a car and abducted by militants. Rami phoned his wife, Pauline, and told her he had been abducted and hoped to be home in two hours. The night passed without his return. In the morning Pauline and their two small children received the terrible news that his broken body had been found in the street about one mile from the bookshop. He had apparently been shot and repeatedly stabbed.[4] No one claimed credit for his shameful murder. Palestinian security forces made no arrests.

Rami's martyrdom was a shock to the Christian community both in Gaza and the West Bank, which had lived for centuries at relative peace with their Muslim neighbors. The residents were now gripped with apprehension. The Bible Society team in Gaza, feeling increasingly threatened, was able to obtain permits from Israel to relocate to the West Bank for several months (a rare exception to restrictive policies that do not allow free movement out of Gaza). The attack was so alarming to Palestinian society that President of the Palestinian Authority, Mahmoud Abbas, addressed Rami's death, calling on Muslims to respect Christian organizations.

BARBARIANS AT THE GATES?

Rami's tragic death is representative of the increasing pressure that Arab Christians are enduring in the Middle East. Christians in Egypt and Iraq have suffered the bombing and burning of their churches, in some cases suffering many deaths. In recent years there have been, as well, a rising number of apparently targeted martyrdoms of Christian workers, such as Rami, including Western missionaries. Beyond the Middle East, militant Muslims have brutally attacked Christians at worship in Nigeria, and burnt their churches in Indonesia.

How should this rise of violence against Christians be interpreted? Is it an historical aberration caused by situational political and militaristic forces? Or does it mean that Islam is fundamentally violent and anti-Christian?

But more important than discerning the rationale for the militant violence against Christians by Muslims, how should Christians respond? Is there an acceptable oppositional stance that is consistent with the teachings

4. Alford, "Christian Bookstore Manager."

of Christ Jesus? Should Islam simply be labeled as a demonic movement that is opposed to God? Should Christian mission to Islam be characterized as seeking to overcome a stronghold of evil in the world? Is the mandate of Christ to love one's neighbor relevant in such a global struggle?

How these questions are answered by the Christian West will determine at least in part whether its mission will have any continuing effectiveness and relevance in the world. Islam, comprising one fifth of the world's population, is a global movement, as is Christianity. The manner in which these two communities treat each other is on display globally and will either support or negate their respective claims to offer a way of peace and hope in an increasingly violent world. The future for both movements will be troubled unless they will overcome their historic hostilities.

When Islam exploded out of the Arabian Peninsula in the seventh century, it rocked the Christian world on its heels. Until that point, it appeared that Christian civilization would continue to expand throughout the world. The young Islamic community understood its role to be a witness "over the nations," calling them into submission to the true god, Allah, and a correction to the errors of Judaism and Christianity.[5] According to Islamic faith, the revelation of a fundamental truth had been given to Muhammad, the final prophet of God, that, "There is no God but God, and Muhammad is the prophet of God."

Islam became the first serious threat not only to Christianity's expansion, but also, it appeared at that time, to its very existence. By 638 CE, only six years after the death of its founder, Muhammad, Islam had conquered Jerusalem, the Holy City. Alexandria, the great center of Byzantine Christianity, fell to Islam in 641 CE. Within one hundred years of Muhammad's flight to Medina from Mecca in 622 CE, which resulted in the formation of the first Muslim community, half of the Christians in the world were under Muslim governance.[6]

Where Islam ruled there would be a steady reduction of Christian presence as Christians converted to Islam for various reasons, not least of which was the effort of Islam—and the inevitable pressure—to bring Christians into the *ummah*, or Islamic community.[7] As David W. Shenk, a long-time Mennonite missionary to the Muslim world and scholar of Islam, has noted, in many countries where Islam has been the majority

5. Shenk, *Journeys of the Muslim Nation and the Christian Church*, 31.

6. Ibid., 32.

7. Ibid.

community, including Yemen, northern Sudan, and Libya, the ancient churches have vanished.[8]

From the first aggressive expansion of Islam, the Christian community generally has assumed a reactive posture toward Islam. The Crusades (1098–1281 CE), which have been discussed, were the nadir of this oppositional response. These failed efforts to expel Islam from the Holy Land deeply antagonized relations between the Christian West and Islam, and coarsened Christian spirituality, further embedding violence in its tradition.

Islamic armies conquered the great Christian center of Constantinople in 1453 CE, and subsequent Islamic expansions would reach to the outskirts of Vienna where they were defeated in 1683 CE. For centuries during the Middle Ages, Europeans lived in fear of Islamic armies overrunning their towns and villages. The father of the Protestant Reformation, Martin Luther, wrote in 1530 CE of the threat of "the Turk" to Europe.[9] These fears were not unfounded in view of the wide Islamic conquests. With trade routes controlled by Islam and its armies at European gates for several centuries, deep roots of fear of Islam were put down into Western Christian cultural soil.

The persistence and subtlety of these fears and prejudices are evidenced even among the intellectuals and artists of the last two centuries in the West as Edward Said (1935–2003) has demonstrated in his landmark work, *Orientalism*.[10] Said, a native Arab Palestinian, was born in British Mandate Jerusalem. He was educated in the United States and was an influential literary critic, author, and professor of English and Comparative Literature at Columbia University for many years. According to Said, orientalism is the manner in which those in the West view the Arab world, inevitably depicting it as other than the West, strange, exotic, and always inferior.[11]

Ironically, contrary to European fears, under Islamic rule in Spain during the Middle Ages a unique society was formed, marked to a certain extent by toleration and the inclusion of Christians and Jews.[12] The Chris-

8. Ibid.

9. Volf, *Allah*, 61.

10. Said, *Orientalism*.

11. Ibid.

12. See Lowney, *A Vanished World*. Lowney, 208, writes, "Muslims, Jews, and Christians sometimes triumphed to forge accommodations with neighbors of different faiths, creating a common life unlike any other achieved or even imagined elsewhere on Europe's continent in the medieval era."

tian Inquisition that followed the *Reconquista*, the reconquering of Spain by Christian armies urged onward by papal directives, drove Jews from Spain or forced them to convert to Christianity. Most of the Jewish refugees who fled Christian rule in Spain eventually found safety in Islamic societies.[13]

The question that might be asked at this point is whether Islamic militarism in the service of its empire in the Middle Ages lessened the Christian obligation to bear witness to the love and humility of Christ? For Francis of Assisi, as has been mentioned, it did not diminish it at all. Islam must confront excess violence within its own community to be sure, but the oppressive actions of other communities, whether the Roman Empire's governance of Jerusalem in the days of Jesus, or Islamic militantism today, do not provide a justification for Christians to abandon the way of the cross. For Rami Ayyad, Islamic extremism in Gaza did not negate Christ's commandment to love and forgive even in the face of threats and attacks against his office.

Forty years ago not many Christians in the West were preoccupied with the Muslim world. The foil for Christian faith was Communism. End times prognosticators warned of the Beast from the north. The first Gulf War (1990–1991) brought Islam to the attention of the West. Yet, enmity in this war was focused on Saddam Hussein and his regime's occupation of Kuwait rather than specifically on Islam. The devastating attack on the World Trade Center on September 11, 2001, perpetrated by Arab men who identified themselves with Islam, brought the West face to face with their centuries-old nemesis.

The reaction of the Christian community to this disaster and to the growing presence of Islam in Western Europe and the United States indicates that little progress had been made in overcoming its historic fear and enmity toward Islam. Far from seeking peace and reconciliation with the Islamic community after 9/11, many American Christians reasserted medieval images of an implacable enemy. One nationally known Christian leader referred to Muhammad as a "terrorist."[14] Another declared Islam to be a wicked, violent, and basically evil religion.[15] These deeply prejudicial comments were instantly transmitted to the Muslim world via the Internet.

---

13. Ibid., 227–46.

14. Ostling, "Falwell Calls Muhammad 'Terrorist.'"

15. These comments were made by Franklin Graham, the son of evangelist Billy Graham. See Charisma News Service, "Preacher's Anti-Islam Remarks Mobilize the White House."

Taking their cues from these leaders and others in the months after 9/11, rank and file Christians expressed their strong convictions that Islam was their mortal enemy. As I was meeting with the mission leader of a local church in the U.S., he confided that he was so wary of Muslims that if he saw a Muslim woman with a head covering walking down the street, he would cross to the other side! When I was speaking to another congregation, a woman, her face contorted with emotion, asked me, "Doesn't the Qur'an say that Muslims are supposed to kill all Christians?" (My response was a challenge: befriend a Muslim for one year, and at the end of that year ask yourself the same question.) My wife, sitting in a lecture at a Christian college was surprised when the seasoned biblical studies professor stated emphatically, "Every Christian should know we are at war with Islam."

For these and the millions who share their fears and prejudices, the death of Rami Ayyad, the attack of 9/11, and images of militants fighting the U.S. in Afghanistan and Iraq, can only mean one thing: Islam is a mortal enemy of Christian civilization. The barbarians are at the gates! Such a perception by Christians leads to an oppositional stance: if they are our enemies, we are theirs.

SEEKING A COMMON WORD

Could there be another reason other than global economic and political forces behind the fact that the Christian West is again face to face with Islam after all these centuries? Could it be that God who "puts down one and exalts another" (Ps 75:7) has a purpose in this? Could it be that God is calling Christians to see this as a momentous day, a day in which we have the opportunity to make a prophetic decision to turn the chapter in our troubled history with Islam; a day in which we may decide, as did Ahmad and Rami, to press deeper into the self-emptying love and the servanthood in humility of Christ, at whatever the cost, so that Islam will finally, on a wide scale, have a chance to encounter the beauty of the grace and mercy of Jesus; a day in which, if we are willing to encounter Islam with the acknowledgement of our shared humanity, an oasis might be created for God's creative hand to heal the wounds between our two communities?

Some Western Christians are indeed seizing the day and exploring new ways forward in Christian and Muslim relationships. In professional theological and ministerial circles, relational and theological bridges are being built that facilitate dialogue. These bridges for dialogue are not being constructed from only the Christian side of the divide. On October 13, 2006, Pope Benedict XVI delivered a controversial lecture at Regensburg University in Germany. The address was a statement on world affairs and included comments on the importance of reason in conversion, rather than coercion.[16] In his remarks the pontiff made reference to negative statements about Islam made by a late fourteenth-century Byzantine emperor, Manuel II Palaiologos, one of the last Christian rulers before the fall of Constantinople. He quoted the following:

> Show me just what Muhammad brought that was new and there you will find things only evil and inhuman, such as his command to spread by the sword the faith he preached.[17]

Although the pontiff noted that these words were not his own, the apparent revival of medieval images of Islam was an affront to the Muslim community. Yet the Muslim response, especially considering that Western armies were fighting in two Muslim majority countries at the time, was unusual. One year to the day after the papal address, scholars representing all branches of Islam issued their reply in the form of an open letter entitled, "A Common Word between Us and You."[18] This document calls for justice and peace between Christian and Muslim communities based on a mutual recognition of their common emphasis on love for God and love for mankind.

Christian leaders responded with numerous official statements.[19] The majority, including the papal response, were strongly affirmative of the thrust of "The Common Word" toward building bridges of understanding between their respective communities. Evangelical leaders have also sponsored dialogues with Muslim scholars to build on this historic Muslim overture. One important response was issued by scholars at the Yale Center

16. "The pontiff was comparing apparently contradictory passages from the Qur'an, one being that 'There is no compulsion in religion,' the other being that it is acceptable to 'spread the faith through violence.' The pontiff argued the latter teaching to be unreasonable and advocated that religious conversion should take place through the use of reason. His larger point here was that, generally speaking, in Christianity, God is understood to act in accordance with reason, while in Islam, God's absolute transcendence means that 'God is not bound even by his own word,' and can act in ways contrary to reason, including self-contradiction. At the end of his lecture, the Pope said, 'It is to the great logos, to this breadth of reason, that we invite our partners in the dialogue of cultures.'" See "Regensberg Lecture."

17. Ibid.

18. "Christian Responses."

19. Yale Center for Faith and Culture, "Loving God and Neighbor Together."

for Faith and Culture at Yale University. Entitled "A Christian Response to 'A Word between Us and You,'" it states:

> We receive the open letter as a Muslim hand of conviviality and cooperation extended to Christians worldwide. In this response we extend our own Christian hand in return, so that together with all other human beings we may live in peace and justice as we seek to love God and our neighbors.[20]

Regrettably, though, these efforts have had little effect in raising the level of discussion in grassroots Western evangelical circles. There are several reasons for this resistance. First, as I will discuss later, evangelicals frequently portray Islam as the evil enemy whom God will destroy at the final battle of Armageddon. To change that narrative would involve rethinking their eschatological expectations, which are a foundational building block in their spiritual worldview. Another reason for the gap between dialogic efforts that are underway and local evangelical churches is that "theology" and "dialogue" are, for many, code words for "liberal," or compromised Christianity. For most conservative evangelical Christians, the culture of Yale Divinity School is remote from their lives, and its arguments unpersuasive.

Perhaps more helpful in overcoming long-held suspicions and hostilities is for Western evangelical Christians to consider the struggles and fears of their fellow evangelicals in the Middle East. These Arab Christians have reason to resent Islam after centuries of marginalization and, at times, oppression, and many do; yet, some are not satisfied with living in hate. Some courageous sisters and brothers are exploring where the way of the cross will lead them in their relationship with their Muslim neighbors. A look back helps us to appreciate the Arab Christian journey and the decisions of some Christians in the Middle East today who are exploring creative paths forward in engagement with the Muslim community.

CHRISTIANS BECOME A MINORITY IN THE MIDDLE EAST

As discussed earlier, the growing community of Islam in the seventh century, when still only decades old, emerged out of the desert cities and wilderness of Arabia with tremendous energy. Islam expanded so explosively that within a decade after the death of its founder, Muhammad, in 632 CE,

20. Ibid.

it had spread across North Africa to present day Morocco, and conquered the Sassanid (Persian) Empire to the east.

Although the weakening of the Byzantine and Persian empires created a space for an emerging empire, the Islamic faith was the motivating force in this expansion. Islam takes its name from the decree of God in the Qur'an:[21] "Indeed the religion in the sight of Allah is Islam . . . " (Qur'an 3.19).

Just as Christianity has the hope that God's reign will be fully realized in this world, that the will of God will be done on earth as it is in heaven (Matt 6:10), Islam envisions that the whole world will come under the dominion of *Allah*, or God in Arabic. When all of creation is submitted to God, it will be at peace, or *salaam* (a word derived from the same basic root, s-l-m, as *Islam*). This peace is spread by bringing people into submission to Allah. As the Qur'an states:

> So if they argue with you say, "I have submitted myself to Allah [in Islam], and [so have] those who follow me." And say to those who were given the Scripture and [to] the unlearned, "Have you submitted yourselves?" And if they submit they are rightly guided; but if they turn away—then upon you is only the duty of notification. And Allah is seeing of [His] servants. (Qur'an 3.20)

The majority of Muslims today regard this process of bringing humanity into submission to Allah as a result of persuasion, not force. A person who has so submitted her/himself to Allah is a *m-islam,* or Muslim, a submitted one. From this perspective, anyone who lived in submission to Allah before Muhammad was a Muslim. Accordingly, Jesus, the second most important prophet in Islam, is regarded as a Muslim; the same as Mary, the mother of Jesus, Noah, Abraham, Moses, and David.

Most in the West understand *jihad*, or striving in the way of God,[22] as only referring to acts of violence against non-Muslims. This perception, though incorrect, has some basis today as Islamic militants speak of perpetrating acts of violence as *jihad*. Indeed, in the early expansion of Islam, its conquering armies were motivated by the concept of *jihad*. But, as the meaning of *jihad* has come to be further articulated in Islam, it speaks first of the personal effort to obey Allah in one's own life; secondarily it refers to the effort to bring all others into Islam.[23]

---

21. Farah, *Islam*, 103.

22. Hourani, *A History of the Arab Peoples*, 66.

23. Farah, *Islam*, 154.

Historically Islam has had a standard for just *jihad* that has developed over time, as have Christian ideas of just war. Among other things, according to Islamic tradition, *jihad*, when it refers to warfare, is to be defensive rather than aggressive, proportionate in its response, and careful not to take the lives of innocents.[24] But, as with Christianity, Islam must practice some contortions in order to justify both its historic and present use of force as legitimate *jihad*, or just war.

Early in its history Islam, like the Christian Byzantine and the later Holy Roman empires, joined faith and empire.[25] The armies of Islam mounted *jihad* against the Byzantine and Persian forces as they expanded, but the popular image of Islam conquering and forcing conversion by the sword is exaggerated. The more typical pattern of a city's conquest, in the case of Christian regions, was that its Byzantine rulers, often resented by local populations, were given a choice to either surrender or face the use of force. Once Muslim leaders were installed, having secured the surrender of the Byzantine leaders, the life of the city went on much as usual with the local Christian and Jewish communities guiding their own affairs, though under new restrictions. Leveraging the potential use of force to effectuate the surrender of a city was regarded as legitimate *jihad*.[26]

It is worth noting that Christians during this early phase of their engagement with Islam had varying interpretations of Islam. Some understood its rapid expansion as a fulfillment of God's promises to Hagar and Ishmael that they would become a great nation (Gen 21:13), a judgment on Christians who would not accept the orthodox Christology, or simply a Christian heretical movement.[27]

Muslims, after an early antagonistic stance toward Christians and Jews, adopted a more conciliatory approach. Regarded by Islam as "people

---

24. As the Qur'an states concerning reciprocity and proportionality in war:
"Fight in the way of Allah those who fight against you, but do not transgress. Indeed Allah does not like transgressors" (Qur'an 2.190).
"And if you punish [an enemy, O believers] punish with an equivalent of that with which you were harmed. But if you are patient—it is better for those who are patient" (Qur'an 16.126).

25. Donald McCurry, a mission leader with long experience in the Muslim world, argues that the influence of the Byzantine Empire's joining of the sword and faith could have been a formative influence on the early Islamic community, and the continuing Christian militarism have continued to establish that paradigm of spirituality up to the present. See McCurry, "Islam and Christian Militancy".

26. Braswell, *Islam*, 74.

27. Goddard, *History of Christian-Muslim Relations*, 48.

of the book" because of their faith in revealed scriptures, Christians and Jews (and later people of other faiths) were given *dhimmi*, or protected, status.[28] This protected and restricted minority status was formalized in a collection of writings that came to be known as the *Covenant of Umar*, after the second caliph, or ruler, after Muhammad, Umar in the seventh century CE. Under this covenant, which was applied with varying degrees of severity in different cities, Christians could lead their own communities, but were required to pay a special tax, and in some cases wear special clothing. They were forbidden to march publicly with the cross, and, of course, could not proselytize Muslims. Although from contemporary standards, *dhimmi* status, or dhimmitude, violates principles of social justice, in the context of the Middle Ages, historians argue that it created better treatment than was usual for minority groups.[29]

How and when did Christians in the Middle East become a minority? Conversion to Islam occurred for different reasons and at different rates in various places. Some converted to Islam to avoid paying the *jizya*, the poll tax. Some converted to advance themselves in Islamic institutions, some to avoid the threat of violence, and some because Christian women married Muslim men. Others, as well, converted because they were persuaded by the Islamic message.[30]

By the tenth century the majority of the population in Egypt was Muslim. It was not until several centuries later, perhaps around the beginning of the fourteenth century, that the same occurred in Syria (that is in the region that includes what is today Syria, Palestine/Israel, Jordan, and Lebanon).[31] During the Middle Ages and afterward, the Christian minority continued to decrease in relation to the Muslim community. Today in Palestine, including the West Bank, Gaza, and East Jerusalem, all Christian traditions amount to less than two percent of the population, although they have much greater influence in Palestinian society than these numbers represent.[32] Tragically, the dwindling presence of Christians in the Holy Land continues. The "worsening economic, political, educational, and social

28. For further discussion of *dhimmi* status see ibid., 41–48.
29. Denny, *Introduction to Islam*, 75.
30. Goddard, *History of Christian-Muslim Relations*, 68–74.
31. Ibid., 70–71.
32. "Palestinian Christians."

conditions are prompting many Christians to consider joining those who have already fled their homeland."[33]

How has this history affected the Arab Christian community in general and Palestinian Christians specifically? As was mentioned previously, Christian and Muslim Palestinians are united in their national aspirations, and work together for that purpose, but patterns of *dhimmi* status remain. For example, on one occasion when Christians processed through the village of Bir Zeit during Easter celebrations, with Boy and Girl Scout[34] marching teams leading the way, I witnessed Muslim youth throwing rocks and taunting some of the marchers as the youth resented the public display of Christian faith. Although the *adnan*, the five-times-daily Muslim call to prayer, is broadcast from mosques with loud speakers, the public witness of Christians to their faith through similar public broadcasts of music or processions is only permitted around religious holidays.

As a result of the centuries of minority status and diminishing numbers, wounds of distrust and resentment still fester. These wounds fuel what one Palestinian Christian leader has characterized as "visceral prejudices" against their Muslim neighbors.[35] Accordingly, the Christian community, in terms of its faith, tends to adopt a bunker mentality toward Muslims. Generally speaking, while Christian organizations liberally extend services to Muslims, there is little thought by the average Christian of welcoming a Muslim into a Sunday worship service.[36]

Western Christians have belittled the historic churches in the Middle East for their lack of mission. The first Protestant missionaries that arrived in the region treated the Roman Catholic and Orthodox communities as false Christians who were doing more harm to the cause of Christ than good (and this disregard was returned in kind!).[37] Today, Western evangelical Christians—if they are aware that there are Christians in the Arab and

33. Ateek, et al., eds., *The Forgotten Faithful*, 17.

34. In Palestine, the Boy and Girl Scouts are located within the Christian community.

35. Khoury, "Living Together," 215.

36. Palestinian law allows for the private practice of religion as long as such practice does not disturb public order. Islam is the official religion of the state of Palestine. Accordingly, although there is no specific prohibition against proselytism, because Islam does not permit Christian evangelism of its community, public proselytism is not permitted. Nevertheless, discussion of religion on a personal basis is allowed. See "Palestinian Law."

37. A useful study (though certainly not sympathetic) of early Protestant mission in the Levant is Makdisi's *The Artillery of Heaven*.

Muslim Middle East—have expressed little regard for Arab Christianity, associating it with the Orthodox and Roman Catholic traditions.

Western Christians who avidly support Israel's right to possess all of the Holy Land fail to acknowledge that their ideology contributes to dispossessing fellow believers in Jesus, Palestinian Christians. Influential author, speaker, and professor Tony Campolo has stated, "Most evangelical Christians in particular, as well as Christians in general, are not even aware that there are Christians in the Arab community, and especially in the Palestinian community . . . which is evidence of massive ignorance on our part."[38]

In the history of Christianity, the long and difficult journey of Arab Christianity and its vital contribution to the faith needs to be appreciated by Western Christians.[39] Indeed, there was an Arab believer in Jesus who was speaking in tongues with Mary on the day of Pentecost, when the followers of Christ were filled with the Spirit of God (Acts 2:11)!

In spite of this difficult history of increasing marginalization by the majority Muslim community, and its self-segregation, some Palestinian Christians are seeking to break through patterns of reactive resentment to listen and learn from their Muslim neighbors, as they seek creative ways to extend by servanthood and friendship the reality of the way of the cross to them. Labib Madanat, whom I have previously mentioned, has been prophetic in his willingness to blaze new trails in working with and serving the Muslim community.

LABIB: "I NEEDED A SECOND CONVERSION TO LOVE"

Although a native Jordanian, Labib was raised in the heart of the Palestinian evangelical community. His father was a pastor in Jerusalem and Ramallah, and Labib remembers being encouraged from the earliest years of his childhood by the warmth of fellowship and the prayers of the older members of the church. In spite of his Christian upbringing, Labib says, "I needed two more conversions: to a love for Muslims and a love for Jews. I carried all the prejudices of a typical Arab Christian."[40]

---

38. Tony Campolo, interview with Andrew Bush.

39. The under-appreciated story of the efforts of Arab Christians to defend their faith theologically during the rise of Islam in the Middle Ages is told by Griffith in his *The Church in the Shadow of the Mosque*.

40. Labib Madanat, interview by Andrew Bush, July 25, 2008.

In 1981, as a university student, Labib had the opportunity to study agricultural science at the University of Mosul in Iraq. There, sharing a room with three Muslim students, his journey into compassion and concern for Muslims began. His university studies coincided with the Iraq-Iran war (1980–1988). The horrible sight of Muslims slaughtering each other, their corpses stacked in piles, was displayed daily on television. In contrast to the brutality of the war, Labib recalls that he began to understand the humanness, sensitivity, and spiritual thirst of Muslims through the words of his roommate, Hussein. He says:

> Toward the end of one of the days, I was sitting on my bed before going to sleep and was reading my Bible. Hussein, my roommate, whose bed was exactly opposite mine, asked me: "Labib, what are you reading?" I answered: "The Bible, would you like to read some?" He said: "No, I am not clean, could you read some for me?" So I read a bit from the story of the crucifixion. Halfway through, he had tears in his eyes, and as I finished my short reading, he said: "I felt my whole body shiver, this must be the word of God!"
>
> The Bible words shook Hussein, but Hussein's words shook me and had a similar effect on me as my Bible reading had on him. The challenge to my worldview had already started. My attitude toward Muslims started to change . . . [41]

Returning to Jordan to pursue a graduate degree, Labib's motivation for mission toward Muslims grew, but it was marred by his attitude about Muslims typical of Arab Christians. He recalls that Muslims became important to him as mission "targets." He states that for most Arab evangelical Christians, evangelism was born out of a sense of duty, and not "out of concern and love for a lost and suffering humanity."[42] Labib says:

> We go telling people *about* his love without feeling the need to practice love and concern in a practical way. In the Middle East most evangelism activities toward our Muslim neighbors are an expression of our anti-Islamic feelings rather than an expression of Divine love incarnated through our humanity.[43]

The evidence of this, he states, is that once a Muslim comes to Christ, he or she is given no place in the Christian community, but rather treated as

41. The references in this section are taken with permission from Madanat's unpublished reflections entitled *Beyond Self*.

42. Ibid.

43. Ibid.

a burden, as a stranger, as untrustworthy. Because evangelism results in inevitable ostracization, "the heart of Christian mission, which is supposed to convey the greatest of God's attributes—love—becomes a graveyard."[44] Labib's inherited—and confessedly cramped—view of mission to Muslims would be shaken again by several other young Muslims who would open their lives to him.

In 1991, Labib returned to the city of his childhood, Jerusalem. Two years later he began serving as the General Secretary of the Palestinian Bible Society. As one aspect of his ministry, he began to correspond with Palestinian prisoners in Israeli prisons. One prisoner with whom Labib exchanged letters was Firas,[45] who was serving three life sentences in an Israeli prison in Ashkelon. Firas spoke of his hope for his future, in spite of his life sentence. Labib continued a deeply personal correspondence with this prisoner over several months, marveling at his courage to hope in spite of his imprisonment.

After some months of correspondence, when Labib was in Beirut visiting the Lebanese Bible Society, he travelled to the Baddawi refugee camp on the border with Syria, where Firas's family lived. Conditions were worse than in many refugee camps Labib had visited in the West Bank. Asking for directions to Firas's family, he was guided to their simple home. The family had experienced the sad journey from frustration and despair to futile resistance shared by many Palestinian refugees: the father's hometown was Safad, in British Mandate Palestine, now in Israel proper; he became a refugee in Lebanon in 1948. Firas was born in Tal Al-Zatar refugee camp for Palestinians near Beirut, which was subsequently destroyed during the Lebanese civil war, at which time his mother and little sister were also killed. Firas and his father became second-time refugees in Baddawi; at the age of sixteen Firas joined the Popular Front for the Liberation of Palestine (PFLP) and, soon after, went on a military mission toward Israel. He was injured, captured by the IDF, and imprisoned.

As Labib read Firas's letters, which they had exchanged, the family wept. Later in their meeting the father confided to Labib that he was a regular reader of the Bible. Labib described his reaction to this revelation:

> I asked myself why he wasn't yet a Christian. But, was it up to me
> to decide what the fruit of the Word should be in his life? I must

44. Ibid.

45. The discussion of the interaction with Firas and his family is drawn from Madanat's *Beyond Self.*

first be a Christian for him, to love and serve and be all that hold-
ing the name of Christ means, before I allow myself the right to
expect him to conform to my Christianity.[46]

This encounter with Firas and his family was an important step in Labib's
journey. He was able to hear the longings of a marginalized Muslim family,
and to experience a real friendship that helped him appreciate their suffering and hopes. After this encounter, Labib sensed a reawakening, a renewed
desire for a different way of mission that broke through old patterns and
attitudes.[47] Although he was living in Jerusalem with its rich spiritual resources, Labib's search for new paths would continue to find inspiration
from the margins of Palestinian society in a refugee camp in Gaza.

Wael, a young Gazan, had seen an advertisement in the local newspaper placed by the Bible Society, offering free New Testaments. He made
the decision to request one. Wael would later explain to Labib the reason
for his interest in the Bible. After having been almost fatally injured during
the first Intifada (1987–1993), Wael became deeply disillusioned with the
stumbling peace process and with what he considered the ineptitude of the
Palestinian leaders. One day, especially discouraged with the hopelessness
of Gazan life and hoping to cheer himself, he went into Gaza City. Wael
recounts his unusual encounter with the gospel that day:

> I was walking aimlessly, tired and depressed. I walked by a Chris-
> tian church and saw the cemetery nearby. It was Saturday, and I
> decided to see the cemetery, since the church was closed on a Sat-
> urday. I was interested to see what Christian graves look like. As I
> walked between the graves, I suddenly stopped in front of a certain
> grave. It was engraved with the sentence: "Jesus said, 'Come to me
> all you who are burdened and heavy laden and I will give you rest.'"
>
> These words sent a shock in my body and took hold of me. I
> said to myself, "This is what I need. I should know more about this
> Jesus who dares give such a promise." So the next day in the morn-
> ing, a Sunday, I decided to visit the church. As I tried to enter, I was
> kicked out because I was discovered to be a Muslim. But this did
> not kill my desire and hunger to know Jesus. When I saw the ads
> in the newspaper, I responded."[48]

46. Ibid.

47. Ibid.

48. Ibid.

After hearing Wael's story, Labib reflected, "Have we been so silent and absent that the stones must speak? Why did all the thousands of church sermons preached never reach Wael? Why did they not mobilize us to reach many other 'Waels'?"

The Bible Society responded to this young man's request, sending him a New Testament, and soon after he requested a visit from Bible Society personnel. When Labib was in Gaza, he found Wael's home, but it so happened that the young man was away at that moment. The effort, however, was not a waste. Labib says:

> Wael's father, with authentic Arab hospitality, insisted that I come in. The father had been a school teacher in the Sinai before it was returned to Egypt. He told me of his fond memories of Egyptian Christian Coptic friends and colleagues. In response to my confession that Wael's desire for a New Testament initiated my visit, he said to me that he was proud that his son was seeking valuable knowledge. He asked me several questions about Christ, and finally asked if I could get him a copy of the New Testament.[49]

This experience again spurred Labib to consider the fact that Christians could only view Muslims through the lens of apprehension, militating against empathy based on their shared humanity. He states:

> I did not leave that house feeling victorious that I had scored a "Bible, 1" for the Christian team against a "Qur'an, 0" for the Muslims. I felt so honored and humbled by the positive, tolerant, and welcoming attitude of this Muslim Palestinian refugee living in the heart of the Gaza Strip. I wondered how many more thousands there are like this man. Why are we hidden from each other? What is blinding our vision to see reality? What preconceived ideas about Muslims have shaped our vision of them in a way which, instead of bringing us together and opening a way for mutual mission, kept us afar and strangers? Can I see through the eyes of Jesus?

As a result of these experiences and in order to facilitate a deeper engagement with the Muslim community so that "mutual mission,"[50] mutually

---

49. Ibid.

50. Labib Madanat, e-mail interview by Andrew Bush, December 6, 2012. Madanat further explains what he means by "mutual mission":

> Within the context of ministering to Muslims, or to any others, we should be humble before the Lord and open to the fact that as we serve Him and take His message of good news to them, He also wants to change us and form us in the image of His son Jesus Christ. He will use the Muslim (or any other!) to uncover

transformative correction, might occur, Labib took the radical step of invit-
ing the Muslim community into the Palestinian Bible Society. This invitation eventually involved welcoming several Muslims onto the PBS staff.
These staff members included Muslims who had recently believed in Christ
and were still very much culturally Muslims; others that joined the PBS
were Muslims both in culture and in belief who were willing to work in
a context that clashed with their views. Another form of inclusion was to
allow Muslim neighbors to inform and shape some of the PBS's programs.

It was a risk for the PBS to partner with Muslim neighbors in this
way. Some would regard it as partnering with the enemy. However, Labib
observed:

> Where friendship and trust and courage are, many fears and ta-
> boos simply dissolve. When we were able to know our Muslim
> neighbours afresh we were able to see through their eyes. When
> we invited our Muslim neighbours to help us see them the way
> they see and know themselves, we were able to see ourselves
> through their eyes.

Rather than ignore the complexity of the context of Israel/Palestine, this
inclusiveness invited the complexity of Palestinian society into the PBS.
This unusual partnership provided a way to deepen its relevancy and provide creative directions in its effort to serve the community. An example of
this partnership was the PBS's work in a small northern West Best village.
There, a former Palestinian militant became the "man of peace" (Luke 10:6)
for Labib and the PBS staff.

Yasouf is a small, lovely agricultural village south of Nablus City on
the West Bank. It is a Muslim village. Once surrounded by hills and fields,
Yasouf is almost entirely encircled—strangled—by an Israeli settlement,
Ariel. The garbage of the settlement has fouled the village's centuries-old
spring. The road into the village passes an IDF checkpoint. In spite of all the
amenities—water, electricity, roads—built by Israel to support Ariel, Israel
refused to allow Yasouf to be serviced with electricity until recently. To help
with the village, the PBS provided for the installation of generators. As the
project began, Labib met Abu Hanan.

Decades earlier, Abu Hanan had been a member of a radical faction
in the Palestinian Liberation Organization (PLO). After Israel occupied

---

wrong attitudes and shame self-acclaimed righteousness within us. Thus, mission becomes mutual; we share with others the message of good news, and they
share with us (actively or passively) good things we may lack!

the West Bank in 1967, he joined a group of militants whose task was to prepare young Palestinians to wage armed resistance. Eventually he was captured by the IDF and given three life sentences. After 18 years in Israeli prisons, he was released as a result of an exchange of prisoners between the PLO and Israel in 1985. Although initially expelled from Palestine, after the Oslo Accords he was permitted to return to his village of Yasouf in 1994.

Turning his back on armed struggle, he directed his energy toward peace and community service. There he had great credibility among his Palestinian neighbors because of his long imprisonment. Labib recalls that while other Palestinian political and Islamic groups held children's summer camps that were focused on glorifying militancy and resistance against Israel, Abu Hanan instead joined the Bible Society's summer camp in Yasouf which emphasized peace and reconciliation.[51]

Through Abu Hanan, doors were opened for the Bible Society in ten other villages, and also several government schools. Not only was he open to Christians, but also to Israeli Jews who belonged to the peace camp. He extended invitations to the latter to come to Yasouf. Out of deep pain and suffering Abu Hanan had developed genuine tolerance and acceptance.

Concerning his relationship with Abu Hanan, Labib reflects:

> He taught me a lot. I did not need to find smart ways to give him a Bible, he asked for it, and for many more to give to his friends. But I never felt that giving him Bibles made my relationship to him a "mission-validated" one. I was truly moving from being self-focused, including the focus on my self-oriented Christianity, to being people-focused. In all my life, other than the experience of following Jesus, this was the most enriching Christian experience I have had.[52]

As a result of Labib's openness to partner with and learn from Muslims, in Living Stones we developed a deeper cooperation with the Muslim community proportionate to their willingness to have us. During the summers we conducted youth camps in Muslim villages near Bir Zeit. This was always by the invitation of the Muslim village's elders. The kids were really hurting for some scrap of normalcy in their lives. During the camps older Muslim teenagers helped with the programs as assistant counselors. Often the women of the villages would come out and help us with some of the really boisterous kids.

51. Madanat, *Beyond Self.*
52. Ibid.

Besides the summer camps, we began to bring Muslims students from all the universities north of Jerusalem on the West Bank to an annual conference in Bethlehem, where they could talk about their hopes and the challenges that Palestinian university graduates face. We began each day with a Bible reading—while at the same time arranging for a room for their daily prayers at the Christian retreat center where we met.

Through these events, as well as the regular evenings at Living Stones that were patronized primarily by Muslim students, it was continually surprising how far Muslims were willing to go in relating to an avowedly Christian organization. They certainly shattered the Western stereotype of an implacably hostile Islam.

At the Christmas season during the Intifada, the parents in Bir Zeit had no money to buy their children even simple gifts. We began having an annual Christmas party with songs, snacks, and a gift for every child to ease the pain of scarcity. "Baba Noel," Father Christmas in full Santa Claus regalia, is a traditional fixture in Palestinian Christmas celebrations. One year during our party I was amused to see four Baba Noels boogying on the stage in the fellowship hall of Bir Zeit's Roman Catholic Church, which we were using for the afternoon. They were getting into the music, hopping around enthusiastically, and the kids were having fun with them. Curious, I asked Ahmad where he found the guys who were the Baba Noels. He answered that they were Muslim boys from a neighboring village! "Why did you get Muslim boys?" I inquired. "In all of our activities I want there to be Muslims," he replied. "Then we will learn to see each other as human beings."

Here was an example of the boundary breaking grace of God: a Muslim believer in Jesus blessing Christian and Muslim kids in a Roman Catholic Church with the help of Palestinian Muslim teenaged boogying Santas!

In Living Stones we were becoming more involved in the local public schools. Their threadbare budgets could not cover any arts programs. The Majida wa Sili School for Girls in Bir Zeit asked if we could help. We wanted to do more than merely provide supplies, but to help them develop an art program with a trained art teacher. Labib took a bold step. He invited a recent university graduate with a degree in fine art, a strict Muslim who wore the head covering of an observant Muslim woman, to join us as a paid staff member. A professional artist, she was the only person available—and willing—that we could find.

My worries for such a partnership was allayed by the parable of the Good Samaritan. Jesus's concern is that the wounded and suffering in this world are aided. Who helped the wounded man in the parable? The good man from Samaria. It was the Samaritan's example of service—the one from outside the disciples' community—that Jesus exhorted them to follow. There were a lot of wounded kids in the Palestinian public schools. Our artist colleague was our Good Samaritan who stood with us in helping these kids whose lives had been so marred by violence.

She worked with us faithfully for several years, sitting through our Bible studies as a regular staff member. Eventually she married and relocated to Jenin. I marveled at the grace she had shown to work in a Christian ministry. Firas, Wael, Abu Hanan, our artist friend, and the boogying Santas: they all demonstrated a willingness to humble themselves, to empty themselves of reactionary attitudes.

This journey changed us. But the cross *should* alter one's life. It should end one's life as one knows it, not just once, but repeatedly. As we follow Jesus, it should end ideas and attitudes that do not represent the fullness of Christ's love. Mission is the adventure in God's love. The further we seek to serve others, the more God's love is revealed to us, perhaps in surprising ways.

Given the long history of Arab Christianity's marginalization as Islam rose to prominence, and the more recent demoralizing diminishment of the Palestinian community, Labib's exploration of the way of Jesus in relating to Palestinian Muslims is prophetic. Labib demonstrates that caring demands a willingness to learn from and be changed by Muslims. Labib says succinctly, "They taught us how to love them."[53]

This humble willingness to learn from others speaks of Christ's emptying himself of the prerogatives of religious aloofness or superiority. This is the way of the cross. Inevitably, with a resurgent global Islam colliding with the West, and the hatreds engendered by the violence of war, there will be tragic deaths such as Rami Ayyad's. When Christians are killed, when people suffer at the hands of Muslim extremists, and when misdirected Christians give voice to historic hatreds, Christians in the West will have to decide if they are willing turn from socially tolerated bitterness and hatred and go deeper into the cross. Firas, Wael, and Abu Hanan are evidence that there are Muslims who are also on a spiritual journey, who are not content to remain in a path of hatred and violence.

53. Ibid.

If Christians also are willing to journey beyond lazy cultural norms, they will find Muslims who also are seeking an authentic friendship with them, as well as earnest spiritual dialogue.

5

Transforming Nationalism

I have other sheep that are not of this sheep pen. I must bring them also. They too will listen to my voice, and there shall be one flock and one shepherd.

JOHN 10:16

If I am called a Christian Palestinian, I have a commitment and obligation toward my Palestinian people and their future and welfare. At the same time I have an obligation to my Lord to love my enemies, to break the circle of hatred and enmity and violence, to be a peacemaker, and to look for practical ways for peace between Jews and Arabs. We as Palestinian Christians can play an important role, and be an avenue of peace.[1]

SALIM MUNAYER, A PALESTINIAN CHRISTIAN LEADER

AHMAD'S GESTURE OF FORGIVENESS and servanthood, Rami's selfless service, and Labib's empathetic understanding are living examples of the way of Christ's emptying, his ministry in lowliness and servanthood. For the Palestinian Christians, this way of Christ provides an opportunity for the acceptance of those who are Other, and to break out of their limiting self-ghettoization in the Palestinian society in order to bring a full-orbed witness of the life and love of Christ.

1. Munayer, "Relations between Religions," 149–50.

This witness of reconciliation between two communities within Palestinian society, while vital to Western Christians long dominated by a paradigm of power, is nevertheless obscured by the larger conflict between Palestine and Israel. The fierce hatreds fueled by the colliding dreams of the Palestinian and Israeli peoples threaten the Christian presence in the land to the degree that they may disfigure the Christian community. If the way of Christ can truly show a way forward in mission it must be relevant to this greater conflict. Can the way of Christ bring healing to these national enmities? The intensity of the conflict that the way of the cross must confront is illustrated not only in the major armed clashes, but in the daily lives of ordinary Palestinians and Israelis.

This was driven home by two jarring encounters during the height of the Intifada. One morning while I was chatting with a university administrator, a Christian, the conversation inevitably turned to the most recent events of the conflict. As we discussed a particularly awful death of an innocent Palestinian civilian, she became increasingly irate. Unable to contain her rage, she exclaimed, "The Israelis are animals!" I was shocked. I had never heard such raw hatred from this very calm and moderate friend.

That very same day, Karen and I traveled from Ramallah to the commercial district of West Jerusalem, the Israeli sector of the city inside Israel proper. We occasionally enjoyed browsing a housewares shop there. It helped us snatch a few minutes of illusory normalcy during the days of violence. We liked the shop owner, a heartily friendly Israeli woman. As we examined the skillets and dishes and such, we began to chat amiably. Again, the Israeli shop owner turned the conversation to the violence of the conflict, which swallowed all other concerns. There had been numerous bombings by Palestinian militants within blocks of her shop. Her face turned deeper shades of red as she became enraged. "The Palestinians are animals!" she finally blurted out.

These two exclamations, not by militants, but from moderate individuals, was a powerful illustration of how the conflict worked to demonize and dehumanize the Other. Hatred not only mutually blinds antagonists to their shared humanity, it reduces one's enemy to a sub-human status. Hatred, in turn, mars each community's human dignity. During the worst months and years of vicious violence, it seemed that both communities were being reduced to their basest instincts.

This dehumanization was fueled by the wounds each community was suffering, but colliding nationalist claims were driving the conflict.

Nationalism exerts overwhelming influence on both Palestinian and Israeli communities. National identity for both the Palestinian and Israeli communities is formed from the earliest years of a child's life. Hanna, a Palestinian Christian, described to me that his mother told him every day from the earliest years of his life, "You are a Palestinian. The Israelis are our enemies." Similarly, many of the children of Israeli settlers on the West Bank are nurtured into the certainty that they are the only legitimate heirs of the promise to Abraham, and the land is theirs. The Palestinians are to be driven out; deep prejudice toward Palestinians is part of their upbringing. A disturbing photograph in a leading Israeli newspaper captured an Israeli child laughing in glee while pulling the head covering off a Palestinian woman from behind, a deep insult.

The conflict engendered by these competing national identities in the same land is heightened by the attempt on both sides to deny the national legitimacy of the other; thus, the claims on the Israeli side that "There is no such thing as a Palestinian people." From the Palestinian side, a few children's school books portray the map of the entirety of Holy Land as "Palestine," denying even the existence and legitimacy of Israel.

In this death embrace of competing nationalisms, Jesus's embrace and affirmation of humanity through his self-emptying unto "being found in appearance as a man" is especially relevant and critical. Whereas the evangelical formulation of the gospel customarily begins with the proclamation that God loves people, an environment of dehumanization requires a more elemental message: you *and* your enemy are human beings, created in God's image.

Just as in our conversations with two normally reasonable acquaintances, the university administrator and the shop owner, emotions in Israel and Palestine during the Intifada were so high, and rage at the deaths of members of their communities was so intense, it overwhelmed reasonable conversation. If Christ's affirmation of humanity, essential to his gospel, was to be heard, what would make it relevant when everyday life and limb hung in the balance? What would make it authentic, and not merely another sectarian religious claim? The idea of a shared human dignity did not seem to stand a chance of being heard against the firestorm of rage that burned in both communities.

Obviously, Palestinians and Israelis cannot easily shed their national identities to embrace a shared human identity. Moderation of their respective nationalisms is viewed as a grave threat to their existence and therefore must be fiercely rejected. How then can a theology of a shared humanity be useful as a means toward reconciliation? How does Christ's self-emptying to share our humanity speak to nationalism in Palestine and Israel?

CHRIST TRANSFORMS NATIONALISM

Christ Jesus's relinquishing of his prerogatives as the Son of God, such as gratuitous demonstrations of power in order to be glorified before the people—a satanic temptation (Matt 4:1–10)—and his subsequent embrace of radical servanthood, offers the possibility of a transformed nationalism that affirms the human dignity and value of the weak and the Other.[2] In his self-emptying to embrace all of humanity, Christ did not deny his national identity. Far from it. By his observance of national feasts, the Sabbath, and his affirmation of the Law of Moses, among other things, he identified himself as a faithful member of the house of Israel. National identity was not a hindrance in his mission of compassion. However, Christ defined a transformed nationalism for Israel—and for all nations—that advanced God's purpose of reconciling all to himself through compassion. This compassion brought healing to the broken among all people, including the weak in his family.

Christ radically redefined what Israel could be, not in a context of idyllic peace, but in an environment of oppression: the occupation of Israel by the Roman Empire. It was a time in which Israel's national existence was under threat; yet, rather than yield to a misdirected national self-interest, Jesus called Israel to a transformed nationalism, characterized by the essential ethical teaching to love one's neighbor as oneself, to bless one's enemies, to forgive, to turn the other cheek. According to Jesus, if the neighbor to be loved happened to be a Roman soldier, the disciple was to carry his gear two miles instead of the required one (Matt 5:40–42); if a Samaritan (John 4:1–41) or Syro-Phoenician (Matt 15:21–8) was in need, Christ's disciples were taught to respond to the pleas for help.

By extension in our day, if Palestinians cry out for help, the disciple should have compassion on their vulnerability as a stateless people; and

2. Ideas related to Christ's *kenosis*, his self-emptying, and transformed nationalism were first explored by this author in a paper entitled "The *Kenosis* of Christ and His Redefinition of Nationalism as a Way towards Reconciliation in Israel/Palestine" presented at the International Association for Missions Studies conference at Balaton, Hungary, August 2008. This paper was subsequently published under the same title in *Mission Spirituality and Authentic Discipleship*, Ma, et al., eds.

if an Israelis are in fear and need of security, the disciple should show empathy, understanding Israel's long and persecuted journey among the nations. In sum, such nationalism is characterized by an inclination toward the well-being of the Other, rather than by a bent toward national privilege and primacy.

This renewed and empathetic nationalism exemplified by Christ Jesus can be understood as a restoration of Israel to the very purpose of its election, the first articulation of which is found in God's promise and commission of Abraham, then Abram, in Genesis 12:1–3:

> Now the LORD said to Abram,
>
> "Go forth from your country,
> And from your relatives
> And from your father's house,
> To the land which I will show you;
> And I will make you a great nation,
> And I will bless you,
> And make your name great;
> And so you shall be a blessing;
> And I will bless those who bless you,
> And the one who curses you I will curse.
> And in you all the families of the earth will be blessed."

Israel's national calling was to be an agent for making the knowledge of the Lord accessible to the nations, and thereby blessing them. How was the Lord to be made known to the nations? Israel under God's law was to be a unique society, reflecting God's justice, mercy, and grace. Stanley Hauerwas states: "For Israel, therefore, to love God meant to learn to love as God loves."[3] Deuteronomy describes this unique and radical calling upon Israel:

> Yet on your fathers did the Lord set His affection to love them, and He chose their descendants after them, even you above all peoples, as it is this day. So circumcise your heart, and stiffen your neck no longer. For the Lord your God is the God of gods and the Lord of lords, the great, the mighty, and the awesome God who does not show partiality nor take a bribe. He executes justice for the orphan and the widow, and shows His love for the alien by giving him food and clothing. So show your love for the alien, for you were aliens in the land of Egypt. You shall fear the Lord your God; you shall serve Him and cling to Him, and you shall swear by His name. (Deut 10:15–20)

3. Hauerwas, *The Peaceable Kingdom*, 78.

If Israel complied with God's law—God's love—by showing mercy to the orphan and the widow, by doing justice with its neighbors, and loving the foreigner in its midst, it would enjoy rich blessings and also illustrate to the nations the character of God and the prospects of life under his authority. If Israel neglected the fatherless, the widow, and the alien or foreigner, it would find that the Lord would defend the cause of the weak and marginalized, even at Israel's expense.

Israel's failure was that it lost sight of its unique national calling to be a righteous people, faithful to the Lord, exercising justice and mercy toward the weakest members of society, and generosity toward the stranger. Mistaking national election for entitlement, and forgetting the marginalized among their own, Israel diverted from its calling first articulated to Abraham. Israel's understanding of its missional calling to the nations became inverted. Instead of seeking to be a blessing to the nations by its example as a just society in which the weak and the alien were not marginalized, Israel presumed that the nations were called to recognize its preeminence. These failures brought upon Israel the rebuke of the prophets and ultimately its loss of national status through captivity. Arthur F. Glasser, in *Announcing the Kingdom*, describes this exclusivity:

> Israel reasoned that nothing it might do would jeopardize its standing with God. Their conviction arose from what was judged to be an unconditional promise made to David concerning the security of Jerusalem, the inviolability of the Temple, and the permanence of the Davidic line (2 Samuel 7:8–16). As a result, Israel largely forgot that it was chosen by God for service and that this was both a privilege and an obligation. Only a few sensed with Isaiah that God was concerned that his people be "a light for the Gentiles" (42:6; 49:6). Almost none of them translated their calling into dynamic outreach. In the postexilic period this concern of the exiles diminished to the point where they sought to preserve their faith and religious practice by living in complete withdrawal from the nations . . . Jewish exclusiveness steadily gained ground during the postexilic period.[4]

The prophets repeatedly called Israel to be the nation that God desired by remembering the widow and the orphan in its midst and by doing justice to the foreigners among it. The prophet Malachi cried:

---

4. Glasser, *Announcing the Kingdom*, 134.

> "So I will come to put you on trial. I will be quick to testify against
> sorcerers, adulterers and perjurers, against those who defraud la-
> borers of their wages, who oppress the widows and the fatherless,
> and deprive the foreigners among you of justice, but do not fear
> me," says the Lord Almighty. (Mal 3:5)

Habakkuk likewise called Israel to do justice:

> How long, Lord, must I call for help,
> but you do not listen?
> Or cry out to you, "Violence!"
> but you do not save?
> Why do you make me look at injustice?
> Why do you tolerate wrongdoing?
> Destruction and violence are before me;
> there is strife, and conflict abounds.
> Therefore the law is paralyzed,
> and justice never prevails.
> The wicked hem in the righteous,
> so that justice is perverted. (Hab 1:2–4)

With their words, the prophets were seeking to restore Israel to its national calling to be a just nation through which God would be known to
the nations.

Similarly the Psalmists of Israel grasped Israel's missional calling to be
a blessing to the nations: "Give thanks to the LORD, call on his name; make
known among the nations what he has done" (Ps 105:1). Walter C. Kaiser
states, "The Psalmist longed and deeply desired that God, the King of Israel,
might be acknowledged as Lord and Savior of the entire world . . . This is
still God's purpose."[5] The end of making the name of the Lord known to the
nations would be that the nations also could serve the Lord and be included
as the people of God.

Christ Jesus as a prophet to Israel continued in the tradition of the
prophets in calling Israel back to its national missional purpose to bless
the nations. Most emphatically, Christ challenged Israel's distorted national
exceptionalism. N. T. Wright states:

> Thus Jesus called Israel to repent of her nationalist ambition and
> follow him in a new vision of God's purpose for Israel. Resistance
> to Rome was to be replaced by love and prayer for the enemy.

---

5. Kaiser, "Israel's Missionary Call," 16.

Israel's plight was radically redefined: sin, not Rome, was the real enemy.[6]

Jesus established his prophetic challenge to Israel in his first sermon in his home synagogue in Nazareth. Luke's Gospel records Jesus's surprising self-identification with the messianic Isaian Servant, his rebuke of Israel's national parochialism, and the violent reaction of his audience to it:

> And He came to Nazareth, where He had been brought up; and as was His custom, He entered the synagogue on the Sabbath, and stood up to read. And the book of the prophet Isaiah was handed to Him. And He opened the book and found the place where it was written,
>
> "The Spirit of the Lord is upon Me,
> Because He anointed Me to preach the gospel to the poor.
> He has sent Me to proclaim release to the captives,
> And recovery of sight to the blind,
> To set free those who are oppressed,
> To proclaim the favorable year of the Lord."
>
> And He closed the book, gave it back to the attendant and sat down; and the eyes of all in the synagogue were fixed on Him. And He began to say to them, "Today this Scripture has been fulfilled in your hearing." And all were speaking well of Him, and wondering at the gracious words which were falling from His lips; and they were saying, "Is this not Joseph's son?" And He said to them, "No doubt you will quote this proverb to Me, 'Physician, heal yourself! Whatever we heard was done at Capernaum, do here in your hometown as well.'" And He said, "Truly I say to you, no prophet is welcome in his hometown. But I say to you in truth, there were many widows in Israel in the days of Elijah, when the sky was shut up for three years and six months, when a great famine came over all the land; and yet Elijah was sent to none of them, but only to Zarephath, *in the land* of Sidon, to a woman who was a widow. And there were many lepers in Israel in the time of Elisha the prophet; and none of them was cleansed, but only Naaman the Syrian." And all *the people* in the synagogue were filled with rage as they heard these things; and they got up and drove Him out of the city, and led Him to the brow of the hill on which their city had been built, in order to throw Him down the cliff. But passing through their midst, He went His way. (Luke 4:16–30)

6. Wright, "Jesus," 348–51.

The first part of Jesus's message pleased the synagogue assembly. "All spoke well of him and were amazed at the gracious words which were falling from his lips." Certainly they did not comprehend the significance of Jesus's self-identification with the Isaian Servant; yet, Jesus's proclamation about the ministry of the Messiah moved their hearts with its hope. It was not to be a ministry of destruction. On the contrary, gracious mercy and relief for the poor, blind, bound, and oppressed were to be the way of the Servant of the Lord, and of all the people of God.

With their warm approval washing over him, Jesus then thrust the surgeon's scalpel into the national rot of exclusivity, the idea that God's blessings were bordered by national identity. God's blessings for the poor and oppressed were not, as it was supposed, exclusive to Israel. Jesus rebuked that assumption in a way shocking to his audience. Recalling the prophets, Jesus stated that during the famine at the time of the prophet Elijah, when many widows in Israel were suffering, God sent the prophet to a Gentile woman in Sidon, in modern Lebanon. Also, during the time of the prophet Elisha there were many sufferers of leprosy in Israel, but it was only Namaan, a leader of the enemy Syrian army that threatened Israel, who received healing.

Jesus was underscoring that the blessing of God was not limited to the precincts of Israel. This was a powerful blow to the underpinnings of Israel's identity, which understood the Lord as *the God of Israel*, their tribal deity. We are so far removed culturally from the context of the first century it is difficult to grasp the shock Jesus's words were to the synagogue that day.

ISRAEL'S NATIONAL IDENTITY
UNDER ROME'S GOVERNANCE

Jesus reminded Israel that God cared for their *enemies*. Imagine the public revulsion if the President of the Unites States in a public speech on the Fourth of July spoke of God's blessing on China or on Iran. That would approximate how obnoxious it was for Jesus's audience to consider God's intentional healing of Namaan, the Syrian.

How angry were the people? They sought to kill Jesus on the spot! His words were traitorous, totally unacceptable. They hauled him to a hillside where they would have thrown him down to his death, but Jesus passed through the angry crowd. It was not time for his death.

At the heart of this rebuke of national exceptionalism was that it was incompatible with God's intention to extend grace to the oppressed, the forgotten. Hardened boundaries create hardened hearts; there is a strict demarcation between those within the perceived sphere of God's blessings, and those without. But exclusion and injustice spread like a cancer. In time, if Israel was unjust to the foreigner, injustice would extend to the weaker members within its own society. Jesus consequently emphasized grace and inclusion to the outcast—the leper, the sinful woman, the unjust tax collector—within Israel (Matt 25:31–40).

Taking this to the present conflict, the Israeli historian and journalist Gershom Gorenberg argues this very idea—that Israel's unjust policies toward the Palestinians are undermining democracy and rule of law *within* Israel. In order to avoid becoming a failed state, Israel, according to Gorenberg, needs a renewal in its policies.[7]

This was clearly the message of Jesus. Israel could not fulfill its destiny as an agent and sign of God's benevolence and justice if it continued in its national exclusivity. Jesus modeled Israel's call to be a blessing to the nations. In the spirit of his Nazareth synagogue message that God's grace is not limited to the Israel, he traveled to the region of Tyre and Sidon and there extended healing to the daughter of a gentile, a Syro-Phoenician woman (Matt 15:21–28). Regarding this encounter, it is argued that his reference to Gentiles as "dogs" is itself a rebuke of popular Jewish prejudice toward Gentiles, and is meant to be instructive to the disciples as they prepared for their mission to the nations.[8]

A central facet in Israel's national identity was the Temple in Jerusalem. It was there that the Lord met Israel in its worship. The Temple, therefore, established Israel's unique relationship to the Lord and to the nations. Yet the Temple was not intended to exclude the nations from access to the Lord; it was intended to advance that access. Jesus's cleansing of the Temple was a prophetic rebuke of a religious institution which had gone awry:

> Then they came to Jerusalem. And He entered the temple and began to drive out those who were buying and selling in the temple, and overturned the tables of the money changers and the seats of those who were selling doves; and He would not permit anyone to carry merchandise through the temple. And He *began* to teach and say to them, "Is it not written, 'My house shall be called a house of

7. Gorenberg, *Unmaking of Israel*.

8. Richardson, "A Man for All Peoples," 105.

> prayer for all the nations'? But you have made it a robbers' den."
> The chief priests and the scribes heard this, and began seeking
> how to destroy Him; for they were afraid of Him, for the whole
> crowd was astonished at His teaching. (Mark 11:15–18)

It was on the cross, though, that Jesus, in the shedding of his blood, made the way for all nations to be reconciled with God directly, without the necessity of Temple worship. By his agony, he also was enthroned as the Son of David, the heir to the throne of Israel who would fulfill the prophecy that king David's heir would reign on the throne forever (2 Sam 7:11b–16). Most important for this discussion of transforming nationalism is that in his passion, Christ Jesus, who was in his person the remnant of righteous Israel, laid aside any means of power and, in complete vulnerability, poured out his life for all. This act, this costly calling to pour out one's life in the world, belonged to Israel and now extended to those who claim Christ Jesus as their Lord.

Finally, through the new covenant, the resurrected Christ heightened Israel's calling to bless and serve the nations, commissioning the first Jewish disciples to take the message of God's forgiveness to all nations. No longer to be a witness by attraction only, now Israel was explicitly commissioned to go out from the land and proclaim the good news of God's salvation through Christ Jesus:

> But the eleven disciples proceeded to Galilee, to the mountain
> which Jesus had designated. When they saw Him, they worshiped
> Him; but some were doubtful. And Jesus came up and spoke to
> them, saying, "All authority has been given to Me in heaven and on
> earth. Go therefore and make disciples of all the nations, baptizing
> them in the name of the Father and the Son and the Holy Spirit,
> teaching them to observe all that I commanded you; and lo, I am
> with you always, even to the end of the age." (Matt 28:16–20)

This sending out is in contrast to the journey toward Jerusalem, the destination of the pilgrims making their way to the Temple. Following the resurrection, salvation was no longer tied to geography, though in truth it never had been so. The presence of God could be enjoyed by faith in Christ Jesus and the gift of the Spirit, wherever a believer may be.

This sending out has other implications. For Israel the nations were the location of judgment, of vulnerability for their people. Security was within the land. The land protected Israel from the existential threat of the nations. But it was out from the land, into the nations, that Jesus sent the representatives of the fledgling messianic community. Did this mean that the land, while still important to Israel, was not to be the basis for its national identity? Did this mean that its security now looked beyond the physicality of this world to an eternal relationship to Christ? As Jesus said in his Galilean commissioning, "And surely I am with you always, to the very end of the age" (Matt 28:20).

The Gospel of Matthew portrays Jesus as the new Moses, the one who brings a new law on a mountain in the Sermon on the Mount, who like Moses was transfigured on a mountain, and ends his earthly journey on a mountain. My colleague at Eastern University, Kenton Sparks, suggests provocatively that this commissioning by Jesus of his disciples to go out to the nations with the message of life stands in an obvious contrast to the commissioning of Joshua and Israel, through Moses, to go into the land *to destroy the nations*. Sparks argues that in the context of the variety of theological voices within scripture, this commissioning by Jesus is a corrective to the triumphal commission to defeat the nations and possess the land by force.[9]

We can thus understand Christ's *kenosis*, his self-emptying to share in the human experience, as including the experience of national identity. Through his perfect love and servanthood, he defined the highest national purpose: to care for the marginalized and to serve all nations by extending the knowledge of God's justice and mercy through the good news of Christ Jesus and by acts of mercy. Arguing, then, from the ministry of Christ and the national identity he embodied, if human identity is molded by such a sense of national purpose it can be a basis for reconciliation and peace.

Does such renewed nationalism sound utopian and idealistic? As Rabbi Michael Lerner states in *Embracing Israel/Palestine*, sometimes prophetic idealism that promotes mutual servanthood is the *only* right response in the face of destruction. He says:

> And yet, it was precisely this kind of prophetic thinking that was necessary for both sides. Indeed, sometimes the only truly "realistic" position is precisely to be prophetic and utopian. But that kind of thinking was dismissed by the mainstream in both the Palestinian and Zionist communities. And so both cocreated the struggle that has plagued both sides for the past sixty-four years (and more by the time you read this).[10]

9. Sparks, "Gospel as Conquest," 4.

10. Lerner, *Embracing Israel/Palestine*, 136.

In any event, what may appear utopian, a nationalism that embraces servanthood, is affirmed by God's ultimate victory by the cross over the satanic claims of dominion that scorn any form of weakness. In other words, the victory of Christ is not *in spite of* servanthood, but it is the victory *of* servanthood. The Gospel of John reflects on this victory through weakness in an important passage which depicts Christ's most profound teaching as he approaches his ultimate destiny:

> And Jesus answered them, saying, "The hour has come for the Son of Man to be glorified. Truly, truly, I say to you, unless a grain of wheat falls into the earth and dies, it remains alone; but if it dies, it bears much fruit. He who loves his life loses it, and he who hates his life in this world will keep it to life eternal. If anyone serves Me, he must follow Me; and where I am, there My servant will be also; if anyone serves Me, the Father will honor him.
>
> "Now My soul has become troubled; and what shall I say, 'Father, save Me from this hour'? But for this purpose I came to this hour. Father, glorify Your name." Then a voice came out of heaven: "I have both glorified it, and will glorify it again." So the crowd of people who stood by and heard it were saying that it had thundered; others were saying, "An angel has spoken to Him." Jesus answered and said, "This voice has not come for My sake, but for your sakes. Now judgment is upon this world; now the ruler of this world will be cast out. And I, if I am lifted up from the earth, will draw all men to Myself." But He was saying this to indicate the kind of death by which He was to die. (John 12:23–33)

In my wife's and my spiritual journey in Palestine we were beginning to see glimpses of this kind of vulnerable servanthood through Ahmad and Labib. The possibility of rising above ethnic hatred and conflict between Israel and Palestine would be shown to us once again by a most unlikely servant of God.

SAMIR: WALKING IN THE SPIRIT OF ABRAHAM

I first encountered Samir late one evening in his village on the West Bank. He had asked me to meet him at the deserted construction site of an office building. A mutual Christian friend had mentioned me, and Samir was curious to make my acquaintance. The mutual friend told me that Samir was interested in the teachings of Jesus. This was unusual because Samir was not a Christian. He was a conservative Muslim.

Arriving after dark, I stumbled through the construction site, strewn with building materials. With no flashlight in hand, I found the unfinished stairway of rough concrete that ascended into the darkness. Samir was supposedly waiting for me on the third floor. Climbing in the darkness, I remembered my mother's constant refrain: "Take care of yourself over there." It didn't seem at that moment I was doing too well on that score, alone in a deserted construction site on my way to meet this stranger!

I had been anxious all day about the evening's meeting. As I carefully felt my way up the stairs, my body tensed. On the third floor, down the darkened corridor, a light shone in the last room. Making my way through a jumble of construction debris, I approached slowly. At the door I peered inside. Samir was reading by a table lamp. "*Marhaba*, Samir!" I called out. He stood, smiling broadly. "*Ahlan wa sahlan! Fut, Fut*? Welcome! Come in, come in!" he replied.

I was immediately struck by the intensity of his personality. His wide shouldered muscular frame was a study in restrained energy. His gaze was steady and penetrating. "This guy means business . . . whatever that business is," I thought to myself.

Samir didn't speak English, and my Arabic was still at an elementary stage. Working together, we slowly communicated. He had been reading the Gospels. He wanted to know more about Jesus. Like my other friends, Christian radio from abroad had intrigued him. When he finally received a Bible he read it voraciously. After that evening's discussion I learned he wanted to meet again.

A few weeks later Karen and I visited Samir in his home. We were greeted at the door by his wife, Rania. She was fully covered in the style of conservative Palestinian Muslim women; her head was wrapped tightly with a scarf, though her face was revealed, and she wore a long *tobe*, a dark coatlike garment that covered her from neck to toes. She was Samir's match, an intelligent and energetic woman who was furthering her university education to be a teacher while she was raising their two young daughters.

Some months later Samir was baptized in a quiet gathering in a home, the fruit of the prayers and efforts of several Christian friends. The account of Jesus's forgiveness in scripture had deeply moved him. He began the difficult walk with Christ of a convert from Islam. A journey also challenged by the intensity of the conflict. In spite of the deep wounds being suffered by the Palestinians, including friends and family, Samir was staying the course in his faith journey. Certainly, he was tapping into deep springs of grace, or he would have been overcome by the fires of hatred that burned around him in the Intifada.

Some months later, after the Intifada had eased, Samir had a life-changing encounter. Two Messianic Jewish men had heard of his spiritual journey and traveled from Jerusalem to Ramallah to meet him, violating Israeli law that forbade its citizens to travel into major Palestinian centers. This was a momentous event for Samir, who had never met a Jew other than an Israeli soldier. He was to speak face to face with those he been raised to see only as enemies.

Afterward, Samir would say to me that there had been four people in the room that day: the two Israeli men, himself . . . and Jesus. Instead of hatred, the presence of God enabled them to open their hearts to each other, as they asked for forgiveness for the hurts their respective communities had inflicted on each other. The meeting ended, Samir said, with a group embrace as they wept together, thankful for the bonds of love they had found.

In recalling this encounter Samir reflected on how much the conversations had meant to him. He said that he had told his new friends that he would be willing to forfeit all of his rights to the land in order to preserve his friendship with them.

What? I couldn't believe that he had said, however rhetorically, that he was willing to forfeit his claim to the land. As a Palestinian who had been raised with an intensely nationalistic perspective, the land was everything to him. The land was the foundation of Palestinian national identity. It was the basis for the Palestinian national movement to have sovereign authority over the West Bank. I had never heard a Palestinian make such a statement, even as a rhetorical gesture.

Samir was willing to *empty himself* of one of the building blocks in the foundation of Palestinian nationalism, their historic relationship to the land. This, perhaps, was an intuitive act. Samir could not find the way of peace unless he was willing to lay down the ideology of entitlement. As the Old Testament scholar Walter Brueggemann observes, the ideology of entitlement to the land and possession of it is intertwined with an ideology of violence.[11] According to Brueggemann, only by dwelling in the land as sojourners, like Abraham, could Israel enjoy the peace and security of the Lord, a theme which will be explored in the following chapter.

Samir was also emptying himself of the prerogatives of anger and judgment that an aggrieved person may normally claim. By setting his face

11. Brueggemann, *The Land*, xv.

toward the priority of reconciliation and the healing of their peoples, Samir, as a prophetic representative of Palestine, was renewing its nationalism. He was walking in the steps of Abraham who lived at peace with the other tribes in the land of Canaan, not seeking exclusive possession of it. He was following the true seed of Abraham, Christ Jesus, who, far from affirming the nationalistic impulses of his day, challenged them, and ultimately demonstrated what the nationalism of Israel was meant to be.

How does the fact that shared human identity, as a basis for mutual understanding, may be frustrated by unchecked nationalism relate to Christianity in the West and its mission? How does Samir's radical statement about those who formerly were perceived as the enemy speak to evangelicals who are deeply patriotic and who have accepted the narrative that affirms that the Unites States is an agent of God, even in its wars?

Just as Constantinian Christianity blurs the distinction between the state and the church, weakening the church and its mission, so Christian spirituality that is molded by nationalism is debilitated in its ability to respond prophetically to injustice. As H. Richard Niebuhr suggests, in such spirituality Christ becomes the figurehead of the culture and its institutions. It domesticates the cross, draining it of its prophetic call to embrace the way of servanthood in humility. Seduced into the idea that there is some way of success other than through the weakness of Christ, a Christian community may fall easily into alliances that provide some appearance of success in mission but which disfigure the full beauty of Jesus.

Many Western Christians have embraced Israeli nationalism with a vengeance. Far from a nationalism of meekness, they have adopted the paradigm of militant nationalism which Rabbi Lerner terms "Settler Judaism," a reference to the Israeli settlers who seek to establish control over all of the land by force, and who embrace an ethos of power in Judaism.[12]

As the next chapter will explore, to promote a nationalism of peace and servanthood will require that Christians find their way out of the culture of militant Israeli nationalism, often referred to as Christian Zionism, in which they have become immersed. That they succeed in escaping this theological/political/cultural/missional movement is critical for the spiritual health of Western evangelical mission.

12. Lerner, *Embracing Israel/Palestine*, 356.

6

Where Are the Peacemakers?

Blessed are the peacemakers, for they will be called children of God.

MATTHEW 5:9

What troubles me is not that the opinions of Christians change, nor that their opinions are shaped by the problems of the times; on the contrary, that is good. What troubles me is that Christians conform to the trend of the moment without introducing into it *anything specifically* Christian. Their convictions are determined by their social milieu, not by faith in the revelation; they lack the uniqueness which ought to be the expression of that faith. Thus, theologies become mechanical exercises that justify the positions adopted, and justify them on grounds that are absolutely not Christian.[1]

JACQUES ELLUL, *VIOLENCE: REFLECTIONS FROM A CHRISTIAN PERSPECTIVE*

THERE IS PERHAPS NO greater evidence that Western evangelical Christians need a fresh perspective on their approach to Israel and Palestine than their absence as peacemakers in the land where the Prince of Peace gave his disciples the gospel of peace. This neglect of peacemaking has consequences that go far beyond Israel and Palestine.

1. Ellul, *Violence*, 28.

The Intifada, which had begun in September 2000, finally ground to a halt more than four years later. The Palestinian uprising had been motivated by the ongoing loss of land on which they hoped to establish a state, and by decades of suffocating Israeli occupation of Palestine. For Palestinians who had hoped to end the occupation and secure their land through the uprising, the Intifada, rather than securing relief, resulted in even greater closures of the roads and the loss of larger swaths of land. More tragic were the deaths from the conflict of more than 3,200 Palestinians and 1,000 Israelis.[2] Thousands more were grievously wounded, and left with debilitating disabilities. Hundreds of children were killed in the conflict on both sides. After the Intifada Israeli settlements in the West Bank expanded at a faster rate.

The violence of the Intifada had wracked the streets of Jerusalem, where women and children, Muslims, Jews and Christians were killed. In Bethlehem, fighting had paralyzed the city during the incursion of Israeli forces. The clashes overwhelmed normal boundaries: a Christian orphanage, with the boys present, was used as an Israeli military outpost; the Church of the Nativity became a refuge for Palestinian militants. For weeks and months, Palestinian Christians in these holy cities hid in their homes, staying away from windows lest they be fired upon.

Still, there was another victim in this violent struggle that so wounded both Palestinian and Israeli societies, and that was the witness of Western evangelical Christians. In the eyes of Arab Christians in the Middle East, the Muslim world, and others globally, the apathy of the Christian West to the ferocity of the conflict in the homeland of their faith was both confusing and appalling. As the city of the birthplace of the Prince of Peace was convulsed by violence, where was the voice of evangelical Christians calling for a better way than bloodshed? As their fellow Palestinian evangelicals in Jerusalem were struggling to survive, their lives daily at risk, why was no hand of help and brotherhood extended to them by Western evangelicals?

On a dark day of violence in Ramallah, when our family was huddled with friends in a darkened room, the electricity cut off, the building shaking from violent explosions nearby, one of the older women cried out into the darkness, "My whole life has been war. Why can't there be peace?"

It seemed that this old woman's cry for peace, and the cry of the bloodstained land, fell on deaf ears. At best, Western evangelicals were silent as

2. "Intifada toll 2000–2005."

this carnage raged. At worst, in their confidence that God was on Israel's side, they added fuel to the fire, cheering them on, and reckoning their military to be an extension of Joshua's army. I recall visiting with American Christian pilgrims in a coffee shop in the Old City near Damascus Gate. They had been on a special tour that had as its highlight a visit to an Israeli outpost in the Golan Heights. They excitedly described how the soldiers had fired an artillery weapon for their tour group. At a time of such violence, a tour that delighted in militarism seemed grotesque.

Many Western evangelicals, immersed in a dispensationalist worldview, had little motivation to be peacemakers. Timothy Weber, in On the Road to Armageddon: How Evangelicals Became Israel's Best Friend, explains the reason for this apathy:

> For the dispensational community, the future is determined. The Bible's prophecies are being fulfilled with amazing accuracy and rapidity. They do not believe the road map will—or should—succeed. According to the prophetic texts, partitioning (of the land) is not in Israel's future, even if the creation of a Palestinian state is the best chance for peace in the region. Peace is nowhere prophesied for the Middle East until Jesus comes and brings it himself. The worst thing the United States, the European Union, Russia, and the United Nations can do is force Israel to give up land for a peace that will never materialize this side of the second coming. Anyone who pushes for peace in such a manner is ignoring or defying God's plan for the end of the age.[3]

Even Israel's political right wing has been more conciliatory to Palestinians than some Western evangelicals. In 2004, Prime Minister Ariel Sharon made the surprising announcement that he would evacuate the Israeli settlements that were inside Gaza. Two reasons motivated this controversial decision. First, it was not feasible that the Israeli residents of these few settlements would ever grow to become a majority of Gaza's population. Second, the defense of these settlements by the Israeli military had been expensive, both in terms of shekels and the loss of life of military personnel. But there was little altruism in this decision, and the condition of the Palestinians in Gaza has not improved. As it is often stated, the jailers (the Israeli military) have simply moved from inside the prison cell (within Gaza) to guarding it from outside. Today, as I write, Gaza remains under strict Israeli closure, impeding commerce, access to work, and consequently strangling this impoverished region economically.

3. Weber, On the Road to Armageddon, 267.

How did many in the evangelical community react to this withdrawal of settlements from Gaza? Were they glad that this decision by Sharon portended the faintest possibility for deeper reconciliation between Israel and Palestine? Were they glad that the evacuation might bring an easing of the plight of the people in Gaza who struggle for the barest essentials in life? On the contrary, before the final evacuation, some American evangelicals joined radical settlers in Gaza to protest this evacuation. From their perspective, the land belonged to Israel unconditionally, and so for Jews to be relocated was an offense. It should be noted that their sense of justice was quite narrow. Traveling into Gaza, these same Americans necessarily passed the cramped refugee camps where Palestinian families suffered a shocking rate of malnutrition. While the Americans traveled freely in and out of Gaza, more than one million people were locked into this dusty stretch of overcrowded desert, unable to pass the Israeli checkpoint.

Even harsher was the response of an American televangelist. After Prime Minister Sharon had accomplished the unilateral withdrawal of Israeli settlers and military from Gaza, and while he was preparing for elections in Israel in which he was going to run on a platform that proposed withdrawing settlements from the West Bank, he suffered a debilitating stroke. The stroke, this televangelist stated, was God's judgment on Sharon for ceding Gaza to the Palestinians. In this astoundingly callous statement, ideology trumped common human compassion for an incapacitated man's plight and ran roughshod over the love that Christ's disciples are called to exhibit.

Why were the Christians who had filled so many tours of the Holy Land silent as peacemakers, but vocal as militarists? Why did Christians in their approach to Israel and Palestine so easily cede the spiritual implications of the place of Christ's life to a hard-edged political perspective that simplistically called for "supporting Israel"? How could Christians—ministers of the gospel at that—so drift from the way of Christ's compassion and mercy that they reckoned the affliction of a dying man to be from God?

Some insight into these disturbing trends can be gained by considering the views of a particularly strident movement that has come to be termed Christian Zionism. Christian Zionism is a Christian theological, political, cultural, and missional movement that supports the goals of political Zionism and the State of Israel's harshest policies toward the Palestinian people. It influences the convictions of many evangelical Christians concerning the modern State of Israel, the Palestinian people, and the status of the land. Exploring Christian Zionism, however, can be a very complicated endeavor.

THE COMPLEXITY OF CHRISTIAN ZIONISM

Critiquing Christian Zionism has become something of a cottage industry, which, in spite of its vigor, has produced scant change in evangelical approaches to Israel and Palestine. Differences between Christian Zionism and the position that opposes it, which has been termed Christian Anti-Zionism, or I think better, Anti-Christian Zionism, often generate intense reaction and misunderstanding. Therefore, some qualifications should be noted before launching into a discussion of Christian Zionism.

First, there are nuances among those who would fall into the broad Christian Zionist movement. Generalizing necessarily homogenizes the discussion, eliminating a consideration of these subtleties. Nevertheless, to speak generally of Christian Zionism is legitimate as the popular values, ideas, and practices of this movement are widely shared. These convictions are secondary outgrowths from the theology of classical dispensationalism. They include the idea that because of God's eternal covenant with the Jewish people and the promise to restore the Jewish people to the Land, any claims to the land or for a sovereign state by Palestinians are illegitimate, and any policy that opposes the modern State of Israel is *de facto* error.

Second, critiquing Christian Zionism does not imply that all the blame for the present conflict should be placed at Israel's feet. Such an approach would perpetuate the simplistic designation of the "good guys" versus the "bad guys" that already burdens the Holy Land. Furthermore, this discussion is meant primarily to address problems in the response of Christians to trends in Israel. As a critique of a Christian movement, it does not in any way discount the need for the Jewish people to have a homeland in which they can dwell securely, nor does it delegitimize the existence of the State of Israel. On the contrary, this critique argues that it is Christian Zionism that is undermining Israel.

Third, critique of Christian Zionism does not imply a rejection of the main theological convictions that undergird this movement, that is God's ongoing purpose for the Jewish people, and the prophecy of their restoration to the land first promised to Abraham (Gen 12:1–3). Such critique does however challenge an understanding of the nature of this restoration that emphasizes forceful nationalism and an exclusion of others in the land.

Fourth, it is important to recognize as well that for a Gentile Christian to even indirectly criticize the national aspirations of the Jewish people as expressed in Zionism, it must be done with the acknowledgement that Christians prepared the soil for anti-Semitism that gave rise to the Holocaust, and thus the present national conflict between Israel and Palestine.[4] From the first centuries after Christ, the church began to portray Judaism as cursed for rejecting the Messiah. These prejudicial views hardened through the centuries in Europe. During the travesty of the Crusades, as had been mentioned, Jewish communities that were in the path of the Crusading armies were decimated.

Fourth, I am convinced that Rabbi Michael Lerner, the editor of the progressive Jewish magazine *Tikkun*, is correct in his assessment that the dysfunction of both Palestinian and Israeli societies is, at least to some extent, due to the fact that both societies are suffering from post-traumatic stress disorder (PTSD).[5] Both peoples need empathetic healers—not harsh opponents—to come alongside and assure them of their safety and acceptance. Yet, by the same token, Lerner states that this societal dysfunction is not a justification for crimes against each other.[6] Where brutality and triumphalism in the name of God are being enshrined, they must be challenged.

Finally, my hope in critiquing Christian Zionism—and Anti-Christian Zionism—is that such critique, however brief, will not harden the unproductive polarization of opinions, but will nudge readers to explore creative theological and spiritual avenues. This, in turn, may produce a richer dialogue between all those concerned with justice and peace in Israel and Palestine. Ultimately such discussion will be helpful for Western Christian mission as well, which is the intent of this book. The following story intends to illustrate popular ideas of God's will for Israel found in Christian Zionism, and how urgently more nuanced discussion is needed.

Ben Yehuda Street is the hub of street life in West Jerusalem. An open pedestrian mall that climbs uphill from Zion Square, it is almost always packed with Israeli families, young people, backpack-toting travelers, representatives of Orthodox Jewish groups selling religious articles, soldiers, street performers, and more who come to enjoy its cafes, pubs, and boutiques. Filipinas, in Israel as caregivers for the elderly, congregate around a few benches on their day off. It is a happy scene that represents the vibrancy and eclectic nature of Israeli society.

One memorable fellow, whom I will call Joe the Prophet, who showed up in Jerusalem around the time of Prime Minister Sharon's announcement

---

4. Chapman, *Whose Promised Land?*, 281.

5. See Lerner, *Embracing Israel/Palestine*, 255–90.

6. Ibid., 271.

of plans to withdraw the settlements from Gaza, was a six-foot-tall American dressed as a theatrical version of an Old Testament prophet, complete with a long, scruffy white beard and a homemade burlap tunic cinched with a rope belt. As Israeli families strolled along Ben Yehuda Street window shopping, enjoying the evening air, Joe the Prophet would admonish them in an American southern drawl—in English—not to yield an inch of land to the Palestinians, lest they be sorely judged by God! His listeners, many of whom didn't speak English, gave him a wide birth. This self-appointed proclaimer was just one more—like those who joined the settlers in Gaza, and the hard-hearted televangelist—to promote with passion the convictions of Christian Zionism.

As a basic definition, Christian Zionism is a movement based on dispensational premillennial theology whose adherents promote uncritically the goals of political and religious Zionism. Zionism is the "national movement for the return of the Jewish people to their homeland and the resumption of Jewish sovereignty in the Land of Israel. [It] has come to include the development of the State of Israel and the protection of the Jewish nation in Israel."[7] For militant Zionists, it is mandatory that Israel reclaim all the land of ancient Israel. The term "Christian Zionism" was first used by the founder of the Zionist movement at the end of the nineteenth century, to describe a particular Christian friend of the movement.[8] It therefore did not begin as a pejorative, nor for many is it so today. Some ministries, such as such as the International Center for Christian Zionism in Jerusalem, use it to identify themselves.[9]

What do these theological terms, mentioned above, *premillennialism* and *dispensationalism,* mean? Premillennialism was advocated by early church fathers. It emphasized the speedy return of Christ, a final battle against the enemies of God, and, based on Revelation 20, that Christ at his (premillennial) return would establish his kingdom on earth that would last for one thousand years. In historic premillennialism, there is not a distinction between Jewish and Gentile followers of Christ, both of whom would participate equally in the millennial reign of Christ.[10]

7. The Jewish Virtual Library, "Zionism."

8. Sizer, *Christian Zionism*, 19.

9. The official website www.israelmybeloved.com is an example of the convictions of Christian Zionists.

10. In early premillennialism the millennium, the one-thousand-year earthly reign of Christ, was described as a time of great sensual delight. In contrast, the influence of Augustine's theology in the fourth century stressed the evil of the physical world, and

Dispensationalism is a theology formed in the nineteenth century by evangelical Protestants in England and Scotland. It maintains that God deals with humanity in different ways during different periods or dispensations in history. Central to God's dealing with humanity is his relationship to Israel. What was viewed in Great Britain as a marginal sect rapidly became widely accepted among many evangelical Christians in the United States. Dispensationalism reinforces the premillennial emphasis on Christ's sudden return to establish his literal one-thousand-year reign on earth.

A foundational concept of dispensationalism is its purported literal hermeneutic, or method of biblical interpretation. Dispensationalism maintains that all references to Israel in the Old and New Testaments are to be taken literally as denoting the nation of Israel. Although there may be references to Israel in the New Testament, such as believers in Christ Jesus who constitute a New Israel (Gal 6:16), according to dispensationalism, these references do not negate the fulfillment of the Old Testament prophecies for the future of the Jewish people, Israel.

Essential among the Old Testament prophecies concerning Israel is the theme of the restoration of the Jewish people to the land of ancient Israel (e.g., Ezek 20:24, Isa 11:11–12), which is regarded by dispensationalists as a condition for the return of the Lord. This restoration involves the possessing of the land promised to Abraham and his descendants (Gen 12: 1–3). (Dispensationalists differ on the boundaries of the restored Israel; some allow for a Palestinian state within historic Israel, most do not. Some argue that boundaries will extend as far south and east as the Nile and Euphrates rivers in Egypt and Iraq respectively.) The return to the land will lead to a rebuilt Temple in Jerusalem, in which worship will be reinstated (Rev 11:1–2). According to this view, the new Temple must replace the presently situated Islamic monument, the Dome of the Rock, and the Al Aqsa mosque, the third holiest place of worship in Islam.

Classical dispensationalism maintains that the church of the New Testament is distinct from Israel and that God has distinct purposes for national Israel and the church, both now and in eternity.[11] God's prophetic

---

an amillennial doctrine that Christ's one-thousand-year reign on earth is effected in the *present* through the church. According to amillennialism the return of Christ will usher in the end of the age and the beginning of eternity. Augustine's influence caused premillennialism to wane until the Reformation.

11. A variation of dispensationalism termed *progressive dispensationalism* softens the distinction between Israel and the church, maintaining that both Israel and the church serve the purpose of the establishment of the kingdom of God on earth, and that in

purposes are ultimately to be fulfilled through Israel. The church, consisting mainly of Gentiles, will be raptured, or removed from the earth before the worst of the Great Tribulation begins. This separation is essential so that God can again use Israel to fulfill his purposes. After the church's removal, the world will be evangelized by a remnant of faithful Jews who have believed in Jesus. Christ will then return to defeat the Antichrist and his forces at a final battle of Armageddon, a plain in northern Israel, and establish his global millennial reign. The millennium reign will have a distinctly Jewish character. It is during the millennium that the Old Testament promises to Israel of a messianic kingdom will be finally and completely fulfilled. While there are varying theological positions within Christian Zionism, generally it is based on these foundational tenets of dispensational premillennialism.[12]

Covenant theology is the most widely accepted alternative to dispensationalism. Instead of different periods of history, it maintains that covenants are the primary theme in God's dealing with humanity. It faults dispensationalism's insistence that the church is separate from Israel. For example, Paul emphasized that through the blood of Jesus, believing Gentiles and Jews were formed into "one new humanity":

> Therefore remember that formerly you, the Gentiles in the flesh, who are called "Uncircumcision" by the so-called "Circumcision," which is performed in the flesh by human hands—remember that you were at that time separate from Christ, excluded from the commonwealth of Israel, and strangers to the covenants of promise, having no hope and without God in the world. But now in Christ Jesus you who formerly were far off have been brought near by the blood of Christ. For He Himself is our peace, who made both groups into one and broke down the barrier of the dividing wall, by abolishing in His flesh the enmity, which is the Law of commandments contained in ordinances, so that in Himself He might make the two into one new man, thus establishing peace, and might reconcile them both in one body to God through the cross, by it having put to death the enmity. And He came and preached peace to you who were far away, and peace to those who were near. (Eph 2:11–17)

According to covenant theology, the thrust of this "one new humanity" is not that it replaces Israel, but rather that it calls Israel into the new messianic

eternity they form one people of God. See Grudem, *Systematic Theology*, 860.

12. Weber, *On the Road to Armageddon*, 19–26.

community. However, the problem for many with the implications of this statement is that to be part of "one new humanity" implies that Jews must become Christians, who by historical and cultural association are Gentiles, and Gentiles have often been the persecutors of Jews. But note that, from the perspective of the followers of Christ in Paul's day, the question was just the reverse: how could Gentiles be part of the predominantly Jewish community of the followers of Jesus?

Perhaps more important for this discussion, than this critique of dispensationalism that it falsely divides the Messianic community, is the problem of how it conceives of the mission of God. Whereas the Old Testament prophets of Israel (e.g., Jonah and Isaiah 40–55), portray an ever widening and inclusive understanding of the people of God who will be included in God's kingdom, dispensationalism argues that the clock of salvation history should be turned backward in the end of the age, again returning God's focus to one people, ethnic Israel. This emphasis on one people with an exclusive claim to the land tends toward the nationalism and triumphalism that the prophets and Jesus opposed (e.g., Luke 4:16–30, as previously discussed).

Finally, although dispensationalism acknowledges that Jesus fulfills the promises made through the Hebrew prophets to Israel, it argues that there nevertheless will be another eschatological fulfillment of these promises for national Israel. The emphasis on this tends to diminish the centrality of Jesus in the salvation of God. For example, dispensationalists argue that Isaiah's prophecy that the nations will be drawn to Israel will occur literally in the millennium. Yet, Jesus declared as he approached his crucifixion, "And I, when I am lifted up from the earth, will draw all people to myself" (John 12:32). It is impossible to ignore how this motif of being "lifted up" is repeated in the Gospel of John (e.g., 2:19), and so obviously parallels and fulfills the Isaian prophecy:

> Now it will come about that
> In the last days
> The mountain of the house of the Lord
> Will be established as the chief of the mountains,
> And will be raised above the hills;
> And all the nations will stream to it (Isa 2:2).

The apostles, in affirming the centrality of Jesus in the purposes of God, as in John 12, are no longer portraying national Israel as the locus of God's salvation. The apostles indicate that the mission of God is now going forward in a surprising way that the prophets could not have comprehended.

The British author, cleric, and long-time resident of the Middle East, Colin Chapman, observes the fundamental shift that occurred with the coming of Jesus, the Messiah, and the problem of Christian Zionism's lack of acknowledgement of this shift:

> Christian Zionism appears to be a well-intentioned but misguided attempt to interpret the recent history of the Middle East and to show sympathy for the Jewish people in their painful dilemmas in the modern world. Basing itself on a profoundly flawed method of interpreting the Bible, it seems to read the New Testament through the eyes of the Old Testament, rather than the Old Testament through the eyes of the New Testament. It fails to grasp how the coming of the Messiah was meant to transform first-century Jewish ideas about the *Torah*, the land, the temple, the Chosen People and how new wineskins were needed to contain the new wine of the gospel of Jesus. It represents a regression to the mentality of the Jewish disciples of Jesus *before* they finally got the point and began to understand the significance of who Jesus was and what he had accomplished.[13]

In wandering from the centrality of Jesus, inevitably Christian Zionist support of Israeli nationalism reflects uncharitable views toward those who oppose it, particularly Palestinians. It routinely promotes the fallacies which I have previously mentioned: that Palestinians are not an authentic ethnic group, but rather are a construct of Palestinian propagandists; that the land was empty when Jewish immigrants arrived in the early twentieth century; and that whoever opposes the State of Israel and its policies, politically or otherwise, is opposing God, and, consequently, is cursed.

Christian Zionism is a reductionist movement that frames issues related to Israel, Palestine, and the land in terms of eschatology and nationalism. In doing so it often neglects the concerns of Christ Jesus. Joe the Prophet apparently was not aware that when Jesus referred to the prophets, it was not to reiterate Israel's claim to the land; rather, when Jesus referred to the prophets, it was primarily to remind Israel of its obligation to social justice—to remember the weak, the widow, and the orphan. In contrast to the nationalistic anti-Roman Jewish radicals in the first century, Jesus asserted that the meek—whoever they may be—will inherit the earth (Matt 5:5).

13. Chapman, *Whose Promised Land?*, 282.

By framing the problems of the Holy Land narrowly, in terms of particular end-times prophecies rather than the more important prophetic values of justice, mercy and peace, not only is the unethical treatment of Palestinians ignored, but the grave social problems Israel faces are not addressed. These social problems pose an equally serious threat to Israel's national existence as does Palestinian claims for statehood, as I will discuss below. Christians who are truly concerned for the modern State of Israel should be concerned with social dysfunction within Israel—human trafficking for sexual exploitation, the unjust treatment of the Bedouin people, Jim Crow-like policies toward Palestinian Israelis who, though full citizens, are not treated equally under the law. These issues are openly discussed in Israeli media, but are rarely mentioned in Western Christian circles.

THE LAND AND SALVATION GEOGRAPHY

As I have mentioned, it is not the purpose of this book to fully develop a theology of the land. Christian Zionism is critiqued as an ongoing example of Western mission allied with power, which must be challenged if mission is to be renewed in its spirituality. However, it is important to note that there are biblical themes that provide a way to support Israel's biblical call to the land while eschewing a triumphal and exclusive understanding of its possession of the same. Biblical scholar Marlin Jeschke notes the importance of land as a biblical theme.[14] (A topic it might be said that covenant theologians tend to spiritualize to excess in their understanding of the implications of the new covenant initiated by Christ Jesus.) Jeschke argues that as part of salvation history God calls his people to a new way of living in the land. Such a way of living sanctifies the land. He writes:

> Salvation geography means a community living out the distinctive style of possession of territory that salvation history teaches, receiving land as a gift from God and stewarding it with respect of neighbors and descendants, extending the reach of holy land.[15]

From this perspective Abraham's call near the beginning of salvation history was a call to live in the land in such a way that God's peace and justice were established in it. All the nations of Abraham's day were to be blessed by this way of living in the land in meekness and peace. The land was to be

14. Jeschke, *Rethinking Holy Land*, 21.
15. Ibid., 23.

a refuge, not just for Abraham and his descendants, but for the foreigner who was to be welcomed into the land and extended justice. The vague boundaries in scripture that define this land of promise and gift (another topic beyond the scope of this book) imply that this call to a new way of living in the land was to spread throughout the world—to every land.

Skipping ahead in salvation history, Christ Jesus did not weaken this understanding of salvation geography. To the contrary, he heightened the call for Israel to live at peace in the land and to understand how God's blessing extends beyond its borders. Ultimately, he points to a day in which humanity will live with their neighbors in the land in a new way—it is worth repeating: "Blessed are the meek," he said, "for they will inherit the earth" (Matt 5:5).

As it can be argued that today Israel still has a call to the land, so it also has this unique call upon it: to demonstrate a way of living with its neighbors and all who are in the land that is so radical in its peacemaking, in its inclusiveness, that the world may learn a different way to co-exist. Also now, as children of Abraham by faith, followers of Christ Jesus inherit the same call. If it is easy to criticize Israel for the harshness of its policies, one might ask how Christians have succeeded at demonstrating the meekness of God in how they have lived in their homes, neighborhoods, and with the nations. The history of Christian conquest that was briefly reviewed in the first chapter answers that question.

Finally on this point, it should be considered that the presence of the Palestinian people in the land represent a gift to Israel, a perhaps final opportunity to live as a prophetic people by making peace. This, as I have mentioned, many in Israel are seeking to do. Hopefully the Christian community will learn from their example, and cease to follow the example of extreme nationalists.

SPECULATIVE ESCHATOLOGY RUN AMOK AND THE UNMAKING OF ISRAEL

Based upon and going beyond the dispensationalist emphasis on the centrality to God's purposes of a restored Israel in the land, Christian Zionism has nurtured ties with the most militant forms of Zionism and the right-wing political parties that support them. Photographs of Prime Minister Benjamin Netanyahu, the leader of the conservative Likud party, are displayed prominently on the website of the U.S. based Christians

United for Israel (CUFI), the largest Christian Zionist organization in the United States.[16] In their involvement in the political process, Christian Zionists have moved from being interpreters of prophecy to, in their perspective, participants in fulfilling it. As Timothy Weber puts it, dispensationalists since the 1967 Six Day War have moved from the bleachers to the playing field of prophecy.[17]

In their zeal to rush history to its close, Christian Zionists have adopted positions that are more radical than those held by most Israelis. For example, consider the settlements of Israeli civilians that are being built with the Israeli government's assistance on the West Bank (discussed in chapter two). As of mid-2011, there were 121 settlements on the West Bank officially recognized by the Israeli government.[18] A report by the Israeli human rights organization Peace Now, based on the records of the Israeli government, determined in 2006 that many of the Israeli settlements are built on land illegally confiscated from Palestinians.[19] In spite of Israeli governmental endorsement, the international community still regards settlements in occupied Palestinian territory as illegal, a violation of the Fourth Geneva Convention, which forbids an occupying power to transfer its own population into the territory that it is occupying.[20]

The constant loss of Palestinian land robs Palestinians of their livelihood and destroys the possibility of a future Palestinian state. In terms of daily Palestinian life, settlements restrict free movement to work, school, and medical care as Palestinian roads near the settlements are often blocked. The settlers routinely attack Palestinians who try to work in their fields, or harvest their olives. These attacks often occur under the gaze of the IDF, which takes little or no action against the settlers.

As a result of their illegality and the oppressive control they exert over Palestinian life, many Israelis refuse to have any involvement with the settlements. The organization Jewish Voices for Peace states that sixty prominent Israeli artists have declared their unwillingness to perform in West Bank settlements. This protest became prominent with their refusal

---

16. Christians United for Israel, http://www.cufi.org/.

17. Weber, *On the Road to Armageddon*, 187.

18. "Settlements & Land." B'Tselem, the Israeli Center for Human Rights in the Occupied Territories, has methodically documented the many methods used to separate Palestinians from their land and confiscate it.

19. Shragai, "Peace Now."

20. "Geneva Convention."

to perform in a newly constructed cultural center in the large settlement of Ariel, which is adjacent to the Green Line.[21] More than 150 Israeli academics supported the actors' boycott of the settlements by a signed and published petition which declared their same intent.[22] The petition read in part:

> "We will not take part in any kind of cultural activity beyond the Green Line, take part in discussions and seminars, or lecture in any kind of academic setting in these settlements," the academics wrote.
>
> "We support the theater artists refusing to play in Ariel, express our appreciation of their public courage and thank them for bringing the debate on settlements back into the headlines," the petition said. "We'd like to remind the Israeli public that like all settlements, Ariel is also in occupied territory. If a future peace agreement with the Palestinian authorities puts Ariel within Israel's borders, then it will be treated like any other Israeli town."[23]

The fact that the government of Israel pursues pro-settlement policies is alarming to many Israelis, not just because it marks an ethical failure, but because they see in it the catastrophic undermining of Israel as a moral, democratic nation. As previously mentioned, the Israeli journalist and author Gershom Gorenberg, argues that the occupation of Palestine and the settlement project are undermining Israel as a democracy, which will ultimately threaten its existence.[24] Robert K. Lifton, the former president of the American Jewish Congress, makes a similar argument. He writes:

> I am a Zionist. Like most Jews living in the United States and elsewhere in the world, I believe in the indispensability of a Jewish state as an ultimate haven and as representative of the Jewish people, whose long history of pogroms, mistreatment as second class citizens, mass expulsions and the extreme horror of the Holocaust demonstrates a need for a state of their own . . .
>
> However, that promise now faces a serious threat. This comes not in the form of foreign militaries, Palestinian terror or economic instability, but in the very persons who purport to support it. The alliance of aggressive nationalists and religious expansionists is endangering the dream of Zionism as conceived of by Theodore

21. "Israel Artists Condemn Settlements."

22. Levison and Kashti, "150 academics, artists back actors' boycott of settlement arts center."

23. Ibid.

24. Gorenberg, *The Unmaking of Israel.*

Herzl and shared by millions of Jews. Through their overzealous efforts toward expansion, in which they seek to extend Israel's jurisdiction over the Biblical "whole land of Israel"—the Territories gained in the 1967 Six-Day War—they are endangering the Zionist foundations of that land.[25]

Mark Braverman, an American Jew, was raised in a family that fervently supported Israel. Several trips into the West Bank proved to be pivotal in his reappraisal of Zionism. He writes:

> Traveling in Israel and the Occupied Territories in the summer of 2006, I experienced first-hand the damage inflicted by the occupation on the Palestinian people and on Israeli society. Witnessing the separation wall snaking through the West Bank on stolen land, the checkpoints, the network of restricted roads, the massive, continuing construction of illegal Jewish settlements and towns, the vicious acts of ideological Jewish settlers, the terrorizing impact of shelling by Palestinian resistance organizations on Israeli border towns, and the effect of militarization and ongoing conflict on Israelis (especially the young), I realized that, no matter what rationales were advanced in justification of Israel's current policies, these actions would never lead to peace and security for Israel. I saw that the role of occupier was leading Israel toward political disaster, and the Jewish people down a road of spiritual peril.[26]

Rabbi Michael Lerner maintains that the settlement enterprise is hijacking contemporary Judaism and distorting its humanitarian values. The influence of the settlement enterprise has become so entrenched that to oppose it is regarded as traitorous. As was mentioned previously, Lerner has coined the term "Settler Judaism," a parallel to "Constantinian Christianity," to describe Judaism that is aligned with power and dominance. He argues that with these values being promoted by the Israeli government in its support of the settlements, Israel should not call itself a Jewish state, as this misrepresents Judaism.[27] Lerner writes:

> Whereas the Bible is filled with prophetic energies that vigorously criticize the distortions of the kings and leaders of ancient Israel, here we have Judaism being appropriated to sanctify the enterprise of building the Jewish State and its military without the slightest

25. Lifton, "Zionism at Risk."

26. Braverman, "Zionism and Post-Holocaust Christian Theology," 31. Braverman describes his remarkable journey in *Fatal Embrace*.

27. Lerner, *Embracing Israel/Palestine*, 360–67.

recognition of the ease with which a state and a military can lose
their way and serve interests that conflict with Jewish ideals. God
is appropriated to serve national interest, thereby demeaning God
and reducing the divine to narrow and self-interested national
purposes.[28]

What is the relationship of Christian Zionism to this settlement enterprise, which is understood by these important Jewish voices as undermining Israel? As if operating in a moral vacuum, there is an organized and
concerted effort by Christian Zionist organizations to support the settlements.[29] The growth of the settlements is understood as fulfilling prophecy
that will speed the return of Christ. Christians were active in raising funds
for the founding of Ariel, the settlement with which the Israeli artists and
academics refused to cooperate.[30] Special tours of the settlements are presently organized by Christian Zionist organizations to show their support.[31]
This endorsement and active participation by Christians in the settlement
movement is out of step with international condemnation of the same,
with important leaders in Israel who argue that the settlements are weakening Israel, and with the ethics of Christ. With this endorsement ideology
trumps reason, not to mentioned compassion and justice.

The Israeli government, although increasing restrictions on Christian
workers in Israel, is happy to partner with Christian Zionists who lobby for
America's support of Israel; yet, it is ironic for Israelis to align themselves
with an expression of Constantinian Christianity, because in so doing, they
are placing their trust in the paradigm of Christianity that has been the
source of anti-Semitic persecution for centuries. Christianity in league with
power drove Jews out of Spain at the end of the Middle Ages, restricted
Jews to ghettos in Czarist Russia, and ultimately laid the foundations for the
Holocaust. While such an alliance may serve Israel's short-term political
goals, ultimately it is aligning itself with a historically oppressive system
that could turn against it.

28. Ibid., 357.

29. For example, see Christian Friends of Israeli Communities, www.cfoic.com/. In
the simplistic approach to scripture, contemporary politics, and law typical of Christian
Zionism, this organization on its website states, *"Judea and Samaria (the 'West Bank') is
not occupied territory. It is the birthplace of the Jewish people."*

30. Weber in *The Road to Armageddon*, 225–27, documents the project of Christian
Zionists to adopt illegal Israeli settlements in the Occupied Palestinian Territories.

31. Rutenberg, et al., "Tax Exempt Funds Aid Settlements in West Bank."

How is it that Christians can passionately pursue programs that contradict the example of Jesus, who did not promote an exclusive nationalism, but rather called for a way of life defined by loving one's neighbor, even if that neighbor was a Samaritan—or a Palestinian? To answer this adequately would require an exploration of social psychology/pathology, national identity and myth, and the nature of religious imagination. But one important contributing factor to this disconnect is Christian Zionism's immersion in a distorted interpretation of scripture that is not supported by a Christ-centered hermeneutic. Such a hermeneutic creates an alternate reality, one which defines nations by the roles they are imagined to play in the events leading to the return of Christ.

A glimpse of this alternate reality can be in an influential book that popularizes Christian Zionism, Hal Lindsey's *The Late Great Planet Earth*, published in 1970. As a premillennial dispensationalist, Lindsey emphasizes the need to interpret prophecy literally rather than allegorically.[32] This purported literalism is problematic for several reasons, but perhaps most difficult is the speculative manner in which Lindsey develops a scenario in which Russia, China, and European, African, and Arab nations are assigned roles in the eschatological finale which will center on the attempted destruction of Israel and the return of Christ. The following passage gives a flavor of speculative dispensational interpretation run amok:

> *The Greatest Battle of All Time*
> With the United Arab and African armies neutralized by the Russian invasion, and the consequent complete annihilation of the Russian forces and their homeland, we have only the two great spheres of power left to fight the final climactic battle of Armageddon: the combined forces of the Western civilization united under the leader of the Roman Dictator and the vast hordes of the Orient probably united under the Red Chinese war machine.[33]

To the enthusiasts of end times prophecy, this speculative certainty is intoxicating. It provides an assurance of exactly how the world will end, and that they will be on the winning side. This hermeneutic, or interpretation of scripture, has the insidious effect as well of portraying various nations in dangerously pejorative ways. The references to the "hordes of the Orient," the "United Arab," and "African armies" as forces that will be opposing Israel and God blatantly fuels Sinophobia, Islamophobia, and racism.

32. Lindsey, *The Late Great Planet Earth*, 176.
33. Ibid., 162.

It is the nations other than North American Caucasian Christians that are conveniently labeled as evil in this popular dispensationalist scenario of the end times.

To render peoples and nations as categorically opposed to God has profound consequences. It strengthens a fabricated worldview that divides the world into the good and the evil. It perpetuates an assumption of cultural superiority and justifies spurning the ethics of Christ to love and to seek peace with all people because certain nations are, presumably, already heading for doom in the end times. It ignores the fact that God is drawing people toward his mercy and forgiveness in all nations.

SEEKING A NEW PERSPECTIVE

A growing number of young—and not so young! —progressive evangelicals and spiritual pilgrims are beginning to question the tenets of Christian Zionism. For seeking Christians who in their spiritual journeys are trying to find their way out of the alternate reality of dispensational premillennialism and into a healthier understanding of Israel and Palestine, it is necessary, like a painter working on a canvas, to step back and get a broader perspective. The esteemed California abstract expressionist, Richard Diebenkorn, once mentioned in an interview that at times he would look at his paintings in progress in a mirror. By viewing them backwards, he could assess flaws that his normal perspective could not detect. So, also, gaining a new perspective concerning Israel and Palestine needs a radically different vantage point that provides a way to correct familiar convictions.

Jesus turned the normal perspective of the people of Israel in his day upside down. He prophetically stated that in God's economy the last will be first and the first last (Matt 20:16), that whoever was least in social status would be the greatest (Luke 9:48). The normal order would be upended. Even the "unclean" Gentile who had faith would be welcomed into Abrahams's company while the "subjects of the kingdom" were cast out (Matt 8:11–12)! We need to consider the upside-down—or rather right side up! —ethic of Jesus, keeping it in the foreground, when considering familiar assumptions about Israel and Palestine. God's ways are not our ways.

Besides reflecting on the teaching and ministry of Christ, to gain a fresh perspective we should also listen to those who are unfamiliar, who live on the other side of the euphemistically designated "dividing wall," Palestinian Christians who have been burdened by Western evangelicals' support of Zionist goals, but who, nevertheless, are seeking to engage these Western friends in constructive dialogue.

A recent effort by Palestinian evangelical Christians to respond explicitly to the oppression of the Occupation and to Christian Zionists who support it has been series of bi-annual conferences entitled "Christ at the Checkpoint." Initiated by Bethlehem Bible College, the conference gathered more than 400 international Christian leaders from thirty nations in Bethlehem in March, 2012. The poignancy and relevance of the conference was evident in that it was conducted just a short distance from Israel's ten-meter high concrete wall, punctuated by watch towers, which pierces into Bethlehem.

The attendance of so many important evangelical leaders suggests both that the evangelical community is ready to reexamine its theology of Israel and Palestine, and that the Palestinian Christian voice has come of age. According to its website, the conference sought to "provide an opportunity for Evangelical Christians who take the Bible seriously to prayerfully seek a proper awareness of issues of peace, justice, and reconciliation."[34] The conference had as its goals to:

> Empower and encourage the Palestinian church; to expose the realities of the injustices in the Palestinian Territories and create awareness of the obstacles to reconciliation and peace; to create a platform for serious engagement with Christian Zionism and an open forum for on-going dialogue between all positions within the Evangelical theological spectrum; and to motivate participants to become advocates for the reconciliation work of the church in Palestine/Israel and its ramifications for the Middle East and the world.[35]

The conference represented a rich engagement of Palestinian Christians and Christian Zionists, some of whom came to observe, while several others, Messianic Jewish leaders, were given the chance to express their views in formal lectures. The presentations of two Palestinian Christians, each of which represented a prophetic cry, were compelling as they called for the need to listen to the Other.

Munther Isaac, a Palestinian evangelical Christian, professor at Bethlehem Bible College, and the Christ at the Checkpoint 2012 conference director, challenged the narrow approach of evangelicals to the Holy Land who can only see Israel and Palestine through the lens of end-times prophecy. In his presentation he said, "The problem with many Evangelical

34. "Palestinian Christians Call On Evangelicals for Action."

35. Ibid.

Christians is that they are prophecy addicts, but not prophetic."[36] This apocalyptic emphasis, he argued, promotes apathy toward moral issues and toward the pain and darkness in the world. Isaac declared that the most common response of Christian Zionists and other evangelicals to the crisis in Palestine that he hears is that it is "unfortunate." This, he stated, was the suggested response of the religious people in the parable of Jesus who walked by the Samaritan who lay wounded in the street. Not wanting to be defiled by this possibly dead man, they ignored him. His condition was "unfortunate." And they did nothing. Isaac challenged this response to Palestinian suffering:

> People look at the conflict, the deaths, the refugees, the Wall, the daily humiliations; tourists pass by the checkpoint and the refugee camp as they go into the Nativity Church, and all they can say is that it is "unfortunate." It is not unfortunate, that is the wrong word. If you have a mug of coffee and spill it, that is unfortunate. People victimized in the name of God and the Bible that is something other than "unfortunate."[37]

In response to this apathy he asked rhetorically, "Have we as Evangelicals lost our conscience?"[38] He noted that the indifference of evangelical Christian Zionists toward Palestinian Christians, their complete lack of reference to them in their theology and conferences, comes from a sense that they represent an inconvenient truth. The fact of the presence of Palestinian Christians destroys Christian Zionism's easy stereotypes that categorize the "axis of good" versus the "axis of evil."[39]

Isaac discussed how believers in Jesus have become equal heirs with Abraham of the blessings (Gal 3:29); how Abraham and his offspring are heirs to the whole world (Ps 2:9, Rom 4:13); how the Christian church did not replace Israel, but rather joined it (Rom 11:17); how Old Testament prophecies point to a restored Israel that would be inclusive of the foreigner who lives within it (Ezek 47:22); how promises to Israel are conditional; and how there is a distinction between the promises of a spiritual and a political restoration of Israel. He closed with a heartfelt appeal:

36. Isaac, "A Palestinian Christian Perspective."

37. Ibid.

38. Ibid.

39. Ibid.

My call to the Church today is "Be prophetic!" We are the light, the salt. Be involved. Let us channel spirit-filled energy in the right direction. Let us promote a culture of peace. Be peacemakers yourselves. We can make a difference. Let us not underestimate what we have. Be radical. There is no hope in the world. And this part of the world looks darker than ever . . . For this we need each other. Will you hold my hand? Will you help me stand? Will you hear my cry? Will you walk next to me? Pray with me? Will you help me shine the hope of Jesus in this dark world?[40]

Sami Awad is a social activist and the director of the Holy Land Trust, which conducts summer programs in Bethlehem to inform young Western Christians about the realities of Palestinian life and the injustices they suffer. Awad addressed the conference on the topic of nonviolence. He called on all the people of the land—Jews, Muslims, and Christians—to embrace nonviolence in their pursuit of justice and peace for all in the land. He described his road to nonviolence, with his own struggles to overcome hate. At one point he sensed that Christ Jesus was calling him to a pilgrimage. He didn't know what this meant, as he lived in the destination of much Christian pilgrimage, Bethlehem! In prayer God spoke to him again that his pilgrimage was to be to Auschwitz, the Nazi concentration camp where thousands of Jews were murdered.[41] He said:

> I went, and I experienced as much as I could the reality of the Holocaust. And I was shocked. This had never been real to me. I began to see the enemy whom I was to love, their history, their pain. Security is the language of Israel. But what is behind security? Fear, deep fear in the Jewish society globally, but in Israeli society specifically.[42]

Awad said that he came to realize that nonviolence was more than a political movement, but also an ethic which challenged his attitudes toward Israel. Ultimately, Awad said, it is nonviolence in the hearts of all the people in Israel and Palestine that will transform lives. This must happen before the wall comes down, or the coming down of the wall will not produce peace.

Usually, Awad said, "Christ at the Checkpoint" is interpreted to mean that Christ is standing with the oppressed Palestinians as they endure waiting for hours to cross the checkpoint every day, the Israeli weapons trained on them. But Awad suggested to the conference attendees who were largely

40. Ibid.
41. Awad, "Non-Violence."
42. Ibid.

sympathetically inclined toward Palestinians that their understanding of God's love must increase. Christ is also standing at the checkpoint with the Israeli soldiers who are suffering as they are forced to victimize others. Christ wants to transform their lives as well.[43]

These two Palestinian Christians, and the several others who spoke, powerfully conveyed the depth and height of the love of God for all in Israel and Palestine, and challenged narrow conceptions of that love which allow the Other to be marginalized.

In the evening after the last presentation, still sitting in the conference hall, I began to weep. I tried to make sense of these tears. The depth of my emotion was evidence of the pain—and lack of forgiveness?—I still carried from the brutality of the Intifada, now exposed by the deep grace expressed by the Palestinian speakers that day.

How many more needed to weep? How many more tears of healing and relief need to be shed by Palestinians, Israelis, and their supporters for the land to become a place of peace?

If there is going to be peace in the Holy Land between Palestinians and Israelis, it should begin with the followers of Jesus. So it was especially disappointing that after the conference, in which so much goodwill and thoughtfulness had been evident, Gentile Christian Zionists and Messianic Jewish leaders began to attack the conference, searching for the phrase or words that would delegitimize the entire effort.[44] This opposition by Messianic Jews was not unexpected. Richard Harvey, a leading British Messianic Jewish theologian who himself spoke in the Christ at the Checkpoint conference, has stated that the Messianic Jewish movement is presently unprepared theologically to dialogue with others. He writes:

> Neither are they [Messianic Jews], with a few rare exceptions, experienced in or equipped to engage with other Christian perspectives on the conflict; they have often developed their thinking within a vacuum of a strongly Christian Zionist perspective. This essay makes a plea for a broader and more realistic engagement with some hard questions. In what way is it possible to work for peace, reconciliation and restorative justice while still affirming the ongoing election of Israel (the Jewish people), which includes the promise of the land of Israel to the descendants of Abraham, Isaac, and Jacob?[45]

43. Ibid.

44. Moon, "Christ at the Checkpoint Rebukes Israel."

45. Harvey, "Toward a Messianic Jewish Theology of Reconciliation," 83.

This unwillingness of Christian Zionism to modify its strident ideology, and engage with greater self-reflection other Christian theologies of Israel and Palestine, has grave consequences, because the effect of this movement is not limited to the Holy Land. It further solidifies Western mission's alliance with agents of power as a *modus operandi*. The question is whether Western mission will continue to yield to the influence of movements such as Christian Zionism that perpetuate "Constantinian mission," or will find the resolve to repudiate it by the fountainhead of mission, the cross of Christ Jesus.

The example of efforts by some followers of Jesus in Israel and Palestine in forging deeper relations in the love of Christ is a hopeful sign the way of the humility in Christ will prevail.

7

Crucified with the Crucified

There they crucified Him, and with Him two other men, one on either side, and Jesus in between.

JOHN 19:18

If anyone serves Me, he must follow Me; and where I am, there My servant will be also; if anyone serves Me, the Father will honor him.

JOHN 12:26

God lets himself be pushed out of the world on to the cross. He is weak and powerless in the world, and that is precisely the way, the only way, in which he is with us and helps us. Matthew 8:17 makes it quite clear that Christ helps us, not by virtue of his omnipotence, but by his weakness and suffering . . . That is a reversal of what the religious man expects from God. Man is summoned to share in God's sufferings at the hands of a godless world.[1]

DIETRICH BONHOEFFER, SHORTLY BEFORE HIS EXECUTION

1. Bonhoeffer, *Letters and Papers from Prison*, quoted in Moltmann, *The Crucified God*, 47.

CHRISTIAN ZIONISM AS MISSION

A FEW QUESTIONS MAY be coming to mind at this point. For those who are not deeply invested in eschatology and the Holy Land, a discussion about the end of the age and scenarios of the return of the Lord to demolish the enemies of Israel at Armageddon may just seem weird and too fringe to be worth spending much time considering. Cannot Christian Zionism be written off as an aberrant sect? Why are Joe the Prophet and the plane loads of Christian supporters of Israel who march in the annual Feast of Tabernacles parade, sponsored by a Christian Zionist organization, of any significance? What does this conversation concerning Christian Zionism have to do with the renewal of Western mission?

In response, we must note that although it is not often evaluated in this light, Christian Zionism is emphatically a missional movement. It seeks the fulfillment of God's purposes for a people group, Jews in Israel, and the establishment of the kingdom of God in a particular land. Christian Zionism strives to hasten the fulfillment of prophecy through its support of Israel in order to speed the return of Christ Jesus. This, in turn, will lead to the end of mission, when the nations are gathered to worship Christ in a restored Israel during the millennium. By its own assessment, therefore, Christian Zionism is of unique missional importance, as it is endeavoring to advance the final chapter in the mission of God.

Because the ideology of Christian Zionism is fundamental to the spiritual worldview of millions of evangelicals, its values, beliefs, and practices—for better or for worse—are of unique influence in mission, if not in scholarly circles. Christian Zionism cannot be written off as fringe movement. It has pitched its tent in evangelicalism, and it is a wide tent. Christians United for Israel (CUFI), for example, claims to include thousands of members.[2] Although its most fervent supporters are conservative evangelicals, this movement spans denominational affiliations as well as nationalities.

---

2. It states on its website:
   Christians United for Israel has grown to become the largest pro-Israel organization in the United States and one of the leading Christian grassroots movements in the world. CUFI spans all fifty states and reaches millions with our message. Each year CUFI holds hundreds of pro-Israel events in cities around the country. And each July, thousands of pro-Israel Christians gather in Washington, D.C. to participate in the CUFI Washington Summit and make their voices heard in support of Israel and the Jewish people.
   See "Christians United for Israel."

Although theology is not a discipline to which many Christians give attention, theology matters! What armchair theologians in Dallas, or London, or Stockholm promote concerning Israel's triumphal mandate, has consequences in Tel Aviv and Ramallah. Bad theology kills. It kills by supporting policies that destroy a people's hopes. By supporting the subjugation of a people by force, it kills physically. When Israel, buoyed by the support—or passivity—of the United States, restricts Palestinian movement along West Bank highways, lives are lost. One Palestinian mother in stressed labor and unable to pass the Surda checkpoint died on the roadside.[3] Wherever it occurs, theology that leads to social injustice must be challenged.

Corrupt theology and its related spirituality cannot be quarantined in one corner of the Christian community's life. In the same way that injustice anywhere is a threat to justice everywhere, as Martin Luther King declared, triumphalism that argues that one people has the right to dominate another in a particular context affects Christian—and Jewish—spirituality throughout the world. Christian Zionism is not only an existential threat to Palestinians and to Israel but, as was discussed in the last chapter, it undermines the integrity of Christian witness globally. If the dispossession of the Palestinian people by military force is accepted as God's will, what does this mean for Christian mission in other places where there is a political bias against a people? If this same dispossession includes the rejection of a religiously motivated claim by Islam of a religious site in Jerusalem, what implications does this have for how Christianity will engage Islam globally?

Christian Zionism is not merely a possible threat to Christian witness, it has, in fact, already worked its damage, obfuscating and distorting the humility and servanthood of Christ that is at the heart of the gospel of God's grace. As will be discussed further, it has hardened Christian attitudes toward the Islamic world, and, conversely, it has marred the central tenet of the Christian faith, God's love, obscuring the beauty of Jesus—to the Jewish people, to the Muslim world, and to young evangelicals already disillusioned by a spirituality of exclusion in the churches in which they were raised. Ironically, Christian Zionist theology reflects an understanding of God that is much closer to the conservative Islamic conception of Allah than Christians are aware, or would care to admit. On the other

---

3. Rana Adel Abdel Rahim Hamad, a Palestinian woman, and her infant died as a result of being detained at the Qalqiliah checkpoint on September 3, 2002. This is one of several similar deaths at checkpoints. See the Palestinian Human Rights Monitoring Group (PHRMG) website, "Palestinians who died at checkpoints."

hand, among Muslims drawn to Christianity, what is often attractive is its emphasis on forgiveness and mercy.

While the historic disaster of colonialism in Christian missions has been acknowledged, the dynamic of colonial practice—the disenfranchisement of an indigenous people, the rejection of their rights to their land, even their very identity as a people—continues to be aggressively promoted and funded by the Christian West in its unequivocal support of Israel's expansionist claim to the land. In spite of denials otherwise, colonialism is alive and well in evangelical Christian mission.

CHRISTIAN ZIONISM AS MISSION OUT OF STEP

It is remarkable that, in spite of all the self-critique of Western mission during the last several decades, the presence of this movement, which departs so extremely from central standards of contemporary mission praxis and theology, has not been acknowledged by mission leaders.[4] For example, as was mentioned in the second chapter, evangelical demographers have scoured the world—at great expense and untold thousands of hours of research—to identify every single ethnic group that is unreached by the gospel of Jesus. The purpose of this is to facilitate sensitive, contextual mission to these ethnic groups, mission that will uphold the dignity and integrity of their cultures. Yet, why has it gone unchallenged that, in contradiction to this established principle and practice, many evangelicals singularly argue that Palestinians—a people with a colloquial language, a national identity, etc.—are the only ethnic group that does not exist? ("There is no such thing as Palestinians.") This produces a schizophrenic mission praxis in local churches, in which contextual mission to all unreached peoples is hailed, while simultaneously one particular people group is suppressed.

As was discussed in the previous chapter, Christian Zionism promotes Israeli nationalism, and this nationalism competes with the teaching of Christ as the locus of Christian ethics. When these two ethics collide, the ethic of nationalism trumps the ethics of Christ. In other words, practically speaking, the ideology that supports disenfranchising Palestinians—even advocating their forcible transfer to another country—is given more authority than Christ's command to love one's neighbor as oneself. While

4. The disjuncture between Christian Zionism and contemporary mission theology and praxis was explored by the author in "The Implications of Christian Zionism for Mission."

healthy nationalism supports a people's identity and sense of worth, nationalism that is at the expense of other nations departs from the principles of the mission of God. If, as Christian Zionists argue, Israel's election does in fact give it a unique status in the world, then the outworking of that chosenness must be left in God's hands. A biblical claim for uniqueness cannot justify political policies of marginalization. We cannot as Christians take the sword of the Lord into our own hands.

Noted academic, author, and speaker Tony Campolo's observation concerning the trend in America to merge religious sentiment, nationalism, and militarism is also relevant to Israel and Palestine. He states:

> Any attempt to cloak nationalism with religious legitimation is bound to lead to militarism in a nation that is a superpower. It then becomes easy to view the armies of that nation as an instrument through which God exercises righteous judgment upon the earth. People who hold this opinion view those who oppose the ideals of the nation as enemies of God who must be held in check, if not destroyed. More than a little bit of this thinking has crept into our rhetoric and our perception of the recent war with Iraq . . . I must declare loud and clear that no nation should ever view itself as the God-ordained instrument of His will.[5]

It should be said that there are also extremes in Palestinian nationalism. When national aspirations are used to justify the suicide bombing of innocent civilians, it makes a mockery of the ethics of Islam and of Christianity, which supporters of such terrorism may espouse. A thoughtful priest, Abuna Aziz, once said to me, "Andrew, there are [Palestinian] Christians who kill too." Munther Isaac has stated, "The issue of faith versus nationalism is an important issue. I just wonder if we Palestinian Christians are sometimes too Palestinian. We could be better Palestinians if we would take the more difficult route and, like Rahab, choose faith over nationalism."[6] Ardent supporters of Palestinian nationalism need to listen to Palestinian voices such as Abuna Aziz, Munther Isaac, and Sami Awad, which challenge their own strident nationalism.

Militarism is an inevitable result of triumphal nationalism.[7] And, as nationalism has colored Western Christianity, as well as Israeli and Pal-

---

5. Campolo, *Speaking My Mind*, 154 and 165.

6. Isaac, "Reading the Old Testament in the Palestinian Church Today," 228.

7. Ideas related to militarism and mission in this section were first presented in a paper entitled "Bullets and Bibles: The Ethical Problem of the Persistent Linkage of

estinian culture, militarism remains stubbornly embedded in Christian culture and mission. During the first Gulf war a Western organization sent unsolicited New Testaments in Arabic to U.S. troops, with an accompanying note that read: "Enclosed is a copy of the New Testament in the Arab language. You may want to get a Saudi friend to help you to read it."[8] The Saudi Arabian government had been complaining that U.S. troops were seeking to evangelize Muslims. The revelation of these evangelistic efforts confirmed their suspicions, and also, regrettably, linked Christian evangelism with military might in the homeland of Islam.

Less direct, but nonetheless controversial, were the efforts of several Christian relief agencies to follow U.S. troops into Iraq at the onset of the war. This opportunistic use of a military invasion as a vehicle to advance their programs confirmed for Muslims in the Middle East that the Christian West was in fact intent on destroying Islam.[9]

Whereas these were efforts to use military engagements to further the gospel in which the use of force was not explicitly linked to the gospel, in Israel and Palestine, this linkage is made more emphatically. There, mission is linked to militarism by Christian Zionism's framing of the Israeli Defense Forces as a modern equivalent of Joshua's army, sanctioned by God. For example, the International Christian Zionist Center has urged Christians to engage in the use of force to combat Palestinians:

> Christian—You too can work in the I.D.F.!
>
> As Israel is forced unwillingly toward a violent, history-making war with its Arab enemies, many Christians who care are wondering what they can do to stand by the Jewish state against its foes.
>
> Some talk about praying, some talk about giving. Others talk about coming over to Israel and giving the Arab enemies what for![10]

Missions and Militarism" by this author at the Evangelical Missions Society in its northeast regional conference in New Haven, Connecticut, March 2009. A revised version of this paper entitled "Bullets and Bibles: The Ethical Dilemma of Marrying Christian Missions to US Militarism" was subsequently published in *Prism*.

8. General Norman Schwarzkopf details this incident in his autobiography *It Doesn't Take a Hero*. This practice was brought to his attention by his Saudi counterpart, a Muslim. As a result of this incident the Pentagon placed restrictions on discussing religion with Saudis and taking Bibles outside of military compounds.

9. For a discussion of the controversy surrounding Samaritan's Purse and other agencies serving in Iraq and Afghanistan, see Begos, "Iraq's Good Samaritans."

10. Goodenough, "Sar-El—Volunteers for Israel's Defense."

Certainly one reason that Christian Zionism is so out of kilter as mission is that it is building on the faulty foundation of a non-contextual theology. Theologically, Christian Zionism has not emerged from within the complex context of Israel and Palestine with its rich history and weave of culture, religion, politics, and inter-communal relationships. Christian Zionism's dispensational theology is distinctly Western, and yet, it attempts to plant this theology wholesale on non-Western soil. It squeezes Israelis and Palestinians into a preconceived idea of God's purposes, and, in so doing, produces hostility and division. Although dispensationalism was developed in Great Britain and the United States before the formation of Zionism at the end of the nineteenth century, it has not altered its foundational precepts during the twentieth century, a period of tremendous advance in mission theology. Also, during the last fifty years, the idealism of Zionism has had to confront the reality of the presence of the Palestinian people in the land, which has produced much reflection that is not noted in Christian Zionism.

The transplanting of Western theology into the Middle East is not new. As has been mentioned, from the first inroads of Western Protestant mission in the Middle East in the nineteenth century, Arab Christians in the region and their theological insights have been given short shrift by Western Christians. Western Christians remain largely oblivious to the long history of Arab Christian contributions to the advancement of Christian mission, theology, and response to Islam. One area of Arab Christian history that is especially unknown to most evangelicals is its effort to make a case for Christianity against the opinions of Islam in the Middle Ages.[11]

This discontinuity between the mission of God through Christ, characterized by love and mercy, and a mission of exclusivity and militarism, is not sitting well with all American evangelicals. Many are straying off their packaged Holy Land tours and actually listening to what Palestinians have to say. Realizing that something is not right with the Christian Zionist juggernaut, they are trying to find their way out of the apocalyptic straitjacket. But where to begin?

As we have seen, the reality of Palestinian life under the now forty-six-year-old Israeli occupation is made even more onerous by the unqualified support of many Western Christians for militant Israeli nationalism. This brings the consequent forceful subjugation of the Palestinians, through what Israeli activist Jeff Halper, co-Founder and director of The Israeli

---

11. For a fascinating exploration of this topic see Griffith's *The Church in the Shadow of the Mosque.*

Committee Against House Demolition, calls the "matrix of control."[12] Many Palestinians—like Munir, the university student who asked me, "Why do Christians in America hate us?"—are discouraged by this one-sided approach to Israel and Palestine.

This discouragement is most pointed for Palestinian evangelical Christians. Alex Awad is a pastor of East Jerusalem Baptist Church and professor at Bethlehem Bible College. As a Palestinian whose family experienced the loss of their land, he has known the pain of Israel's policies.[13] For Awad, Christian support of Israel's oppressive policies is deeply troubling. He writes:

> Palestinian Christians are, for the most part, appalled by the great flood of support that numerous Western Christians have poured in the Zionist project during the last 120 years . . . How long will the Bible be used as a manual to promote military occupation? And how often must the Palestinians be subjected to the cruelties and brutalities of military conquests sanctioned by theories of divine involvement?[14]

Certainly, many American Evangelicals would be disturbed if they knew the implications of their avid backing for Israel—that people's hopes and dreams for a better future are being crushed by their enthusiasms, including those of their fellow evangelicals in the Holy Land. I recall speaking with a pastor in California, a sincere man and an ardent backer of Israel. He was deeply saddened when I told him of Munir's query. He had no idea that this is how Palestinians, even Palestinian Christians, viewed his fervent support of Israel. In subsequent visits, as I shared stories of the Palestinian people and their plight, I could tell that something was shifting in his thinking. He was exploring whether his spiritual worldview could withstand the radical overhaul of some of its convictions, and he was beginning to ask important questions. Did Israel have to occupy *all* the land? Could peace be a valid pursuit for Israelis and Palestinians? What is the history of the Palestinians? In brief, he did not want to be an oppressor.

Speaking widely in the United States during the last fifteen years, sharing the accounts of the faith of Ahmad, Labib, and Rami, and their testimony that the grace of God is not limited by the ten-meter high dividing wall that is being built to separate Israel from the Palestinian territories, I

12. See The Israeli Committee Against House Demolitions website.

13. For his account of his family's experience see Awad, *Palestinian Memories*.

14. Awad, "A Palestinian Theology of the Land," 200 and 204.

have found that many evangelicals are similarly dissatisfied with a theology that locks them into marginalizing an indigenous people. They are looking for a way out of the theological straitjacket that negatively influences their perspective of other peoples. They are seeking a way to support justice for the Palestinian people, while at the same time not abandoning their love and support for Israel. In this light, the challenge of Dietrich Bonheoffer to persevere in finding our way to renewal as Christians is relevant today:

> We have been silent witnesses of evil deeds; we have been drenched by many storms; we have learnt the arts of equivoca-tion and pretense; experience has made us suspicious of others and kept us from being truthful and open; intolerable conflicts have worn us and even made us cynical. Are we still of any use? What we shall need is not geniuses, or cynics, or misanthropes, or clever tacticians, but plain, honest, straightforward people. Will our inward power of resistance be strong enough, and our honesty with ourselves remorseless enough, for us to find our way back to simplicity and straightforwardness?[15]

The way out of a culture of dominance—be it American, Israeli, or Palestin-ian—is not easy. It begins with a confrontation with the most significant event in the history of the land, a reacquaintance with a death—taking into account all the blood that has been shed and all the lives lost in the Holy Land—and a decision about what that death will mean in one's life. The cross is not easy, as the fact that it keeps drifting to the periphery of Chris-tian spirituality indicates.

THE CROSS AND THE CRUCIFIED

In the Louvre museum in Paris hangs "The Crucifixion," a remarkable painting completed around 1457–1459 C.E. as part of an altar triptych by the Italian renaissance artist, Andrea Mantegna.[16] Having admired this great work for years, I was surprised on viewing it in person that its dimen-sions (sixty-seven by ninety-six centimeters) were not greater. Its impact, though, was not diminished.[17] The artist's portrayal of the physicality of the crucified Christ and the two thieves heightens the sense of the brutality of the Roman Empire's method of execution. The physical torment of the

15. Bonhoeffer, *Letter and Papers from Prison*, 16.
16. See "*Crucifixion* (Mantegna)."
17. Ibid.

cross has drained Christ's body of all color. Mantegna's crucifixion is no ethereal mystic event, but a cruel, tortuous extinguishing of human life. His rendering of this group execution heightens the poignancy of Jesus's prayer, "My Father, if it is possible, let this cup pass from Me; yet not as I will, but as You will" (Matt 26:39). To endure the cross was Jesus's ultimate act of obedience to the Father, and utter act of love for the world. As has been mentioned, Paul marvels at the extremity of the death Jesus would suffer, "He humbled Himself by becoming obedient to the point of death . . . *even death on a cross*" (Phil 2:8).

Mantegna's painting portrays several groups of people at the crucifixion. Women stand behind the cross supporting Mary who, draped in black, is collapsing in grief. The Roman centurions, their grisly work complete, are now oblivious to the crucified men and the grief of the onlookers. Some soldiers are engaged in conversation; others walk away. Three centurions sit on the ground, intent on casting lots for Jesus's garment. Another, standing, holds the garment on his outstretched arm, displaying its quality. The Gospel of John describes this scenario:

> So they said to one another, "Let us not tear it, but cast lots for it, to decide whose it shall be"; this was to fulfill the Scripture: "They divided My outer garments among them, and for My clothing they cast lots" (John 19:24).

These Roman soldiers, who are casting lots for Christ's garment, are intensely focused on *something* that has to do with Jesus, but in their attention to the garment, the fate of *Jesus himself* on the cross becomes of no concern. As I have considered how Palestinian Christian sisters and brothers identify with the cross—Subha's forgiveness of her unknown assailant, Ahmad when he sought to serve celebration candies to those who had firebombed Living Stones, Labib's overcoming the prejudices of Arab Christianity to learn to love Palestinian Muslims and Israelis, Samir's willingness to lose the bedrock of Palestinian national identity for his friendship with Messianic Jewish men, Sami Awad's pursuit of the gentle nonviolence of Jesus—I have realized with sadness a fundamental distraction from the cross in my journey in mission.

Like the Roman soldiers intent on winning the outer garment of Jesus, I too often have been distracted from the essential work of Jesus on the cross by so much missional clutter. Pentecostal/Charismatic concerns such as spiritual warfare, which seeks to identify the prevailing demonic "strongholds" in a country and dismantle them through prayer; an endless preoccupation with spiritual gifts and with making worship more spiritual (what some call worshiping worship); missional issues such as mission strategy (people group movements, church planting theory, etc.); cross-cultural dynamics (cultural bonding, enculturation, the bi-cultural life); the challenges of raising a family overseas; and relational issues with other missionaries—all these were a constant source of busyness. This missions *stuff*, like the garment, had *something* to do with the crucified Christ, but it effectively shifted *Jesus himself* from the centrality of my spirituality and mission praxis.

As an inexperienced missionary preparing to live in Manila, the Philippines, almost twenty-seven years ago, I was crammed with these concerns, some of them very important if kept in the right perspective, but, collectively, they became an obscuring haze. My predicament has been shared by many others. The recent, and very belated, inquiry by evangelical mission leaders into the relationship of spirituality and mission indirectly discloses the paucity of such reflection during the last thirty years, which focused on what could be termed mission technocracy.

For almost twenty years, I busied myself with missional tasks, and these tasks were advanced with varying degrees of apparent success. I preached about the cross as a legal concept by which forgiveness is obtained; yet, the cross as an example of and call to radical servanthood and mercy drifted to the periphery. I could understand the emptying implied by the cross intellectually, but my entering into that emptying as a living spiritual journey had not yet begun.

Without the centrality of the cross, mission theology and practice are left to drift, susceptible to the influence of other ideas, values, and practices that are chosen for their usefulness in achieving a shallow success. Such misplaced agents of influence may include persuasive marketing skills, utilized, for example, by Western evangelists to stage mass conferences in Manila, which, in the estimation of Filipino leaders, have the effect of manipulating and then wearing out the local people who are left disappointed and disillusioned from countless promises unfilled. They may include militarism and the use of the U.S. military presence as a mission strategy to distribute gospel tracts, effectively associating the gospel with the use of force in the minds of millions of Muslims. They may include the use of Western higher education to qualify—and thus eliminate—national brothers who are rich in the education of hospitality and concern for others, but not in graduate degrees. They may include materialistic theologies which sanction greed.

And finally, they may include the uncritical promotion of nationalism that oppresses the Other. Once mission is drawn into the orbit of the disfiguring influence of something other than the radical self-emptying of Christ, it becomes almost unrecognizable as an expression of Christ, as the previous discussion of Christian Zionism makes clear.

The challenge for Western evangelical spirituality and mission is for the cross—more specifically Jesus in his crucifixion—to become its benchmark. Jesus calls us to this. He said, "Where I am, there My servant will be also" (John 12:26). Considering that one place where Christ was found was the cross, this promise has sober implications. Paul spoke of the cross as the subject of the gospel of God's salvation, but also as the locus of spirituality, a way of life. To the Corinthian church he wrote, "For I determined to know nothing among you except Jesus Christ, and Him crucified" (1 Cor 2:2). And returning to Paul's exhortation in the foundational passage of this book, Philippians 2:5–8:

> In your relationships with one another, have the same mindset as
> Christ Jesus:
> Who, being in very nature God,
> did not consider equality with God something to be used to his
> own advantage;
> rather, he made himself nothing
> by taking the very nature of a servant,
> being made in human likeness.
> And being found in appearance as a man,
> he humbled himself
> by becoming obedient to death—
> even death on a cross!

How can mission be grounded in the cross? How can the meekness and servanthood of the cross be realized in missional theology, praxis, and spirituality? How can agents of mission meet people in their humanity, seeing them not as objects to receive ministry—as Muslims, or Hindus, or disaffected youth—but as their brothers and sisters in a shared journey? Is there one priority we could set before our eyes to move us toward these goals? There is in the crucifixion of Jesus a clear missional act that provides practical direction to those who see to make the cross foundational to their lives and mission.

Considering Mantegna's tableau of the crucifixion from the perspective of God's redemptive mission, one might ask, who was in the most urgent need at Golgotha? Among the soldiers gambling for the garment, the soldiers departing the scene, the women with Mary, and the male disciples standing at a greater distance, who was in most urgent need of God's salvation in that very hour? Actually, it was none of these, but instead the thieves crucified on either side of Christ who were on the precipice of eternity, suffering the agony of a brutal execution, cut off from any human consolation.

Christ's crucifixion was for all people of all time. He was the Lamb who takes away the sins of the world (John 1:29). But at the same time, the mission of Jesus on the cross was immediate. He was crucified with the crucified. By his willingness to accept the cross, Jesus also was accepting the company of the thieves. He was joining them in their disgrace and pain. The crucifixion was a radical act of empathy for two Jewish men who were bearing the Roman Empire's most brutal punishment. In the act of joining these men in their suffering, Jesus was the only one at Golgotha who could speak words of forgiveness and hope to them. He did this in spite of their taunts. Luke 23:39–43 unfolds the drama:

> One of the criminals who were hanged there was hurling abuse at Him, saying, "Are You not the Christ? Save Yourself and us!" But the other answered, and rebuking him said, "Do you not even fear God, since you are under the same sentence of condemnation? And we indeed are suffering justly, for we are receiving what we deserve for our deeds; but this man has done nothing wrong." And he was saying, "Jesus, remember me when You come in Your kingdom!" And He said to him, "Truly I say to you, today you shall be with Me in Paradise."

Although Christ in his crucifixion was joining all of humanity in its failure, in its doom, He especially identifies with the "crucified," the despised, the marginalized, the Other in this world. As Jürgen Moltmann states:

> By His suffering and death, Jesus identified himself with those who were enslaved, and took their pain upon himself. And if he was not alone in his suffering, nor were they abandoned in the pains of their slavery. Jesus was with them. And there too lay their hope of freedom, by virtue of his resurrection into the freedom of God. Jesus was their identity with God in a world which had taken all hope from them and destroyed their human identity until it was unrecognizable.[18]

This gospel of the one crucified with the "crucified" has been abused by those who seek to dominate the poor. The poor have been told that their

18. Moltmann, *Crucified God*, 47.

poverty and marginalization is their cross to bear in this world. In this way the oppression of the marginalized is justified. But the cross was not intended to affirm people in their poverty; rather, Christ, in joining the abandoned in their sufferings, sought to break the power of despair, to open a future and a hope for the forgotten. As Paul declared, "For you know the grace of our Lord Jesus Christ, that though he was rich, yet for your sake he became poor, so that you through his poverty might become rich" (2 Cor 8:9).

The cross is rightly portrayed in Christian theology both as the basis of salvation in Christ's substitutionary death and as an example of God's love. Paul further exhorts, as has been discussed, that we are to enter into the cross by following Christ's example of self-emptying of the prerogatives of position, privilege, and power, and by embracing servanthood toward the Other, those deemed despised, the crucified. We enter the cross by coming alongside the weak, the condemned, identifying with them in their humanity, sharing their shame, seeking to impart the hope there is in Christ.

It is difficult, though, to side with the marginalized and not resent those who marginalize. Week to week in Israel, Messianic Jewish leaders speak of the grace of Yeshua, sensitive to history of the Jewish people's suffering through the centuries. Similarly, Palestinian evangelical pastors weekly seek to encourage their congregations whom they view as the oppressed. Yet, the nationalism these Christian communities cherish in Israel and Palestine may convey a message of exclusion and hostility toward the Other. Likewise, the Christian Zionists and the Anti-Christian Zionists in their bordered mercies may portray a limited Christ to the communities they seek to serve. But, Christ Jesus can never be reduced to a tribal deity—either Palestinian or Israeli!

These observations suggest that the cross will always be confrontational to the Christians who seek to enter into it. Even as one seeks to stand with a marginalized community, serving it empathetically, the cross will confront one's limitations in grace and compassion toward those who are outside this community. Ultimately, however, we can never own the cross, domesticating it so it fits comfortably in our lives at the service of our agendas. The challenge will always be to push beyond the borders we put on grace, allowing its depth and height, length and breadth to open our hearts and bring us to our knees.

THIS IS HOW WE SHOULD LIVE

From December 27, 2008 to January 18, 2009, Israel unleashed a massive invasion of Gaza. Known as Operation Lead by Israel, and the Gaza Massacre by the Palestinian residents of Gaza, this fierce assault by land and air killed between 1100 and 1400 Palestinians. It is estimated that as many as 750 of these fatalities were innocent civilians, including children. Thirteen Israeli soldiers were killed in the invasion, four reportedly by inadvertent friendly fire.[19]

Israel's justification for the invasion ostensibly was to respond to the ineffectual rockets fired by militants from Gaza into southern Israel. The international community protested the disproportionate scale of the invasion, and the excessive deaths of civilians. A U.N. special mission led by South African Justice Richard Goldstone produced the Goldstone Report in 2009, which determined that Israel had committed war crimes, intentionally targeting civilians, a finding strongly opposed by Israel. The same report also faulted Palestinian militants for war crimes.

During the invasion, the daily toll of civilian deaths enraged and grieved the Palestinian community on the West Bank. Of those days, Labib Madanat said:

> It was a terrible time. The photographs in the media of the Palestinian children were just awful. With the images and news of the invasion was filling my mind, I still had to submit every day to the indignity of passing through Israeli manned checkpoints within the Palestinian Territories. I was faced with the question of whether as a Christian I could escape being destroyed by hate.[20]

Labib then decided that he must do something radical to advance the cause of Christ, and to escape being consumed with bitterness. He loaded his car with small gifts, and with a Messianic Jewish leader he drove to the hospital in the Negev where the Israeli soldiers, wounded in the invasion, were being treated. There he began to go from bed to bed, offering the small gifts and extending his concern and prayers. I asked Labib what the reaction of the soldiers had been when he shared with them that he was a Palestinian. He said that some of the soldiers wept, as they expressed their hope for peace.

19. "Gaza War."

20. Labib Madanat, interview by Andrew Bush, January 8, 2012. The account of this incident in the following paragraphs is taken from this interview.

Labib recounts approaching one mortally wounded soldier. The soldier's family was gathered around him as he clung to life. The elderly patriarch in the family asked Labib, a Palestinian, to pray. Lifting his voice in Hebrew, Labib beseeched God for healing and comfort. Moved by his heartfelt supplication, a white-haired Israeli gentleman, grieving for his son, took Labib's hand and, pointedly speaking in Arabic, said "Shukran," or "Thank you," and with tears in his eyes added, "This is how we should live."

Honestly, this act might trouble many Palestinians who would judge it as yielding too much to their oppressors. So it stands as a prophetic challenge as much to Palestine as it is to Israel, and their respective Western supporters. In this act, Labib was not abandoning his hope for Palestinian freedom and the realization of national sovereignty, but, as one representative of the Palestinian people, he was demonstrating what the only kind of nationalism that will nurture life and hope will look like.

By joining this Israeli family, he was crucified with the crucified. He was willing to share the pain and tears of those who were despised. He met the wounded soldiers as a prophet standing in the midst of the conflict and calling for people to turn to the love of God as ultimately revealed in the Messiah Jesus. In that love is a refuge from the fires of hate that can invade not just a land, or town, or house, but one's heart, ravaging it by its bitterness and lust for revenge.

The Western evangelical Christian community has come to an historic, prophetic day of decision. Will it find the resolve to look squarely at the contradictions in its spirituality and mission, which, while espousing a gospel of mercy, peace and justice, have also embraced coercive power, the paradigm of Constantinian Mission, to accomplish the mission of God?

Will it turn from the essential cruelty of pushing the children of Israel into a nationalism that is even now morphing from a nurturing mother into a brutal taskmaster, requiring of Israel that it surrender its merciful humanness, and thereby rapidly effecting the "unmaking of Israel"?

Can it hear a Palestinian student's plaintive question, "Why do Christians in America hate us?" and decide to do the hard work of rethinking its approach to Israel and Palestine, forming a new theology that begins with the greatest event in the history of the land, the cross of Jesus?

Will it yield itself anew to such an immersion in the grace of God, so that it can turn the page on Christianity's historic hostility toward Islam, and serve its Muslim neighbors in humility, emptying itself of the prerogatives of assured religious superiority, so that Islam can finally receive a witness to the full-orbed beauty of Jesus—a witness it has largely been denied for fourteen centuries?

Can the Western Christian, as Moltmann says:

> . . . no longer adapt oneself to this society, its idols and taboos, and its imaginary enemies and fetishes; and in the name of him who was once the victim of religion, society and the state . . . enter into solidarity with the victims of religion, society and the state at the present day, in the same way as he who was crucified became their brother and their liberator . . . ?[21]

There are sisters and brothers who are going before us to show the way. They are experiencing the pain of Western triumphal mission in the Holy Land, and yet are willing to speak of peace and reconciliation. They know the pressure of living as a minority in a majority Muslim society, and yet are willing to walk in such meekness that they can say that their Muslim neighbor is teaching them how to love. They are learning to be crucified with the crucified.

These sisters and brothers may have been reckoned to be least, but are we willing to let them teach us the way of the cross?

21. Moltmann, *Crucified God*, 40.

8

Someone Else Will Lead You

Thomas said to him, "Lord, we don't know where you are going, so how can we know the way?"

JOHN 14:5

True mission is the weakest and least impressive human activity imaginable, the very antithesis of a theology of glory.[1]

DAVID J. BOSCH, *A SPIRITUALITY OF THE ROAD*

WHY WESTERN CHRISTIANS SHOULD CROSS BORDERS TO LEARN FROM THE LEAST

NICODEMUS, A RELIGIOUS LEADER of Israel, a Pharisee and a member of the Sanhedrin, came by night to Jesus to search out Jesus's true identity and purpose (John 3:1–2). In the terminology of the Gospel of John, night speaks of spiritual darkness. "I am the Light of the world; he who follows Me will not walk in the darkness, but will have the Light of life," Jesus said (John 8:12). Nicodemus was in spiritual darkness when he came to Jesus. Although a spiritual leader, he needed a spiritual renewal. That renewal,

---

1. Bosch, *Spirituality of the Road*, 76.

Jesus said, could only occur by looking to the Son of Man lifted up (John 3:14). The Son of Man, Jesus said, must be lifted up for the healing of all people as Moses lifted up the bronze sculpture of a serpent, during ancient desert sojourn (Num 21:8).

From that dark night when Nicodemus first approached Jesus, the Gospel of John portrays his pilgrimage to the cross and to faith. It is the longest account in the New Testament of the progress of a skeptic to the cross. Some months after his first encounter with Jesus, Nicodemus is mentioned in the biblical narrative again. During the Feast of Tabernacles, which commemorated Israel's pilgrimage in the wilderness, and at the moment in which the priests in the Temple poured out water in remembrance of the water that sprang forth from the rock in the wilderness (Exod 17), Jesus cried out in the Temple, "If anyone is thirsty let him come to me and drink," (John 7:37). At this exclamation, some claimed he was the Messiah. The religious leaders then sought to arrest Jesus to put him to death, but Nicodemus spoke up and challenged them: "Our Law does not judge a man unless it first hears from him and knows what he is doing, does it?"(John 7:51). With this challenge, Nicodemus began to move out of the spiritual darkness as he took a stand, however tentatively, for Jesus. He now has put his reputation in jeopardy; he begins to empty himself for the sake of Christ.

Later we see Nicodemus at the cross. The lifeless body of Jesus is hanging there. Joseph of Arimathea, a member of the Sanhedrin as well as a disciple, requests permission from Pilate, the Roman Prefect who had given the order for Jesus to be crucified, to take the body of Jesus down (John 19:38). The Gospel of Mark states that Joseph had to work up his courage to face Pilate. The Gospel of John describes Nicodemus's participation in retrieving the broken, bloodied body of Jesus:

> Nicodemus, who had first come to Him by night, also came, bringing a mixture of myrrh and aloes, about a hundred pounds weight. So they took the body of Jesus and bound it in linen wrappings with the spices, as is the burial custom of the Jews. Now in the place where He was crucified there was a garden, and in the garden a new tomb in which no one had yet been laid. Therefore because of the Jewish day of preparation, since the tomb was nearby, they laid Jesus there. (John 19:39–42)

Nicodemus openly comes to the cross. Jesus is now disgraced in death. The voices of the mockers are quieted; the drama is over. The business of

Jerusalem resumes. This is a remarkable step in Nicodemus's spiritual journey. His growing faith and perhaps nagging conscience had led him back to care for Jesus. By tending to the lifeless body of Jesus, he is associating with the shame and apparent utter defeat of the one who had taught him about life that dark night.

The journey to the cross is one that calls us to share in the shame of Christ Jesus. We do so as we are crucified with the crucified, as we identify with the pain and shame of those who have been cast out, considered cursed, unclean. For many Western Christians, their love for Israel—however the expressions of that love may go awry—is born out of a deep empathy for the suffering of the Jewish people, their marginalization and persecution for centuries in Christendom. Other Western Christians, as they have sojourned among the Palestinian people, have been moved with an equally profound empathy. For such concerned friends of either Israel or Palestine, identification with a suffering community may cause them to harbor hostility toward the other.

This limitation—that in loving the outcast an enmity is fostered toward the one who is perceived to be the oppressor—is a constant reminder of how far short every Christian falls on their journey to the cross. How can we as Christians keep moving, and not become settled, pleased with our advocacy for the particular estranged community that we are comfortable to love?

The mystery of grace is that it works in each individual uniquely. There is no pattern or plan by which we can guarantee that we will move deeper into the love of Christ. The cross demands an emptying of that which is our false security, our certainty of our special worth, our status that may separate us from the weak, from the broken—from humanity. Such a false sense of security and superiority may be found in the pride of intellect, the satisfaction of an intense spiritual experience, the assurance of cross-cultural skill, confidence in theological acuity, or one's national or religious identity, etc. How can we move past these hindrances? How can we put them in their rightful place in our lives? This book advocates for the importance of learning from the least.

In the first chapter, I described a coarse American who reacted brutishly to a baptism of Palestinian Christians in the Jordan River. We encountered another equally boorish American in the Philippines on a journey into the back country of the island of Palawan. The trail that had to be hiked to reach a very remote tribal group was marked by many crossings of a winding river. The American and his friends did not want to keep taking their shoes on and off every few minutes to cross the winding river, nor did they want to slog along in wet shoes. A very goodhearted Filipino brother, Telly, who had been sharing the gospel with this rural tribe, was leading the way. He was walking without shoes. Not wanting to be slowed down by the Americans at the river crossings, Telly invited the foreigners onto his back.

One by one he piggy-backed them across the river several times. At the third crossing, the absurdity of this sunk into even the densest—myself! I can still feel Telly's strong back and arms carrying me—the boorish American!—through the waters. The assumption of privilege that allowed me to get on that brother's back was a sense of privilege at odds with the way of Christ. Telly's servanthood was a glimpse of the cross.

It is through such experience that we may reflect on life and spirituality. Experience may reveal that something is essentially wrong with our theology, if we find that the outworking of such theology is the careless disregard, or even the oppression, of others. Allowing experience to shed light on our theology and spirituality is rejected by some as humanistic, as not sufficiently biblical. From this perspective, theology is something that must be worked out solely by weighing the scriptural text and theological tradition. According to this perspective, if the Palestinians are suffering, that's too bad, but it doesn't change God's mandate for Israel to take the land; to alter one's theology as a response to the suffering of the Palestinians is merely humanism, and a deception.[2]

This ignores the obvious fact that we always bring to the reading of scripture our life experience: the teachers we have had, the multitude of radio programs and magazines we have read, the casual conversations we have enjoyed with other Christians, the travel we have experienced, etc. The opinion that experience should not be a source of theology also ignores the fact that the scripture is an account of individuals reflecting on their experiences of God and of their interactions with those around them. In the introduction I mentioned Sister Teresa Okure, SHCJ, an important majority world theologian from Nigeria. She argues for the importance of experience in biblical interpretation:

> Life as the starting point and abiding context of hermeneutics is
> not only important; it is a reality that imposes itself. Emerging and

2. For an example of this dismissal of human experience in biblical interpretation as it relates to Israel and Palestine, see Juster, "A Messianic Jew Looks at the Land Promises," 68.

liberative trends in biblical studies (Third World, women's feminist, womanist, reader-response hermeneutics, and inculturation hermeneutics) require that readers address their life situation as part of interpreting Scripture. The biblical works themselves are records of people who struggled to understand the meaning of their life in relation to God. Contemporary historical critical studies have assiduously combed the biblical texts, aided by imagination, to discover the life situation of the authors and their communities. The implication is that these texts grew out of, and addressed the life situation of the persons concerned, and that if we knew more about their lives, we would understand their texts better. Yet, we have no corresponding effort to relate these same texts to our contemporary life concerns and those of our communities. By leaving ourselves out in the search for meaning we missed an important key for discovering the biblical message.[3]

HOW WESTERN CHRISTIANS CAN CROSS BORDERS TO LEARN FROM THE LEAST

This suggests that deepening one's theology of Israel, Palestine, and the Land requires experiencing these communities, getting off the well-beaten and often ideologically bent path of Holy Land tours and listening to those one would not otherwise hear. Those unable to travel to the Middle East may read the excellent autobiographies of Palestinians. One of the best of these is *Blood Brothers,* by Father Elias Chacour.[4]

Richard Harvey, a Messianic Jewish scholar whom I previously noted, underscores the importance of allowing the practical issues of how people are living together in the Land to inform what may seem to be inviolable doctrine of Israel in prophecy. He states:

> The future of Israel, as part of the eschatological map, relates to the broader issues of a theology of land and the land of Israel in particular. A vital task for Messianic Jewish theology is to link eschatology with a practical theology of reconciliation with Arab Christians and the Arab population in the light of the Israel-Palestine conflict. This has yet to be attempted by those who expound a specific eschatological scheme . . . Those who see the State of Israel as a fulfillment of prophecy must still give opportunity for

3. Okure, "First Was the Life, Not the Book," 209.

4. Chacour, *Blood Brothers.*

self-critical reflection on present issues of justice, peace and reconciliation whatever their understanding of the future.[5]

Recently, I was guiding some friends through the desert on a back road
from Ramallah to Jericho. They had spent the previous days getting to
know Palestinian professionals. Along the way, I pointed out several remote
settlements, dug in like medieval towns in the fastness of the desert. One of
my acquaintances, a staunch supporter of Israel from a continent away, was
bewildered at the checkpoints we passed along the road. These checkpoints
did not separate Israel from Palestine, but rather punctuated Palestinian
territory, controlling the movement of Palestinians. At one point he said,
"There is just no way to understand the situation here, unless someone
comes here and sees it for himself." He couldn't have been more right. In
light of what he was experiencing, he was beginning to be troubled by his
triumphal theology of Israel.

A theology of triumphalism, of national exclusivity enforced through
military force, becomes difficult to reconcile with the biblical themes of
mercy and justice when Palestinians cease to be stereotypes but are known
as the people who have invited you into their homes, who have prayed with
you, who have laughed with you. As a result of experience one may begin
to consider whether an interpretation of scripture is fundamentally flawed
if it supports the marginalization of such people. This isn't humanistic. This
is recognizing that God values all of humanity, and that one's entrenched
theology may contradict this fundamental value. Again, those unable to
journey to Palestine may access various sources—books, films, dialogue
events—which can open up the humanity of the Palestinian community.

This same journey and possibility of change applies to Palestinians
and their supporters as well. A Palestinian friend with strong political
views began to soften in his attitude toward Israel after he was treated for
a serious illness by an Israeli physician. For hours during the Intifada, as I
drank coffee with him, he would rail on about Israel and its injustice. But
after his interaction with the Israeli physician, he began to recall biblical
verses that spoke of peace. His ability to hear Christ's voice in scripture was
sharpened. His posture toward Israel began to change, if ever so subtly.[6]

5. Harvey, "Toward a Messianic Jewish Theology of Reconciliation," 100.

6. During the writing of this chapter I visited with this friend again. He had recently
made an appointment to visit the Israeli doctor who has cared for him for the past twelve
years. Reaching the checkpoint that he had to cross to go into Jerusalem, he was informed his pass was revoked. As he told this story to me, about the relationship he had

Thus, one step Western Christians who are only familiar with the narrative of Israel can take is to abandon their packaged Holy Land tours, go beyond the tourist sites and meet Palestinians Muslims and Christians, and Israelis Jews. Travel with Palestinian Bible Society workers up to Living Stones in Bir Zeit, or down to their office in Jericho or Bethlehem (www. pbs-web.com). Spend a summer living in a Palestinian refugee camp in Bethlehem and working in a summer program with Sami Awad and the Holy Land Trust (www.holylandtrust.org). Help with a summer camp for kids at Bethlehem Bible College (www.bethlehembiblecollege.edu). For the brave of heart, join Rabbis for Human Rights as they act as human shields, protecting Palestinian farmers from the attack of Israeli settlers during the October olive harvest (http://rhrna.org/get-involved/volunteer.html),[7] or join Christian Peacemaker Teams (www.cpt.org) in nonviolent direct action protests. The Fellowship of Reconciliation (http://forusa.org) facilitates conversation on its tours with both Israelis and Palestinians on both sides of the Green Line.

The most important thing is to engage not only programmatically but also on a personal level, enjoying meals together while listening to one's host's stories. Ask questions and listen closely to the answers. During these encounters, wounds may surface. As representatives of the Christ, it is important not to react defensively, feeling the need to defend the United States and its policies, Western Christians, Israel, or Palestine as the case may be. Opportunity certainly exists to interact with Palestinians in the United States as well. There are more Palestinians from the village of Bir Zeit who reside in the United States than in the village itself! It is estimated that there are as many as 250,000 Palestinians residing in America.[8] It would not be

---

formed with his doctor, he began to weep, unable to grasp why he could no longer visit his doctor of so many years.

7. See T'ruah: The Rabbinic Call for Human Rights; Formerly Rabbis for Human Rights—North America. The invitation of Rabbis for Human Rights to volunteer in Israel reads:

> Volunteer in Israel
> If you are visiting Israel and the West Bank, our colleagues at Rabbis for Human Rights offer volunteer opportunities during olive harvest and planting seasons to accompany, assist and bear witness to Palestinian farmers who face harassment and violence by Israeli settlers and security forces. You may also join Rabbis for Human Rights every Friday for non-violent demonstrations in the Sheikh Jarrah neighbourhood of East Jerusalem, protesting settler takeovers of Palestinian property . . .

8. "Palestinian American."

unusual to find that your Middle Eastern neighbor down the street is actually Palestinian!

Inquiry that begins to build bridges with another community should lead to becoming salt in one's sphere of influence. Paul exhorted, "Let your speech always be with grace, as though seasoned with salt, so that you will know how you should respond to each person" (Col 4:6). To be filled with grace certainly includes challenging statements that dehumanize and belittle another people. Although Christians are meant to love and follow truth as embodied in Christ Jesus, it is remarkable how willing they may be to give voice to prejudicial fallacies.

For example, a commonly heard statement is that Jews and Arabs have been at enmity with each other since Sarah cast out Hagar and Ishmael. This enmity, it is said, will not end until Christ returns, precluding reconciliation as futile. First, historically this is simply not true. Jews and Arabs—Muslim and Christian—have coexisted peacefully in the Middle East for centuries. Much of the tension between Jews and Arabs is a result of political tensions in the modern era. Particularly useful is Chris Lowney's discussion of the manner in which Jews, Christians and Muslims lived and worked together in Medieval Spain until the defeat of the last Muslim kingdom in the Iberian Peninsula in 1492 CE.[9] More important is the biblical account of the burial of Abraham. Where is Ishmael at this burial? Cast out? Estranged? No. Isaac and Ishmael were both present together and part of the burial of their father: "Then his sons Isaac and Ishmael buried him in the cave of Machpelah, in the field of Ephron the son of Zohar the Hittite, facing Mamre . . . " (Gen 25:9). The presence of Ishmael at Abraham's funeral is indicative of reconciliation between the brothers.

When Christians try to legitimize hostility, their attention should be drawn to examples of reconciliation today. Last summer I was in a remarkable meeting. It was a gathering of Palestinian Christians, Israeli Arabs of Palestinian descent, and Israeli Messianic Jews. During the Intifada there had been scarce fellowship between these groups. Some encounters were quite difficult as people brought the pain of their communities to their attempt to relate.

In spite of these challenges, this group had come together under the auspices of the Palestinian and the Israeli Bible Societies for the dedication and launching of a marvelous book of daily devotions entitled *My Brother's*

---

9. Lowney, *A Vanished World.*

Keeper: Daily Devotions in the Faith that Unites Us.[10] The devotions were written by various representatives from the Israeli Messianic Jewish and Palestinian Christian communities in Israel and Palestine. A particularly poignant aspect of the book is that the authors of the daily devotions are not identified. As one reads the devotions, one's heart may be moved by the writings of those who were formerly viewed as enemies.

At the end of the dedication celebration, all joined together in prayer. As one visitor commented to me afterward, it was such an historic, powerful moment she expected the heavens to open and the Spirit to be poured out again as on Pentecost!

Similar to the need to discover the humanity of the people of Israel and Palestine is the need for Christians to pursue more meaningful engagement with the Islamic community, to move past stereotypical views of Muslims as haters-of-the-West and of Christianity. Increasingly Muslims, who once sought to identify with mainstream American life by becoming less visible, are growing more confident in their status as American citizens and so are increasingly more visible through clothing, prayer during the day at their work place, etc. Consequently one may notice Muslims at one's workplace, school, or neighborhood. These encounters in the flow of life are an opportunity to be neighbors as Jesus called us to be: to listen to their concerns and needs, and to offer friendship, help, and prayers.

In fact, one may find it difficult to be a better neighbor than a Muslim as Islam places great importance on serving one's neighbors. One snowy day at our home near Philadelphia I was shoveling our driveway. No sooner had I started than our Muslim neighbor's twelve-year-old son showed up with his shovel, his youthful cheeks rosy from the cold. He came to help me, he explained. I insisted on paying him; he as determinedly refused to accept anything from me! This exchange went back and forth until I relented. He said it was his responsibility to be a good neighbor to me.

As my wife and I became acquainted with this young man's family, they described the fear they experienced after the tragic attack of the World Trade Center on September 11, 2001. For weeks they stayed indoors, afraid even to go to the grocery store. Their openness to share their fears helped us gain a more empathetic understanding of the American Muslim community.

Besides such informal encounters, there are opportunities to engage with Muslims during their annual religious events. During Ramadan

10. *My Brother's Keeper*.

many mosques in the United States welcome non-Muslim visitors to their *iftar* meals, which break their fast at the end of the day. These meals are rich opportunities for Christians to sit with Muslims and get to know them on a personal basis, to learn more of how they understand their faith and their spiritual journey. President George W. Bush hosted *iftar* meals at the White House during his tenure. During one such event in 2005 he cited the concern and compassion of Muslims for their neighbors as evidenced during the rebuilding of American communities following their devastation by hurricanes.[11]

During an *iftar* dinner that I attended at a mosque near Villanova, Pennsylvania, an African American gentleman explained to me why he left Christianity to embrace Islam. As a Christian it was painful to listen to his story, yet it helped me understand why so many African Americans are making the same decision. (About 40 percent of Muslims in the United States today are African American.[12]) He said that the close community that he found in Islam had been absent from his previous experiences in Christian congregations. This gentleman's story underscored the need for local churches to be supportive communities in which members are aware and responsive to each other's needs, and open to welcome those whom they may consider Other.

In the same way, Christians often have stereotypical views of Jews and of Judaism. In their biblical eschatology, they may see Jews only within the confines of an ambivalent role—of being cursed and blessed. A role, by the way, which ends in another holocaust according to dispensational eschatology.[13] The Jewish community, although almost universally deeply loyal to Israel, affirms a wide range of political views and of understandings of nationalism. As I have mentioned, nationalism based on militarism and the suppression of the Palestinians is vigorously challenged. In the United States one might explore events sponsored by Jewish Voices for Peace (http://jewishvoiceforpeace.org/), or the writing of

11. U.S. Department of State, "President Bush Hosts Iftar Dinner at the White House."

12. Braswell, *Islam*, 241.

13. Weber in his *The Road to Armageddon*, 129, quotes Jewish historian Yaakov Ariel, who comments on the contradictory themes in dispensational theology:

> On the one hand they are God's chosen nation to whom the biblical prophecies refer. They will be restored to their ancient land and serve as the central nation in the millennial kingdom. On the other hand as they have refused to recognize Jesus as their messiah, their character reflects obnoxiousness and rebellion. Their road to glory is paved with suffering and destruction.

Rabbi Michael Lerner, especially his book, which I have previously cited, *Embracing Israel/Palestine*, or visit the synagogue he leads, Beyt Tikkun, in Berkeley, California. Mark Braverman, raised in a home deeply dedicated to Israel and Zionism, recounts his journey away from unqualified support of Israel's expansionist policies, and challenges Christians' promotion of the latter as a result of the guilt they feel for the holocaust in his book *Fatal Embrace*. A particularly fascinating documentary directed and produced by Danae Elon, entitled *Another Road Home*, explores an unusual relationship spanning decades between a Jewish and Muslim family in Jerusalem.[14]

THE EFFECT OF CROSSING BORDERS
TO LEARN FROM THE LEAST

In this same effort to affirm the humanity of others in Israel and Palestine, in Islam, Judaism, and beyond, Christian leaders should look closely at the missions they support, and make clear decisions not to fund ministries that promote bigotry and the subjugation of others. For Western mission to be transformed, for the triumphal culture of Western Christianity to change, pastors and other Christian leaders must be the first to follow in the way of Christ's humility and reconciliation. This demands that they turn away from what is hateful and demeaning. For many leaders this will necessitate costly decisions. Pastors who lead congregations that are heavily indoctrinated in a pro-Israel or pro-Palestinian perspective must be willing to call their congregations to the cross, to God's acceptance of all of humanity. To do so is to identify with Jesus in his vulnerability on the cross. If leaders do not show the way to the cross, what value is their leadership? In a recent book on leadership, John Perkins, the well-known Christian social activist states: "In the end, all good leaders and good followers must lead to Christ and the freedom found in His cross."[15]

Western mission is an expression of Western Christianity's spirituality, lived out week to week in local congregations, communicated through its media, acted out in its outreaches and service projects. To build just and Christ-like relationships with its neighbors—Muslim, Jewish, Hindu, agnostic—step by step, community by community will help to transform the culture of Western Christianity, furthering it in the way of Christ, and

14. *Another Road Home*, directed by Danae Elon, 2004.
15. Perkins and Claiborne, *Follow Me to Freedom*, 7.

thereby tilling the soil out of which mission will occur. However, the task of working out the practical implications of walking in the way of humble servanthood for mission organizations remains. I recall the frustration of the director of a mission agency, at a conference in which a new paradigm of partnership was exhorted. While accepting this idea, he was frustrated with the lack of practical steps offered.

What are practical steps toward such a partnership? How can mission become a partner with majority world brothers and sisters, serving them not from a posture of wealth and privilege but rather out of humility and lowliness? This book has argued that such a successful partnership must begin with a renewed spirituality, not merely reworked theory and strategy.

Spirituality brings together our conception of God and understanding of how God works in the world, with how we live out our faith practically day to day. The importance of spirituality in mission must not be assumed, but must be clearly enunciated; although, as one mission scholar has stated, it rarely is:

> Spirituality is somewhat like the air we breathe. It is so familiar to us that it is only when we stop and reflect on our experience of faith that we begin to grasp something of its richness and depth . . . Therefore, in the perspective of missiology and mission studies, the communication of a distinct perspective on what it means to live the Christian life was and is implicit in every proclamation of the Gospel. However, the recognition of the foundational importance of spirituality is seldom explicit in the works of evangelization and mission.[16]

For mission leaders and practitioners, then, the reflection upon spirituality should be an intentional part of mission training and retooling throughout their service. Theology and experience inform spirituality, and therefore how one goes about the engagement with other faiths and learns from these encounters, as has been discussed above, will have an important effect on spirituality in mission. Participants in mission should become deeply involved in engagement with communities other than their own as a prelude to formal mission service. This will assist them in the discipline of embracing and valuing the humanity of the Other, of confronting their ethnocentrism. It will help them to develop the habit of learning from the Other.

At the same time, preparation for those who serve in mission should include deep reflection on Philippians 2:5–11, and on the teaching of Jesus

---

16. Rakoczy, "Spirituality in Cross-Cultural Perspective and Mission Studies," 73–74.

that calls his disciples to deny themselves. Mission candidates should ask themselves what it means to empty oneself unto vulnerability and servant-hood. To what extent are they willing to make themselves vulnerable? They should consider why Christ sent the first apostles in mission without extra money or garments (Matt 10:9–10). How should such a sending inform their life among other peoples? Are they willing to be dependent on the Muslims among whom they live, for example?

What does it mean to serve? What are their expectations in service? Is there an unspoken *quid pro quo*? What respect do they expect? Jesus taught his disciples to love their enemies by giving to them without expecting anything in return (Luke 6:35). Mission candidates should ask themselves if they can realistically accept such a proposition. Serving in humility and vulnerability should be a growing characteristic of persons in mission.

Jesus seems to be communicating this to Peter after his resurrection:

> He said to him the third time, "Simon, son of Jonah, do you love Me?" Peter was grieved because He said to him the third time, "Do you love Me?"
>
> And he said to Him, "Lord, You know all things; You know that I love You."
>
> Jesus said to him, "Feed My sheep. Most assuredly, I say to you, when you were younger, you girded yourself and walked where you wished; but when you are old, you will stretch out your hands, and another will gird you and carry you where you do not wish." This He spoke, signifying by what death he would glorify God. And when He had spoken this, He said to him, "Follow Me."
>
> Then Peter, turning around, saw the disciple whom Jesus loved following, who also had leaned on His breast at the supper, and said, "Lord, who is the one who betrays You?" Peter, seeing him, said to Jesus, "But Lord, what about this man?"
>
> Jesus said to him, "If I will that he remain till I come, what *is* that to you? You follow Me."
>
> Then this saying went out among the brethren that this disciple would not die. Yet Jesus did not say to him that he would not die, but, "If I will that he remain till I come, what is that to you?"(John 21:17–23, NKJV)

Linked to Jesus's query of Peter as to whether he loves him, and his exhortation to "Feed My sheep," Jesus interjects the unusual statement about Peter's independence in his youth, that he dressed himself and went wherever he wanted; but in time this would yield to a dependence on others who would dress him and lead him to where he did not want to go.

Although this is often interpreted as pointing to Peter's future martyrdom, in the symbolic language of the Gospel of John, this might also speak of what it means to love Jesus and to care for those he loves, to be part of the mission of God. Such love calls Peter into the progressive vulnerability that Jesus had accepted in his life, culminating in his crucifixion. This progressive vulnerability—a progressive dying as Peter takes up his cross—would also enable Peter to feed those whom Jesus loves, "his sheep," all of humanity. In this daily dying to independence, God is glorified, Jesus says.

In this same passage, it is amazing how quickly the disciples turn away from the topic of becoming dependent and vulnerable to speculation about "the disciple whom Jesus loved" and what Jesus meant when he said that he wanted this disciple to remain alive until he returned. How quickly eschatology of a sort overshadows the topic of the cross! How quickly human curiosity turns to a secondary topic, away from the sobering teaching of loving through becoming vulnerable!

To be allowed into the vulnerability of the marginalized is a gift. In the second and third chapters, I discussed the vulnerability our family experienced as our support systems were stripped away from us during the Intifada. This led me into a contemplation of Philippians 2:5–11, the emptying of Jesus. Another unique experience that helped me on my spiritual journey was suffering a critical illness in Ramallah a few years after the Intifada had ceased. Moments of personal spiritual experience are notoriously difficult to communicate; nevertheless, allow me to share a few details pertaining to this illness.

A few years ago after returning to Bir Zeit from a trip to the United States, I noticed I was experiencing chest pain. A cold, I thought. The pain intensified during the next several days until one afternoon I could not walk because the pain was so intense. I sat down on a stone, and wondered if that would be the last step I ever took. The sky was blue and there was a lovely breeze that moved the branches in a nearby olive tree orchard. It would have been a good day to die. After I waited for some time, not seeing anyone who could help, a lone car passed my way. I hailed the driver, and he took me immediately to my cardiologist in Ramallah. I had to drag myself up three stories to reach the doctor's office, as the elevator was broken. The cardiologist quickly ascertained that I was having a major heart attack.

He asked me to which hospital I would like to be taken. Arab Care Hospital in the center of Ramallah was popular. It cared for the average Palestinian. It had no heart center, as I was to discover. In that moment, though, I wanted to be taken to the hospital that ordinary Palestinians used. I wanted to accept their limitations. (In this hospital Palestinian Muslim nurses would eventually care for me, and with a surgery, my health was restored.)

I will never forget being rolled on a stretcher into the ambulance that would take me to the hospital. So many Palestinians had suffered, bled, and died in that ambulance during the Intifada. To share that place of suffering was a profound experience. In some way I felt that God was allowing me into his love for the Palestinian people. I was being allowed a fresh glimpse of God's love.

The journey into a spirituality of vulnerability is a mysterious work of grace. From this perspective, the mission agency director's frustration at the lack of practical guidance in entering into a partnership of servant-hood with majority world brothers and sisters was inevitable. There is not a manual for this journey other than scripture, and the story of the lives of the brothers and sisters in the majority world, "the least of these my breth-ren," such as Brother Tony in India, Lyn in Manila, the young Palestinian woman, Subha, and Palestinian followers of Jesus, Ahmad, Rami, Samir, and Labib. They are a living testimony that servanthood out of weakness is transformative. The radical servanthood of the cross is the means of revela-tion by which the love of God is made known.

In the end what difference does it make if the spirituality of Western mission is renewed or not? It matters because God loves this broken world so filled with suffering, with longing for life. It matters because he calls his people to "Tend My sheep," to care for those who are hungry, hoping for life.

Ultimately, to be a part of the mission of God, we must cry to God to save us—to save us from the trivial, from lust for power, from achievement, from the casual acceptance of violence. A prayer written by the biblical scholar Walter Brueggemann, a reflection on Jeremiah 50–51 entitled "Vic-tims . . . and Perpetrators," is such a cry that God will save us and make us vessels of life rather than death.

> Mighty God, giver of Peace, slogan for war,
> We watch while cities burn and
> children cry and
> women weep.
> We listen while tanks roll and
> missiles zizzle, and
> mobs assemble.
> We smell while

flesh burns and
old tires smoke and
oil wells flame
out of control.
We dare say,
We dare imagine,
We dare confess, that yours is the Kingdom and the power and
the Glory.
We come to you as victims of terror and
mass death.
We come as perpetrators of death and massacre.
We come as citizens and patriots and taxpayers
and parents and children.
We come bewildered, anger, sorry.
You, you beyond the smell and the din and the smoke.
You, beyond our hopes and our hates.
You, our beginning before time
our end beyond time.
Be present—save us from our power
save us from our violence,
save us from our fear and hatred,
save us as only you can do.
Save us as you have before saved us . . .
In love and power
In compassion and justice
In miracle and in waiting.
Save us because we are your people
and because this is your world.[17]

17. Brueggemann, *Prayers for a Privileged People*, 125–26.

Epilogue

A Postcard from Ramallah

ONE JULY AFTERNOON, JACK Sara and I meet for lunch in Ramallah. It is Ramadan and most of the restaurants are closed, but we find a café that caters to the international community. It has been almost thirteen years since the night of violence at the outbreak of the Intifada, when Jack braved his way up from Jerusalem to rescue us. Jack, now the president of Bethlehem Bible College, speaks widely internationally. He speaks as a representative of the college; he speaks as a Palestinian Christian; he speaks as a voice for Christ Jesus from the margins, as one of the "least."

The question that I have as we sit down together is whether anyone in the West is listening. Are there indeed those in the West who are *learning from the least*? Are they gaining new insights into God's love that will effectively be seeds of transformation for their mission? Are attitudes changing towards the Palestinian people, and thus about what mission to Israel and Palestine might look like?

After we had ordered our meal I raise these questions with Jack; he ponders quietly, and answers thoughtfully:

> Wherever I have spoken I have told people about the story of Palestinian Christians. I have told them about their suffering for Christ, about our desire to see the kingdom of God come to the Holy Land, that is God's justice, peace, and reconciliation, and our effort to see that become a reality.
>
> I have asked people to consider their responsibility to love. I have challenged them concerning their attitude toward my

Palestinian community: when the Lord asks, "What are you doing for your Palestinian brother?" are you going to say, "Am I my brother's keeper?" or will you say, "Here I am Lord, send me?"

What has been the response? It has been very moving. In some meetings, people in large numbers have come up to me after the service weeping, really in tears, asking for forgiveness for their attitudes. Some have said, "We never knew about your Palestinian Christian community." Others have said, "What can we now do to help you?"

From 1999 when I first began to travel to the U.S. there has been a distinct change. A new openness and acceptance of the Palestinian community. I hear people speaking of "Palestine" who a few years ago would be shocked to even hear that term.

I probe a bit more: weren't there some negative responses? What has been your experience when you were invited to conferences sponsored by avid supporters of Israel? Jack answers:

There was a conference in New Mexico, that I had to really ask myself whether I wanted to attend or not. Some of the leaders of the conference have stated very hurtful things about my people. But I had to decide to intentionally put aside these ideas and go in the love of Christ. If I had not made this decision I would have reacted in anger to them.

When I went in this way, and interacted in an attitude of love—because they are still my brothers even if we disagree—I felt their respect, and that some relationship was built. I know that many still disagreed with my ideas, but what was important was that we started a good relationship. Some might begin to think differently about the Palestinian people.

I ask Jack if this acceptance by congregations in America has affected him, healing the hurts he has felt from the attitudes he previously encountered.

Yes, it gives me hope to go on. It gives me hope that the will of God can be done in Israel and Palestine, that people will make their priority God's love. But still forgiveness is something I must decide for every day.

Jack's report of how people are receiving him, honoring him, learning from him, and being changed in the process, underscores how important it is to listen and learn from those on the margins who walk in a posture of servanthood in humility. This is not the mock humility of a supplicant's request for funds, but rather a humility that has been formed by the difficult choice, as Jack said, to lay aside the consideration of ideas and words that are hurtful.

The welcome, the tears, the request for forgiveness, the searching question, "What should I do?" on the part of Jack's audiences are like olive branches moving in the breezes, signs that faint winds of the Spirit of God are blowing, bringing a day of renewal for Western mission. This is renewal characterized by a commitment to servanthood that is willing to lay aside cherished ideas and triumphal traditions—so much missional clutter—and to embrace the way of servanthood in the weakness of the cross.

Andrew Bush
Ramallah, July 17, 2013

Bibliography

Abu El-Assal, Riah. *Caught In Between: The Extraordinary Story of an Arab Palestinian Christian Israeli*. London: SPCK, 1999.

Alford, Deann. "Christian Bookstore Manager Martyred in Gaza City." http://www.christianitytoday.com/ct/2007/octoberweb-only/141–12.0.html?start=1.

Another Road Home: The Personal Story of an Israeli's Quest To Find Her Palestinian Caregiver. Directed by Danae Elon. New York: QI. Film, 2004.

Ansary, Tamim. *Destiny Disrupted: A History of the World Through Islamic Eyes*. New York: PublicAffairs, 2009.

Associated Press. "Google lists Palestinian territories as 'Palestine.'" http://news.yahoo.com/google-lists-palestinian-territories-palestine-163931951.html.

———. "Palestinians angry over Gingrich's 'invented' people comment." http://www.washingtontimes.com/news/2011/dec/10/palestinians-angry-over-gingrichs-invented-people-/.

Ateek, Naim, et al., eds. *The Forgotten Faithful: A Window into the Life and Witness of Christians in the Holy Land*. Jerusalem: Sabeel Ecumenical Liberation Theology Center, 2007.

Awad, Alex. "A Palestinian Theology of the Land." In *The Land Cries Out: Theology of the Land in the Israel-Palestinian Context*, edited by Salim J. Munayer et al., 200–216. Eugene, OR: Wipf and Stock, 2012.

———. *Palestinian Memories: The Story of a Palestinian Mother and Her People*. Bethlehem: Bethlehem Bible College, 2008.

Awad, Sami. "Non-Violence." http://www.christatthecheckpoint.com/index.php/blog/117-videos-day-4-presentations.

Bainton, Roland. *Christian Attitudes Toward War and Peace: A Historical Survey and Critical Re-evaluation*. Nashville: Abingdon, 1960.

———. *Early Christianity*. Princeton, NJ: D. Van Nostrand, 1960.

Begos, Kevin. "Iraq's Good Samaritans." http://www.christianitytoday.com/ct/2003/november/5.64.html.

Bonhoeffer, Dietrich. *Letters and Papers from Prison*. London: SCM Press, 1971.

Boorstin, Daniel. *A History of the United States*. Lexington, MA: Silver Burdett Ginn Religion, 1981.

Bosch, David J. *A Spirituality of the Road*. Eugene, OR: Wipf and Stock, 1979.

Braswell, George W. *Islam: Its Prophet, People, Politics and Power*. Nashville: Broadman & Holman, 1996.

Braverman, Mark. *Fatal Embrace: Christians, Jews, and the Search for Peace in the Holy Land*. New York: Beaufort, 2010.

———. "Zionism and Post-Holocaust Christian Theology: A Jewish Perspective." *Holy Land Studies* 8:1 (2009) 31–54.

Bruce, F. F. *The Spreading Flame: The Rise and Progress of Christianity from Its First Beginnings to the Conversion of the English*. Grand Rapids: Eerdmans, 1979.

Brueggemann, Walter. *The Land: Place as Gift, Promise, and Challenge in Biblical Faith*. Minneapolis: Augsburg Fortress, 2002.

———. *Prayers for a Privileged People*. Nashville: Abingdon, 2008.

Bush, Andrew. "Bullets and Bibles: The Ethical Problem of the Persistent Linkage of Missions and Militarism." *Prism* 16:5 (September 2009) 11–15, 27.

———. "The Implications of Christian Zionism for Mission." *International Bulletin of Missionary Research* 33:3 (July 2009) 144–50.

———. "The *Kenosis* of Christ and His Redefinition of Nationalism as a Way towards Reconciliation in Israel/Palestine." In *Mission Spirituality and Authentic Discipleship*, edited by Wonsuk Ma et al., 98–109. Oxford: Regnum Books International, 2013.

———. "A Profile of Harvesters Christian Fellowship Tondo: A Contextual Filipino Mission in Inner City Manila." Denver: Evangelical Missions Society Annual Conference, September 2008.

Campolo, Tony. Interview with Andrew Bush, February 20, 2012.

———. *Speaking My Mind: The Radical Evangelical Prophet Tackles the Tough Issues Christians Are Afraid to Face*. Nashville: Thomas Nelson, 2004.

Carey, Roane, and Jonathan Shanin, eds. *The Other Israel: Voices of Refusal and Dissent*. New York: New Press, 2002.

Chacour, Elias. *Blood Brothers: The Dramatic Story of a Palestinian Christian Working for Peace in Israel*. Grand Rapids: Chosen, 1984.

Chapman, Colin. *Whose Promised Land?: The Continuing Crisis Over Israel and Palestine*. Grand Rapids: Baker, 2002.

Charisma News Service. "Preacher's Anti-Islam Remarks Mobilize the White House." http://www.beliefnet.com/News/2001/11/Preachers-Anti-Islam-Remarks-Mobilize-White-House.aspx.

Christian Friends of Israel Communities. http://www.cfoic.com.

"Christian Responses." http://www.acommonword.com/category/site/christian-responses/.

Christians United for Israel. http://www.cufi.org/.

"Christians United for Israel." http://www.cufi.org/site/PageServer?pagename=about_aboutCUFI.

Courage to Refuse. "Combatant's Letter." http://www.seruv.org.il/english/combatants_letter.asp.

"*Crucifixion* (Mantegna)." http://en.wikipedia.org/wiki/Crucifixion_(Mantegna).

Denny, Frederick Mathewson. *An Introduction to Islam*. Upper Saddle River, NJ: Pearson Prentice Hall, 2006.

Ellison, Ralph. *The Invisible Man*. New York: Vintage, 1952.

Ellul, Jacques. *Violence: Reflections from a Christian Perspective*. New York: Seabury, 1969.

Escobar, Samuel. *The New Global Mission: The Gospel from Everywhere to Everywhere*. Christian Doctrine in Global Perspective. Downers Grove, IL: InterVarsity, 2003.

Farah, Caesar E. *Islam*. Hauppauge, NY: Barron's Educational Series, 1994.

Fasheh, Munir. "Reclaiming Our Identity and Redefining Ourselves." In *Faith and the Intifada: Palestinian Christian Voices*, edited by Naim S. Ateek et al., 61–70. Maryknoll, NY: Orbis, 1995.

"Gaza War: Casualties." http://en.wikipedia.org/wiki/Gaza_War#Casualties.

"Geneva Convention Relative to the Protection of Civilian Persons in Time of War (Fourth Geneva Convention)." *International Committee of the Red Cross (ICRC)*. http://www.unhcr.org/refworld/docid/3ae6b36d2.html.

Glasser, Arthur F. *Announcing the Kingdom: The Story of God's Mission in the Bible*. Grand Rapids: Baker Academic, 2003.

Goddard, Hugh. *A History of Christian-Muslim Relations*. Chicago: New Amsterdam, 2000.

Goodenough, Stan. "Sar-El—Volunteers for Israel's Defense." http://israelmybeloved.com/sar-el-volunteers-for-israels-defense/.

Gorenberg, Gershom. *The Unmaking of Israel*. New York: HarperCollins, 2011.

Griffith, Sydney H. *The Church in the Shadow of the Mosque: Christians and Muslims in the World of Islam*. Princeton, NJ: Princeton University Press, 2008.

Grudem, Wayne. *Systematic Theology: An Introduction to Biblical Doctrine*. Grand Rapids: Zondervan, 1994.

Guder, Darrel L, ed. *Missional Church: A Vision for the Sending of the Church in North American*. Grand Rapids: Eerdmans, 1998.

Gutierrez, Gustavo. *Las Casas: In Search of the Poor of Jesus Christ*. Maryknoll, NY: Orbis, 1993.

Harnack, Adolph von. *The Mission and Expansion of Christianity in the First Three Centuries,* vol. I. Translated and edited by James Moffat. New York: Putnam's Sons, 1908.

———. *The Mission and Expansion of Christianity in the First Three Centuries,* vol. II. Translated and edited by James Moffat. New York: Putnam's Sons, 1908.

Harretz Service and News Agency. "Livni: National aspirations of Israel's Arabs can be met by Palestinian homeland." http://www.haaretz.com/ news/livni-national-aspirations-of-israel-s-arabs-can-be-met-by-palestinian-homeland-1.259321.

Harvey, Richard. "Toward a Messianic Jewish Theology of Reconciliation in the Light of the Arab-Israeli Conflict: Neither Dispensational nor Supercessionist?" In *The Land Cries Out: Theology of the Land in the Israel-Palestinian Context*, edited by Salim J. Munayer et al., 82–103. Eugene, OR: Wipf and Stock, 2012.

Hauerwas, Stanley. *The Peaceable Kingdom: A Primer in Christian Ethics*. Notre Dame, IN: University of Notre Dame Press, 2002.

Hourani, Albert. *A History of the Arab Peoples*. Cambridge: Harvard University Press, 1991.

Hutchens, James. "What about the Palestinians?" http://www.tjci.org.

In the Press. "Mahmoud Darwish spoke in the name of the Palestinian people." http://www.mahmouddarwish.com/english/spoke.htm.

International Christian Zionist Center. www.israelmybeloved.com.

"Intifada toll 2000–2005." http://news.bbc.co.uk/2/hi/middle_east/3694350.stm.

"Israel Artists Condemn Settlements." http://jewishvoiceforpeace.org/campaigns/making-history-support-israeli-artists-who-say-no-normalizing-settlements-4.

Isaac, Munther. "A Palestinian Christian Perspective." http://www.christatthecheckpoint.com/index.php/blog/108-video-a-palestinian-christian-perspective.

————. "Reading the Old Testament in the Palestinian Church Today." *The Land Cries Out: Theology of the Land in the Israeli-Palestinian Context*, edited by Salim J. Munayer, et al., 217–33. Eugene, OR: Wipf and Stock, 2012.

Jeschke, Marlin. *Rethinking Holy Land: A Study in Salvation Geography*. Scottdale, PA: Herald, 2005.

Jordan, Clarence. *The Cotton Patch Gospel: The Complete Collection*. Macon, GA: Smyth & Helwys, 2012.

Juster, Dan. "A Messianic Jew Looks at the Land Promises." In *The Land Cries Out: Theology of the Land in the Israel-Palestinian Context*, edited by Salim J. Munayer et al., 63–81. Eugene, OR: Wipf and Stock, 2012.

Kaiser, Walter C. "Israel's Missionary Call." In *Perspectives on the World Christian Movement*, edited by Ralph D. Winter et al., 10–16. Pasadena, CA: Carey, 1999.

Khalidi, Rashid. *Palestinian Identity: The Construction of Modern National Consciousness*. New York: Columbia University Press, 1997.

Khoury, Rafiq. "Living Together: The Experience of Muslim-Christian Relations in the Arab World in General and in Palestine in Particular." In *The Forgotten Faithful: A Window into the Life and Witness of Christians in the Holy Land*, edited by Naim Ateek et al., 210–15. Jerusalem: Sabeel Ecumenical Liberation Theology Center, 2007.

Kimmerling, Baruch, and Joel S. Migdal. *The Palestinian People: A History*. Cambridge: Harvard University Press, 2003.

"Koinonia Partners." http://en.wikipedia.org/wiki/Koinonia_Partners.

Lerner, Michael. *Embracing Israel/Palestine: A Strategy to Heal and Transform the Middle East*. Berkeley, CA: North Atlantic, 2012.

Levison, Chaim, and Or Kashti. "150 academics, artists back actors' boycott of settlement arts center." http://www.haaretz.com/print-edition/news/150-academics-artists-back-actors-boycott-of-settlement-arts-center-1.311149.

Lifton, Robert K. "Zionism at Risk." http://www.huffingtonpost.com/robert-k-lifton/zionism-at-risk_b_890427.html.

Lindsey, Hal. *The Late Great Planet Earth*. Grand Rapids: Zondervan, 1970.

Lowney, Chris. *A Vanished World: Muslims, Christians, and Jews in Medieval Spain*. Oxford: Oxford University Press, 2005.

Maalouf, Amin. *The Crusades Through Arab Eyes*. Translated by Jon Rothschild. New York: Schocken, 1984.

Madanat, Labib. *Beyond Self: The Story of the Palestinian Bible Society, 1993–2005*. Unpublished Material, July 2006.

————. Interview with Andrew Bush. Jerusalem, July 25, 2008.

————. Interview with Andrew Bush. Skype interview. Amman, Jordan, January 8, 2012.

————. Interview with Andrew Bush. Email interview. December 6, 2012.

Makdisi, Ussama. *The Artillery of Heaven: American Missionaries and the Failed Conversion of the Middle East*. Ithaca, NY: Cornell University Press, 2008.

Mallouhi, Christine A. *Waging Peace on Islam*. London: Monarch, 2000.

McCarthy, Justin. "Palestine Population: During the Ottoman and British Mandate Periods." http://www.palestineremembered.com/Acre/Palestine-Remembered/Story559.html.

McCurry, Donald. "Islam and Christian Militancy: How Christianity Has Fueled Muslim Violence." *Mission Frontiers* (December 2001). http://www.missionfrontiers.org/issue/article/islam-and-christian-militarism.

Moltmann, Jürgen. *The Crucified God: The Cross of Christ as the Foundation and Criticism of Christian Theology*. Translated by R. A. Wilson and John Bowden. Minneapolis: Fortress, 1993.

Moon, Luke. "Christ at the Checkpoint Rebukes Israel, Demands Empathy for Islamists." http://www.thejerusalemconnection.us/blog/2012/03/22/christ-at-the-checkpoint-rebukes-israel-demands-empathy-for-islamists.html.

Munayer, Salim. "Relations between Religions in Historic Palestine and the Future Prospects: Christians and Jews." In *Christians in the Holy Land*, edited by Michael Prior et al., 143–52. London: The World of Islam Festival Trust, 1994.

Murphy-O'Connor, Jerome. *Paul: A Critical Life*. Oxford: Oxford University Press, 1996.

My Brother's Keeper: Daily Devotions in the Faith that Unites Us. Jerusalem: Palestinian and Israeli Bible Society, 2012.

Neill, Stephen. *A History of Christian Missions*. London: Penguin, 1990.

Niebuhr, H. Richard. *Christ and Culture*. New York: Harper & Row, 1951.

Noll, Mark A. *Turning Points: Decisive Moments in the History of Christianity*. Grand Rapids: Baker Academic, 2012.

Okure, Teresa, SHCJ. "Enkindling Fire in the Mission." In *To Cast Fire Upon the Earth: Bible and Mission Collaborating in Today's Multicultural Global Context*, edited by Teresa Okure, 2–31. Pietermaritzburg, South Africa: Cluster, 2000.

————. "First Was the Life, Not the Book." In *To Cast Fire Upon the Earth: Bible and Mission Collaborating in Today's Multicultural Global Context*, edited by Teresa Okure, 194–214. Pietermaritzburg, South Africa: Cluster, 2000.

Ostling, Richard N. "Falwell Calls Muhammad 'Terrorist.'" http://www.beliefnet.com/News/2002/10/Falwell-Calls-Muhammad-Terrorist.aspx.

"Palestinian American." http://en.wikipedia.org/wiki/Palestinian_American.

"Palestinian Bible Society Building Bombed in Latest Gaza Incident." http://www.abpnews.com/archives/item/2203-palestinian-bible-society-building-bombed-in-latest-gaza-incident.

"Palestinian Christians Call On Evangelicals For Action." http://www.christatthecheckpoint.com/index.php/blog/82-palestinian-christians-call-on-evangelicals-for-action-.

"Palestinian Christians." http://en.wikipedia.org/wiki/Palestinian_Christians#Demographics_and_denominations.

Palestinian Human Rights Monitoring Group (PHRMG). "Palestinians who died at checkpoints." http://www.phrmg.org/PHRMG%20Documents/Freedom%20Of%20Movement/Tables/Died%20at%20Checkpoints-%20English.htm.

"Palestinian Law." http://en.wikipedia.org/wiki/Palestinian_law#cite_note-USAID-5.

"Palestinians: IDF kills woman, 95." http://articles.cnn.com/2002-12-03/world/mideast.violence_1_israeli-forces-palestinian-cabinet-member-israeli-military-sources?_s=PM:WORLD.

Pappe, Ilan. *The Ethnic Cleansing of Palestine*. Oxford: Oneworld, 2007.

Perkins, John M., and Shane Claiborne. *Follow Me to Freedom: Leading and Following As an Ordinary Radical*. Ventura, CA: Regal, 2009.

Pew Research Center. "Global Christianity: A Report on the Size and Distribution of the World's Christian Population." http://www.pewforum.org/uploadedFiles/Topics/Religious_Affiliation/Christian/Christianity-fullreport-web.pdf.

Rah, Soong-Chan. *The Next Evangelicalism: Freeing the Church from Western Cultural Captivity*. Downers Grove, IL: InterVarsity, 2009.

Bibliography

Rakoczy, Susan. "Spirituality in Cross-Cultural Perspective and Mission Studies." In *To Cast Fire Upon the Earth: Bible and Mission Collaborating in Today's Multicultural Global Context*, edited by Teresa Okure, 73–86. Pietermaritzburg, South Africa: Cluster, 2000.

"Regensberg Lecture." http://en.wikipedia.org/wiki/Regensburg_lecture.

Richardson, Don. "A Man for All Peoples." In *Perspectives on the World Christian Movement*, edited by Ralph D. Winter et al., 104–7. Pasadena, CA: Carey, 1999.

"Riwaq wins the Prince Claus Award." http://www.riwaq.org/2010/awards-prizes.php.

Rutenberg, Jim, Mike McIntire, and Ethan Bronner. "Tax Exempt Funds Aid Settlements in West Bank." http://www.nytimes.com/2010/07/06/world/middleeast/06settle.html?pagewanted=all&_r=0.

Said, Edward W. *Orientalism*. New York: Vintage, 1979.

Samuel, Dilbin. "Church in China Experiencing Explosive Growth." http://www.christiantoday.com/article/church.in.china.experiencing.tremendous.growth/26420.htm.

Sara, Jack. Interview with Andrew Bush. Jerusalem, July 30, 2011.

Schwarzkopf, General Norman. *It Doesn't Take a Hero: The Autobiography of General H. Norman Schwarzkopf*. New York: Bantam, 1993.

"Settlements & Land: Land Expropriation and Settlements Statistics." http://www.btselem.org/settlements/statistics.

Shenk, David W. *Journeys of the Muslim Nation and the Christian Church: Exploring the Mission of Two Communities*. Scottdale, PA: Herald, 2003.

Shragi, Nadav. "Peace Now: 32% of land held for settlements is private Palestinian property." http://www.haaretz.com/news/peace-now-32-of-land-held-for-settlements-is-private-palestinian-property-1.215530.

Sizer, Stephen. *Christian Zionism: Road-map to Armageddon?* Leicester, UK: Inter-Varsity, 2004.

Smith-Park, Laura. "Attacks on Arabs in Israel Prompt Soul-Searching." http://www.cnn.com/2012/08/30/world/meast/israel-arab-racism-concerns/index.html.

Sparks, Kenton L. "Gospel as Conquest: Mosaic Typology in Matthew 28:16–20." *The Catholic Biblical Quarterly* 68 (2006) 651–63.

Sylvano, Lyn. Personal interview with Andrew Bush. Manila, Philippines, December 2007.

T'ruah: The Rabbinic Call for Human Rights; Formerly Rabbis for Human Rights—North America. http://www.truah.org/.

The Israeli Committee Against House Demolitions. http://www.icahd.org/?s=matrix.

The Jewish Virtual Library. "Zionism: A Definition of Zionism." http://www.jewishvirtuallibrary.org/jsource/Zionism/zionism.html.

The Joshua Project. "Tajik, Afghan of Afghanistan." http://www.joshuaproject.net/people-profile.php.

The Sayings of the Desert Fathers: The Alphabetic Collection. Translated by Benedicta Ward. Kalamazoo, MI: Cistercian, 1984.

Tucker, Ruth A. *From Jerusalem to Irian Jaya: A Biographical History of Christian Missions*. Grand Rapids: Zondervan, 2004.

U.S. Department of State. "President Bush Hosts Iftar Dinner at the White House." http://newsblaze.com/story/20051018080359nnnn.nb/topstory.html.

Volf, Miroslav. *Allah: A Christian Response*. New York: HarperCollins, 2011.

Walker, Williston. *A History of the Christian Church*. New York: Scribner, 1970.

Walls, Andrew F. "Converts or Proselytes? The Crisis over Conversion in the Early Church." *International Bulletin of Missionary Research*, January 2004, 2–6.

———. *The Cross-Cultural Process in Christian History: Studies in the Transmission of Faith*. Maryknoll, NY: Orbis, 2002.

Weber, Timothy P. *On the Road to Armageddon: How Evangelicals Became Israel's Best Friend*. Grand Rapids: Baker Academic, 2004.

Wright, Christopher J. H. "An Upside Down World: Distinguishing Between Home and Mission Field No Longer Makes Sense." http://www.christianitytoday.com/ct/2007/january/30.42.html.

Wright, N. T. "Jesus." In *New Dictionary of Theology*, edited by David F. Wright et al., 348–51. Downers Grove, IL: InterVarsity, 1997.

Yale Center for Faith and Culture. "Loving God and Neighbor Together: A Christian Response to 'A Common Word Between Us and You.'" http://www.yale.edu/faith/acw/acw.htm.

Yoder, John H. "Is There Such a Thing as Being Ready for Another Millennium?" In *The Future of Theology: Essays in Honor of Jürgen Moltmann*, edited by Miroslav Volf et al., 63–72. Grand Rapids: Eerdmans, 1996.